CORPORATE MANAGEMENT

Encyclopaedia of Modern Management Series

CORPORATE MANAGEMENT

Edited by
R. K. Malhotra
Nachhattar Singh
S. D. Sharma

ANMOL PUBLICATIONS PVT LTD
NEW DELHI-110002 (INDIA)

ANMOL PUBLICATIONS PVT LTD
4374/4B, Ansari Road, Daryaganj,
New Delhi - 110002

Corporate Management
First Edition, 1997

ISBN 81-7488-394-0

PRINTED IN INDIA

Published by J. L. Kumar for Anmol Publications Pvt Ltd, New Delhi, and Printed at Mehra Offset Press, Delhi.

PREFACE

A major trend virtually in all areas of business is the increasing utilisation of 'management science' concepts, models, techniques and approaches in the organisations. Rapid advances in management concepts and techniques and changes in the climate in which business organisations, institutional enterprises and governments operate call for a more comprehensive and authoritative information on all modern arts and science of management. The Encylopaedia of Modern Management is an attempt in this direction. The encyclopaedia is designed on the lines of systematic reading—a programmed reading of subjects in a planned sequence.

It is more than a reference work covering over 1000 topics related to management. Each topic has been selected carefully and recognition has been given to new development and innovative approaches. In addition to the new dimensions in the information processing and communications technology, the changes in taxation, employee-employer relations, mergers and acquisitions, enhanced moral responsibilites regarding environment and acceptable norms of business, modern techniques in production, marketing and office administration and new insights of the behavioural sciences into human motivations and group effectiveness are some of the topics covered. Elaborate discussions and illustrations have been given as the complexity of the subject matter demands. The book has been designed so that it may be used by top management, department management, executive, executive aspirant, accountant, teacher, student of business and management and, indeed, all those concerned with the conduct of business. The scope of this treatise differs in many respects from any reference books, handbooks and deskbooks dealing with business management.

The writing effort has been assited by many individuals. We gratefully acknowledge all the contributions made by various individuals which made this encyclopaedia possible. Constructive suggestions to help improve the book are welcome.

Editors

CONTENTS

1

THE FUNCTIONS OF CORPORATE MANAGER

IN essence the Art and Science of management is practised by corporate manager. The corporate manager has been described vastly in the literature of management in every conceivable style. Numerous surveys, serious as well as facetious have been undertaken. Sincere ones have investigated in depth while others have ridiculed. Still others have given glamorous accounts in the fiction of our times.

This proves the great interests in the Corporate Managers (also called presidents). It is fitting that this should be the case. After all they are the leaders. Further in a tepid era when security rides high and self-reliance often seems on the wane, those willing to make the sacrifice of assuming leadership are, at the least, a curiosity.

Apparently, from a low at the time of the Great Depression, the corporate manager has risen to new highs in every line of endeavor. Civic groups and church groups seek him out, perhaps with mixed motivations but certainly with energy. Government ask his counsel and advice. And even the most militant of unions no longer try to depict him as an ogre.

There are other reasons for this interest in presidents. Seventy-five million TV sets, as many or more radios, and every form of mass communications daily extol a very narrow and material form of the way of living, namely, that the hard-working and self-sacrificing husband and father who brings home the bacon to "mom" and the kids, the upright and staunch breadwinner, is somehow a proper sort of hero. The idea is matriarchal in concept, but many people, especially women, have vague imaginings that the president of a firm is a kind of super-soap- opera leading man. The idea may be an unconscious one, but I have run into it countless times.

Because a company president not only brings home more bread and butter but also makes it possible for others to do likewise, it is no wonder that he is a subject of fascination to the public at large, to the student who hopes to follow in his footsteps, and to just about everyone, including, of course, other company presidents.

This is not said lightly. The great sweep of history and economics will show that it was always thus. The men at the top, the leaders of any society in any time, are the ones who have been vested with whatever the people have considered the most important attributes at any given time. Revival of the arts swept the imagination of the Renaissance. Money was the idol of the capitalistic era. In our time, the successful company president epitomizes our quest for material things, but with social consciousness; our enthusiasm for machine-age progress, but with a respect for our past; our preoccupation with the age of space, but with a pride in our "breadwinning" ways which have virtually licked the old battle for sufficient food, clothing, and shelter for all our people. And, as always, this civilization of today is still resplendent with the leadership of a few. The truth is that there just are not very many company presidents.

DEFINING PRESIDENTS

Statistics are very misleading as to presidents. They vary from one chamber of commerce to another. It all depends upon whether you classify an owner of a business in the same light as you might a president of a company. If we include typical owners, then we include a much, much larger group who "keep store", which is not here our purpose. This is not meant to disparage in any way the thousands of storekeepers who "do" rather than "manage", because these small stores have a way of growing into large corporations, and sometimes very quickly. Even if they do not grow, they are still a part of the strong backbone of society. But most could not exist without the hard core of successful larger and more basic enterprises.

But if we are to talk about the president's job, we should have some ground rules for recognizing him. The company president we shall discuss is the "president who is actively engaged in managing the activities of others."

If we accept this concept, we can say that there are somewhat more or less than 1,00,000 men and women in this country who fit into the category. If we add to this others who are doing top-level management or executive work, those working toward doing it, and those planning actively to do it, then we are talking about approximately an additional 5,00,000 at the most.

It challenges the imagination to realize that upon a small group of less than a half million people depends much of the economic future of a nation soon to be starting upon its third hundred million population.

It is little wonder that there is an abiding curiosity about these few presidents upon whose success so much depends. Perhaps it is relevant to know what they do in their personal lives. Perhaps we should stop for a moment before becoming amused at people who ask questions about the size of the presidential shirt, the size of his shoes, and his favorite food. The truth is, of course, that the shirt size is average, as compared with any random group, as is the shoe size, and presidents, too, along with more than 100 million other people, name curry rice as their favorite food.

But before even trying to define and describe the president's job, we should also examine some of the tasks being done by the less-than-a million managers or executives who do similar work, because the president's job concerns them almost as much as it does the chief executive himself.

Presidents and Executives

The big difficulty encountered when we try to discuss the president's job is the varying size of the companies of our 1,00,000 presidents. Often, a vice-president's work in a large company will be far more important and require more responsibility and decision making than will the job of the chief executive of many of our smaller firms. As a result, there is a tendency to dismiss the smaller firms. We hear so much about the 500 largest firms, the 50 biggest executives, and so on. This can be a trap for a good many people who would write about the profession of management. Countless surveys show that size alone is not necessarily a criterion for much of anything.

In an effort to narrow our scope of whom are we discussing, let us consider a definition of an *executive* covered in *Fortune* magazine:

> "An 'executive' is a relatively high-level member of the management family whose work is largely in the area of decision-making and policy formulation. His capacity is such that his judgment, perspective, and skill in properly delegating responsibility will weigh heavily in the long-term success or failure of the business."

It seems that this definition can be used to describe the work of presidents of companies of every size as well as executives of larger companies whose management activities are of comparable nature to those of smaller company heads. Although the definition is most general, it gives us a ground rule for discussion. It should be fairly easy, through surveys, investigations, and observations, to take a close look at company presidents, learn something of their motivations, what they do with their time, their similarities and differences, and then, perhaps, draw some conclusions.

CHARACTERISTICS OF PRESIDENTS

The company president or true executive has:

1. Less time for his family.

2. Less time for recreation (and even the leisure hours are often spent with business acquaintances, rather than friends).

3. A work week ranging from 60 to 80 hours, rather than the 40 to 50 hours of most people.

4. A travel schedule which is approximately 10,000 times greater than the national average and ten times that of lesser executives.

These facts are borne out in innumerable surveys. What possible advantages and what inner drives force a man to put up with such a life? The truth is that most presidents, according to AMA, think it is fun and would have it no other way. But we can search for deeper motivations.

What are the qualities of leadership that are supposedly the mark of the successful president, or true top executive, which set him apart from others doing management work? Naturally, there is no one answer. However, that the man who worked up through the ranks, often in the face of cruel circumstances, from a laboring position; the bright young executive who started well soon after graduation from the right school; and the man who inherited his mantle of authority through family affiliation (after all, the latter could hire "management" if he chose and become an absentee owner) do have some motivating characteristics in common.

There are three such characteristics. They are (i) assume control, (2) sense of self, and (3) sense of identity. Let us examine these in detail.

Assume Control

I have seen a definite desire to take control, on the part of most successful presidents, rather than to be controlled by the forces of economics, time, and the activities surrounding them. This could be labelled drive or aggressiveness, but it goes much deeper. It is more resistance to being at the mercy of the decisions of others, coupled with complete willingness to accept full responsibility for the success or failure of any project or the entire enterprise. And there are no patterns as to how he accomplishes his objectives; for example:

1. I know a desk-pounding head of an appliance firm. He literally shouts for acceptance and gets it with resounding success.

2. I know a stay-behind-his-closed-office-door president of a large service organization who achieves remarkable success, quietly, by indirection, through others.

3. I know a pat-on-the-back oil-company president who uses his charm to infuse great team spirit into his executives. And he promptly gets everyone to do exactly what he wants done in the exact way he wants it done—most profitably!

Sense of Self

There is a sense of self in all men who are successful presidents and in those who will become successful presidents. It is not too unlike the inner forces that make men successful artists, musicians, poets, or even actors. Although self-expression is part of sense of self, it is not all of it. It also takes something of the ego and far more, a sense of having a contribution to make. We may define this sense of self as "an ego which expresses itself by making a contribution, or the giving of its talents." Sense of self is the opposite of selfishness. It is not money-motivated. Presidential management requires some ego; it is one of the most articulate forms of self-expression; and there must be the feeling with all this of making a contribution. The following men are examples.

1. The foregoing may sound frothy if we consider a crusty, recalcitrant, hard-bitten president hypothecial who always handles his own union negotiations. He loves to win. He is articulate to the point of being known as the "bald legal-eagle" by union leaders and their attorneys. His own personal contribution to nation is to lick inflation by giving no raises except for a commensurate production increase. It is a crusade for him. And it is also a sense of self.

2. A chairman of a large retail chain, who began his rise to success by selling coffee door to door, confesses that his principal reason for starting his chain (even today, they will beat anyone's price) was to help people during the Depression. This man had known privation in early life.

3. A management consultant once originated a new technique which would save industry uncharted millions if accepted. On the surface, at least, it would have been much more profitable for him to keep the technique captive or secret and sell it company by company. Instead, he gave it away even to competitors, and then formed an association to control its application and use. It was his way of expressing himself, making a contribution, and letting the widest possible audience know what he had done.

Lest this account gives the impression that management is a form of idealistic pap, it might be well to insert right here that in all the above cases the profits were far greater, as it turned out, than if other courses of action had been followed. But is this not always true? Henry Ford once said something to the effect that if managers do all they possibly can to give the customer the best possible thing they can, profits can't help falling into their laps.

Sense of Identity

A "sense of identity" covers a number of things, including responsibility, but also the feeling that you belong to something, that you are a part of what is happening to it, and that it is part of you. The "it", of course, is the company. At the extreme range, it is almost a feeling that you and the company are one and that you are creating jointly something of lasting value. It is not quite dedication, but it borders on it. Now I do not mean that all presidents are, or even should be, zealots. But a tinge of this enters into the thinking of the great managers. If the sense of identity is there, all else follows: responsibility, integrity, loyalty, steadfastness. Why? In a sense of identity there is love, too. Love for a thing called a company? A man may have many loves: for a woman, for his children, for the sea, for the plain, for the desert, for animals—even for the fine grain-fed cattle which he has laboriously raised and yet knows he must eat. And have you ever heard a farmer wax poetic over his cornfield? He is not boasting. It is because it is his, and the sense of identity is there. Examples are easy to find:

1. Why does a man who knows that his policies no longer quite work still resist retirement? A sense of identity.
2. Why does the president insist on putting in longer quite working hours? And whether necessary or not, in general, he does insist on it.
3. Why do approximately 98 per cent of all presidents interviewed by AMA in one of their surveys say that they do not believe that they are working too hard, and then admit that everyone else that they are, including their doctors?

Actually, this sense of identity is present in everyone to some extent. We hear so often of the man who damns his company to his associates within the company, but who points with pride to where he works when talking to outsiders. So pride too is part of the sense of identity. But in successful presidents, it goes further and means so much more than this.

Other Characteristics

Perhaps there are other identifiable characteristics common to company presidents and top-level managers. One such characteristic may well be the ability to synthesize information. Synthesizing has to do with creative imagination. It is the piecing together of bits of information in order to arrive at a complete picture on which to base a decision. It is the opposite of analysis. It is a somewhat new concept.

Synthesis is a combination of creativity and timing. It is also the most important presidential characteristic having to do with profit. Profits depend not only on day-to-day decision making, but on long-range decision making as well. Day-to-day synthesis might affect pricing, production, purchasing, and selling policies. Long-range synthesis might affect improvements in a product line, new products, acquisitions or mergers, the building of new facilities, and so on. Synthesis is undoubtedly related to the sense of identity which have been just discussed.

Little has been said about profits in trying to describe the presidential motivating characteristics. Yet every top manager will insist that profit is the motivating factor of business itself. It is the motivating factor of business. But doubt exists that it is the motivating factor of the president as an individual. He must show a profit, and the bigger the better! His own share is pitifully little of it. How then can profit be the personal motivating factor?

As nearly as one can evaluate it, these elusive qualities of leadership have changed little through time. The ancient tribal chiefs who become kings had "take control", a "sense of self", and a "sense of identity", and many, no doubt, had a "sense of synthesis", too. The pioneers who hewed out the community wilderness, making organized states out of what were limitless and uncharted forests, streams, lakes, and mountains, had the same motivations. And let us admit, unsavory as the word is when used with business, the buccaneers who plundered and plagued the nations of the world for 1,000 years had them too.

GENERAL OBSERVATIONS ON PRESIDENTS

In their day-to-day work, we can find similarities and differences in presidents. Also, we can find certain general truths which may commented upon briefly.

1. Presidents of larger companies are usually older than presidents of smaller companies. In part this stems from the fact that the larger company has a slower work-up-through policy than do the smaller organizations. Also, the larger companies are usually older and better established.

2. More and more companies, large and small, are making retirement at sixty-five mandatory. Whether or not this is good is debatable. Some executives believe that it is a waste of talent, especially today when new advances in medicine have so greatly increased the life span. Again, the trend toward forced retirement is most apparent in the larger organizations. Along this same line, however, there is another paralleling trend which makes use of retired executives by placing them on special boards to guide and counsel younger executives.

3. One very significant difference between the presidents of larger companies and smaller ones is that the larger company head spends more time on external relations. To define objectively, external relations as public relations, community relations, stockholder relations, and so on.

4. Presidents today, on the average, have a better formal education than did their fathers. This fact is so pronounced that we can also state that younger presidents today have more formal education than older ones. And we can be certain that the president of tomorrow will have more formal education than does the president of today. It is a trend of the times. It is noteworthy to mention that several surveys show that the vast majority of presidents feel that their schooling did little to prepare them for their role in business. This may be due to the fact that our schools give degrees in specialized areas such as engineering, finance and science while there really is no one course which prepares a man to be president. But the presidents themselves blame their educational inadequacies on the educational system.

5. More company presidents rise to the top through the sales field than any other area. This is more pronounced in small organizations, but it is true in the bigger companies, too. One reason for this is that the sales area is one where personal performance is always noted more quickly. Another, less scientific reason is that the type of personality usually found in the sales area is more outgoing in nature, and so usually does a better job in day-to-day meetings and contacts with others, as well as in general human relations.

6. Promotion from within is still the route most presidents of companies follow on their road to the presidency. But in a survey of one hundred presidents conducted by a well-known manage-

ment periodical, fully 20 per cent of those queried feel that there is too much inbreeding in their companies. Collectively, their opinion is that if the president must come from within, there must be fresh blood brought in at other management levels. An indication that many companies, particularly larger ones, question the promotion-from-within policy has evidenced itself since World War II. Many successful military men have been named company heads. Also, there are many other cases where lawyers, bankers, and other professional men have been brought in to serve as president. It seems to me that this is a definite indication that many of our companies are thinking in terms of professional management.

7. Presidents, in general, work far longer hours than do lesser executives, or their contemporaries in the professions, such as law or medicine. Surprising as this latter comparison may seem, it is the regularity of work both in the office and out which makes up the difference. Both lawyers and doctors may have longer single periods of activity, but this is made up for the vacations and days off. A 5-day work week is common in the professions, surprisingly enough. This refutes the TV and motion-picture concept of the heroic physician. It also points up a weakness in public-information policies of the businessman.

8. The motivations of the president of a company are usually more dynamic than are the motivations of others working within the company. This all comes back to the take-control, sense-of-self and sense- of-identity elements discussed earlier.

9. Most presidents are copyists of other presidents. Although successful presidents are directly responsible for many business and management innovations, they still rely on tried and proved concepts in much of their work. This should not be interpreted as a weakness, but rather intelligence. In the medical profession, doctors make free use of the results of the research work done by others. In this sense, they are copyists. The businessman copies industrial-engineering procedures, management-development programs, packaging, labor-relations policies, and other management techniques. In this sense, he is a copyist. Certainly, it is sound business practice.

10. While there is much discussion regarding professional management, only two out of forty personally interviewed presidents

felt that they were in any sense professional managers. Many thought it would be a fine idea and that some day there would be such a thing. Seven, however, did not like the concept, thought it presumptuous, and in effect stated that being a successful businessman meant a lot more than being a "professional anything."

11. The biggest single problem that all presidents, surveyed personally and checked through other surveys, have in common is that of handling people. All admit it, and all are trying to do something about it, they say. What they are trying to do to solve this problem defies uniformity. It ranges from one president who is privately studying psychology from a psychiatrist to a president who has virtually abdicated his chief executive's role by delegating everything except the signing of papers. And in between are hundreds of committee management solutions. One president even admits that 90 per cent of the meetings he calls are unnecessary but that he calls them for human-relations reasons. Still another, tired of the emphasis on human relations, admits that he has become a martinet and literally shoves his decisions down the throats of his subordinates.

Presidential Age

The AMA states that its typical company president is "a footloose, energetic man around 50, earning an income that is pleasurably nigh." MEC pegs its average age of presidents around 55, but states that he could be in his early forties, especially if the company is fairly small. This pretty much bears out *Fortune's* survey on executives, in general. *Fortune's* exact tabulation is given in Table 1. It should be noted that in this survey, as in the other surveys used, all the executives did not answer all of the questions. The response to all the surveys was, however, extremely good; for the most part, over 90 per cent of those contacted supplied all the information requested.

It can be seen that the great number fall in the 40 to 60 range, but there are a surprising number in the 60 to 70 age bracket. There was no break-down here, but the majority are actually found in the 60 to 65 bracket.

The results of the YPO survey with regard to age are not given purposely because the requirements for membership in this organization limit the age of the member group. The YPO, however, states that the majority of its members head smaller companies, thus supporting the MEC survey, which points out that younger presidents usually head up smaller companies.

Table 1

The Executive Age

Age	*Number of Men*
40 and under	3
40–50	100
50–60	340
60–70	325
70–80	60
80–90	5

Presidential Income

The income before taxes of the presidents surveyed by AMA ranged from $ 13,5000 to $ 400,000 a year, which is another one of those statistics that is impossible to reconcile. Its "average" company president's income is pegged at $ 60,000 per year, two- thirds of which is derived from salary.

The YPO survey reports incomes of its presidents considerably lower. This is quite easy to understand, since most of the YPO members are in their thirties and head smaller organizations. YPO reports a median salary of $ 36,160.

AMA states that a president's salary usually varies with the size of the company as measured by its annual sales, but it is quick to admit that this is not an exact relationship. AMA also reports that the president of one of its companies surveyed with a multi-billion-dollar sales volume earns considerably less than do a great number of other presidents heading companies one-tenth that size.

AMA also says that it has found that presidential income and company size tend to increase with the age of the president, except that men of 60 and above usually preside over smaller companies, on the average, than do those aged 50 to 59. Nevertheless, it points out, the older men earn the higher incomes. The results of the AMA survey are shown in Table 2.

Table 2

Income of Presidents

Age group	*Range*	*Average (for those who replied)*
30–39	$ 15,000–$ 160,000	$ 47,000
40–49	13,500–235,000	61,200
50–59	15,000–265,000	70,200
60 and above	16,000–400,000	83,300
Overall.........	$ 13,500–$ 400,000	$ 68,000

Now let us take a look at the YPO survey results regarding income which are shown in Table 3. Bear in mind that many of the YPO members head up smaller companies and that most of them are under 40.

Table 3

YPO Members' Incomes
(Median income $ 36,160)

Income	*Per cent*
Under $ 15,000	3
$ 15–20,000	13
$ 20–25,000	12
$ 25–30,000	18
$ 30–50,000	31
Over $ 50,000	22
No answer	1

There is a definite disagreement between both the AMA table and the YPO table and the table of *Fortune's* 900 executives from the largest of companies. As *Fortune* points out, these 900 earn "the hardly princely compensation of $ 70,000 to $ 80,000 before taxes." Chief executive officers, they point out, do an average of $ 30,000 better.

Educational Backgrounds of Presidents

As mentioned previously, there is more and more a trend toward presidents having a college degree than has been true in the past. It is getting to be a prerequisite, but as the following tables will show, there are still a goodly number of freewheeling, non-college graduates around; and there always will be those who work up through organizations, found their own companies or inherit their companies who, for many reasons, do not get beyond the high school level.

Table 4

Median Compensation

All top executives.........	70	Metals.........	80
Chief executive officer.........	100	Oil.........	80
Railroads.........	40	Textile.........	80
Utilities.........	40	Auto and auto parts.........	90
Food.........	60	Building materials.........	90
Pulp and paper.........	70	Machinery and equipment......	100
Transportation equip. and metals fabrication.........	70	Retail sales.........	100
		Steel.........	100
Aircraft.........	80	Miscellaneous.........	110
Chemicals.........	80		

MEC found that 76 per cent of its presidents surveyed had college degrees, and all but 8 per cent had some college-level training. Of this group 22 per cent held master's degrees or the equivalent.

AMA's survey (Table 5) shows that only 2 out of 41 younger presidents did not have at least some college.

The figures from the AMA survey are also borne out by a YPO survey which shows that less than 10 per cent of its members have not at least attended college. The *Fortune* survey shows similar educational trends, although they do not record those who might not have at least graduated from high school (Table 6).

Table 5

Educational Background of Company Presidents

Age range	*Below high school graduate*	*High school graduate*	*Some college*	*College graduate*	*Graduate school*
30–39	...	2	11	24	4
40–49	2	5	10	59	24
50–59	5	8	17	60	30
60–69	6	9	20	28	7
70–79	...	...	...	2	2
Overall...	13	24	58	173	67

Other findings, however, indicate that although college seems to be a badge which most presidents wear, many make little use of what they actually study. The AMA found that less than 5 per cent of its 335 presidents actually rose to the presidency through the practice of the specialty in which they were educated.

Table 6

Extent of Formal Education of 900 Executives

	Executives under 50 (%)	*All executives (%)*
Postgraduate study......	36.0	22.1
College graduation......	48.0	42.9
College attendance......	11.0	16.0
High school......	5.0	19.0

Almost all its 335 presidents surveyed actually feel that the principal benefits of their college training, or their educational training, were in the field of personal development rather than any form of technical training. Of the AMA presidents surveyed 79 felt that their principal gain in education was learning how to think, analyze, and solve problems. Of these presidents 51 say that the main thing they learned in formal education was how to get along with others. Only 39 said that the specific subjects taken helped them in *any way* in their business. More than one-third of the AMA-surveyed people advised a straight liberal arts program as the best means of learning about management. Another sixth (which takes us to over half of those surveyed) advised liberal arts plus work in a graduate school of business. Very few advised the practice of any form of engineering or science as a means of rising to the presidency of a company.

Almost all the presidents surveyed by AMA advised the broadest preparation available, the objective being to arouse interest in all types of knowledge and to develop the habits of effective thinking in every area.

Of further interest is the listing of the actual majors which the presidents of the 335 companies reported on. The great majority (over half) majored in either economics or English. Here is the complete listing in order:

1. Economics
2. English
3. Mathematics
4. Engineering
5. Psychology
6. Accounting
7. History

Routes to the Presidency

One of the things most important to the man who would learn more about presidents is to find out what route they took to reach the presidency. Before examining various surveys, it might be well to point out that there are still a large number of presidents who reach the top job through family inheritance and ownership. This is prevalent especially in medium-sized and smaller companies.

In MEC's survey, we find slightly over 20 per cent of the companies owned by the family of the president. And MEC's average presidential age is fifty-five. This all probably indicates that in spite of our preoccupation with "professional" management, there is still a considerable blend of old-fashioned capitalism in our society.

Fortune's survey gives us the best breakdown of what routes lead to the presidency in the larger companies. Table 7 lists the first job each man held in the company. Table 8 shows the job each held immediately before his present job.

In spite of the addition of much science to the art of management over the past several decades, *Fortune* admits that "luck obviously plays a part in the rise of top executives… and they (the executives) seem to manage to meet luck better than half-way."

Table 7

First Job in the Company

Job	*No. of top executives*	*Per cent of:* *Top executives*	*Chief executive officers*	*Retail sales executives*	*Railroad executives*	*Top executives under 50*
Founder……	10	1.3	2.2			
Chief executive……	64	8.2	18.2	6.1	8.1	2.0
Vice president……	79	10.1	11.2	6.1	6.8	10.2
Other executive……	98	12.5	11.2	15.1	8.1	13.2
Total executive……	251	32.1	42.8	27.3	23.0	25.5
Production……	66	8.4	4.8	6.1	6.8	10.2
Laborer……	69	8.8	10.0	…	8.1	8.2
Total production……	135	17.2	14.8	6.1	14.9	18.4
Administration……	59	7.5	5.9	6.1	6.8	6.1
Clerical……	121	15.5	14.9	45.5	36.5	13.3
Total administration……	180	23.0	20.8	51.6	43.3	19.4
Legal……	43	5.5	5.2	6.1	10.8	8.2
Financial……	40	5.1	3.3	6.1	5.4	3.1
Sales……	79	10.1	9.7	3.0	…	16.3
Engineering……	54	6.9	3.3	…	2.7	9.2

Fortune states that "the types of work that lead up to the top jobs have obvious variations by industry and a few aberrations. (More than one-fourth of metals managers come up through finance). There is nonetheless a consistent pattern: less law experience than generally supposed, not much engineering or research, and among younger executives, a lot of sales."

Some of the *Fortune* comments regarding the routes to the presidential chair are most helpful and revealing. They report that one man in twenty started in law, and while he found limited opportunity in most industry, his chances were better in oil, utility, railroad, and food companies, 10 per cent of whose top managers joined their companies in a legal capacity. One man in twenty started in finance with equal opportunity to rise to the top in all industries. One in fourteen started in engineering, looked upon with special favor by the older utilities and the newer aircraft industries. One man in ten started in sales, upping his chances for the executive class by more than half in machinery or equipment and doubling his chances if he entered the food or building-materials fields. One in six went into production—best chance if he entered transportation equipment and metals fabricating. Nearly one in four men went into administrative work, often clerical. Here chances were best, *Fortune* reports, if the man went into machinery and equipment, 30 per cent of whose present top executives started in paper work. Among railroad executives 43 per cent began in paper work; and 52 per cent of retail sales executives began in paper work as opposed to only 3 per cent in direct selling.

Table 8

The Job That Preceded the Top Job

Job	*No. top executives*	*Per cent of:*				
		Top executives	*Oil executives*	*Steel executives*	*Utility executives*	*Top executives under 50*
Law......	63	8.2	13.1	3.0	15.4	18.6
Sales......	192	24.9	23.0	24.2	4.6	34.7
Finance......	127	16.5	8.2	12.1	16.9	10.5
General management......	123	15.9	8.2	27.3	33.8	12.6
Production and operations......	176	22.8	41.0	24.0	9.2	18.9
Engineering and research......	84	10.8	4.9	6.1	20.0	9.5
Other......	7	0.9	1.6	3.0	—	1.1

Oddly enough, most of the executives did not leave their starting areas of management in their rise. One in twelve went on in law, one in ten through engineering and research, one in six through general management, and one in six through finance.

Meanwhile, they reveal, one executive in four was climbing the sales ladder, and one in four in production. They point out that the big increase in chances went to the salesmen. And they show that the trend today for younger men wishing to rise to the executive level is best found in the sales area.

In all the surveys used, there seem to be few discrepancies present except those which occur as a result of company size. There are few exacting paths to follow to the presidency, but certainly chances are better in some areas than others. Also, it would seem that the importance of sales, being what it is, indicates the area a younger man should concentrate upon if he has talent in this area at all.

The President's Work

Little research has been done on what an executive actually does with his time, once he succeeds to the top job. Interesting beginnings have been made by the University of Minnesota and MEC.

The University of Minnesota spent a great deal of time trying to find out exactly what the typical executive-manager does with his time (Table 9). They find that he works about 42 hours a week at the office and 5 hours away from the office at home, or a total work week of 47 hours. (In most surveys, presidential hours are usually calculated longer, but this is for all executives).

Table 9

Work Week of a Typical Executive

PLANNING	9 HOURS
SUPERVISING	12 HOURS
COORDINATING	7 HOURS
EVALUATING	6 HOURS
INVESTIGATING	5 HOURS
NEGOTIATING	5 HOURS
STAFFING	2 HOURS
REPRESENTING	1 HOUR
TOTAL	47 HOURS

This study shows that he devotes about 9 hours a week to planning and almost 12 hours to supervising the activities under his direction. Only a small part of the typical executive's job is spent directly on staffing and maintaining a work force or on representing the organization as such.

The President and Various Management Activities

MEC's survey on what part a president actually plays in different management activities is one of the best and also one of the few of its kind, I have seen. The tables that follow 10–16 are from the MEC survey.

Participation in Sales. There is little doubt that sales is the key function, based on both the time devoted to this activity and on the fact that so many presidents are chosen from the ranks of those who have had heavy sales experience. Because of the importance of this activity let us consider it first. Table 10 gives the degree of participation versus delegation in the sales activity.

Table 10

Sales Participation Versus Delegation

Considers sales his primary job and actively engages in it:	%
Average of all presidents.........	28
Presidents of companies with sales of:	
$ 5 million or less.........	50
$ 6–10 million.........	33
$ 11–50 million.........	19
Over $ 50 million.........	0
Handles some favorite accounts personally.........	12
Cultivates sales relations but handles no accounts.........	46
Delegates rather completely.........	14

It can be seen that very few presidents (14 per cent) do not participate rather actively in the sales activity. It is also interesting to note that so many presidents of companies with annual sales of $ 10 million or less consider sales to be their primary job.

Participation in Manufacturing. Very few of the presidents surveyed by MEC take an active part in directing manufacturing operations, and large company heads seem to have divorced themselves almost completely from participation in this activity. Most companies have come to the conclusion that low-cost manufacture, efficiency, and cost reduction are areas for specialists and technicians. Production, in recent years, has become more and more scientific and less and less "art." Probably the field of production is where most of the professionalism we have in management occurs. Table 11 gives the results of the MEC survey.

Table 11

Participation versus Delegation in Manufacturing

	%
President takes active part in directing manufacing as main part of his job:	
Average of all presidents.........	6
Presidents of companies with sales of:	
$ 5 million or less.........	14
$ 6–10 million.........	8
$ 11–50 million.........	0
Over $ 50 million.........	0
Actively reviews progress, but does not participate in daily problems:	
Average of all presidents.........	44
Presidents of Companies with sales of:	
$ 5 million or less.........	57
$ 6–10 million.........	50
$ 11–50 million.........	50
Over $ 50 million.........	0
Delegates direction of manufacturing rather completely:	
Average of all presidents.........	48
Presidents of companies with sales of:	
$ 5 million or less.........	29
$ 6–10 million.........	42
$ 11–50 million.........	50
Over $ 50 million.........	100

Participation in Financial Management. The results of the survey on presidential participation in the area of finance (Table 12) shows just how much the business picture has changed since the era of the capitalist. Time was when finance was the main interest of most presidents. In the times of freewheeling capitalism, it was often about the only interest. Perhaps this is an indication of just how far management has progressed toward a professional concept.

Table 12

Participation in Financial Management

President takes active part in day-to-day workings of the accounting-financial function:	%
Average of all presidents.........	8
Presidents of companies with sales of:	
$ 5 million or less.........	14
$ 6–10 million.........	8
$ 11–50 million.........	6
Over $ 50 million.........	6
President delegates the function rather completely:	
Average of all presidents.........	92
Presidents of Companies with sales of:	
$ 5 million or less.........	86
$ 6–10 million.........	92
$ 11–50 million.........	94
Over $ 50 million.........	100

When a top manager states that he is in business to make a profit, it certainly bears out a contention made earlier that this was the object of the business but not a great motivation for the president himself; otherwise, he would be watching finance much more closely.

The Organization Function. MEC reports that 70 per cent of its presidents said that the hardest part of their job was handling people (AMA reported nearly 100 per cent on this), yet only 10 per cent thoroughly recognize organization as a function and how it fits together with people. This is borne out by the fact that 56 per cent stated that they take an active part in certain aspects of organization, such as management development. Judging from the results of the MEC survey (Table 13), larger companies require greater participation in the organization activity on the part of the president.

All companies are basically organized in the way the chief executive wants them to be organized. In organization charting, usually the president indicates to a subordinate what he wants done, the plan is put into effect, and then is promptly violated by the president himself. All of which indicates that there is some entrepreneurism still going on. There is a big trend afoot, however, for larger companies to create such positions as "vice president for administration", "vice president in charge of organization", and the like.

Table 13

Presidents and the Organization Function

President thoroughly recognizes organization as separate function and carries on almost all aspects, such as charting company objectives, future organization planning, development of men to fill organization, and training in selling organization changes:	
Average for all presidents.........	10
Presidents of companies with sales of:	
$ 5 million or less.........	7
$ 6–10 million.........	0
$ 11–50 million.........	13
Over $ 50 million.........	25
President carries on a few aspects, such as management development:	
Average for all presidents.........	56
Presidents of companies with sales of:	
$ 5 million or less.........	28
$ 6–10 million.........	58
$ 11–50 million.........	69
Over $ 50 million.........	75
President doesn't recognize this as function and uses various aspects only as occasion arises:	
Average for all presidents.........	34
Presidents of companies with sales of:	
$ 5 million or less.........	65
$ 6–10 million.........	42
$ 11–50 million.........	18
Over $ 50 million.........	0

The President and Public Relations. It has been a long time since J.P. Morgan said something to the effect that "We are going to do this, and the public be damned." Yet, this was the prevalent feeling of the early twentieth century. Today, most presidents realize that business exists only because of public acceptance. Thus the great interest in this area of management.

Almost half of the presidents surveyed by MEC (Table 14) are active in this area, and this probably accounts for some of the long working hours that presidents have reported. "You are never completely free from public relations activities", comments one MEC president. Another: "Wherever I go, even if it is on personal vacation, I find occasions being thrust on me such that whatever I say or whatever I do will have some effect on the company's reputation."

Table 14

How the President Participates in Public Relations Activities

	%
President is actively public-relations-minded and participates vigorously:	
Average for all presidents.........	44
Presidents of companies with sales of:	
$ 5 million or less.........	63
$ 6–10 million.........	17
$ 11–50 million.........	56
Over $ 50 million.........	38
President strongly interested, encourages others, but doesn't participate very actively in public relations activities:	
Average for all presidents.........	46
Presidents of companies with sales of:	
$ 5 million or less.........	14
$ 6–10 million.........	67
$ 11–50 million.........	38
Over $ 50 million.........	62
President not much concerned with public relations; neither participates nor especially encourages, handles matters as they arise:	
Average of all presidents.........	10
Presidents of companies with sales of:	
$ 5 million or less.........	23
$ 6–10 million.........	16
$ 11–50 million.........	6
Over $ 50 million.........	0

Even company size does not enter in too much here, although it would appear that presidents of small companies do more aggressively put the company's name before the public. But even the heads of the largest of companies do not escape activities of this sort. Some larger company presidents even admit that public relations is their most important function.

If there is any question at all about this, we only need look at the fees being paid to public relations consultants: they are second only to advertising in gross billings for outside services, far ahead of legal services, management consultants, and others.

Participation in Union Negotiations. The results of the MEC survey, as shown in Table 15, are somewhat misleading in this area. Although only 12 per cent take an active part in negotiations, most presidents are kept informed of progress at all times and participate most actively behind the scene. Almost invariably they spend many hours weighing the pros and cons of settlement.

Table 15

President's Part in Union Negotiations

	%
President takes part directly in negotiating with unions concerning contracts, wages, and the like:	
Average 42 presidents of companies with unions.........	12
Presidents of companies with sales of:	
$ 5 million or less.........	40
$ 6–10 million.........	0
$ 11–50 million.........	8
Over $ 50 million.........	0
President stays out of direct negotiations:	
Average 42 presidents of companies with unions.........	88
Presidents of companies with sales of:	
$ 5 million or less.........	60
$ 6–10 million.........	100
$ 11–50 million.........	92
Over $ 50 million.........	100

Participation in the Engineering Function. Table 16 shows that only 10 per cent of the presidents interviewed by MEC take an active part in problems of design, research, and product development. This is another indication of how much the practice of management has changed since the turn of the century. At that time, it was not uncommon to find that the president of a company was primarily an inventor or a "tinkerer." There still are, of course, some company presidents that fit this characterization, particularly in smaller companies, but for the most part few presidents have the time to do creative engineering work or even to supervise such work closely.

Table 16

President's Participation in the Engineering Function

	%
President takes active part in problems of design, research, and product development:	
Average for all presidents.........	10
Presidents of companies with sales of:	
$ 5 million or less.........	7
$ 6–10 million.........	17
$ 11–50 million.........	13
Over $ 50 million.........	0
President delegates this rather completely, except for review, discussions on major projects, amount to be budgeted, and the like:	
Average for all presidents.........	90
Presidents of companies with sales of:	
$ 5 million or less.........	93
$ 6–10 million.........	83
$ 11–50 million.........	87
Over $ 50 million.........	100

It should be pointed out that even though only 10 per cent of the presidents interviewed take an active part in the engineering function, fully 70 per cent said that they are vitally interested in new products as one of the principal ways of achieving growth.

SUMMARY

We have examined the president from the theoretical standpoint, and we have examined many of his characteristics, his background, and what he does with his time. This may be of help to others, but it is obvious that few conclusions can be drawn. The successful president of a company is an uncommon species in an era whose collective heart beats for the ever-present common man.

We may recall the president's job description of one of our largest corporations: "He may delegate portions of his responsibilities, consistent with sound operations and authorized policies and procedures, together with proportionate authority for their fulfillment, *but he may not delegate or relinquish any portion of his accountability for results.*" This, then, is the crux of the president's job.

Let us face the fact that there is no such thing as a typical company president. One may be a man from sales; another from research; still another from engineering and production; and still another rises slowly through many corporate activities, with no badge of education upon which to rely.

The challenge offered to one who aspires to be a company president, a leader, is a great one. There are no road maps because there are no roads.

Perhaps this, then, is the challenge. A manager can read about many things, he can become expert on many things, but this does not mean that he will become a company president. He must, as did our early pioneers in exploring the great forests which stretched westward almost unendingly, blaze his own trail.

2

CORPORATE ORGANISATIONAL MANAGEMENT

THE concept of management which has been discussed in earlier volume, the functions of managers and the environment within which managers operate, we now discuss the types of organizations within which managers work.

Ours is a mixed economy, i.e. it has both a private and a public sector. Most private sector organizations supply goods and services with the aim of making a profit. Some public sector organizations supply goods and services, while others undertake purely administrative activities. We discuss both sectors in turn, beginning with the larger, private sector.

PRIVATE SECTOR ORGANIZATIONS

About two thirds of all workers (employees, self-employed and employers) are found in the private sector. This sector comprises several types of organizations. There are about 2 million unincorporated businesses—one man business and partnerships, making this the most important type atleast numerically. These businesses or enterprises are genertally managed single-handedly or at the most by two people.

The One Man Business

By far the most popular type of organization is the one man business or sole trader. They are especially common in agriculture, retailing and the provision of local services such as building repairs, plumbing, window cleaning etc. Because the business is owned by one person, the management style is usually compact and personal and the owner is able to exercise his entrepreneurial skills to the full, e.g. by branching out into new lines of business.

In practice, most sole traders keep to the business they know well and remain small. For example, the typical small trader in retailing has one shop which he runs on his own or with the help of his immediate family. However, there are some outstanding exceptions to this rule.

The main source of funds for the one man business are the owner's savings and ploughed back profits. These are often sufficient, but may well be inadequate if the owner wishes to expand rapidly. He may be able to obtain short-term credit from his suppliers, and equipment on hire purchase. He is also likely to approach a bank for a loan or overdraft facilities, but the bank will probably require what it considers to be adequate collateral (e.g. by means of a charge on equipment). Our banking system is not well known for its entrepreneurial spirit, although in recent years it has modified its 'safe is sure' attitude. (The financial problems facing small businesses, and the steps taken to counteract these problems, are considered in greater detail below).

The freedom to exercise the owner's entrepreneurial skills, may not be an unmixed blessing. In the early years of a business or when it is expanding, a wide range of managerial skills—financial, marketing, production etc.—may be required and these skills are seldom found to the same extent in one person. The danger is that in following his entrepreneurial nose, e.g. in finding new markets, the owner may disregard other areas that are equally vital to the health of the business, e.g. planning and controlling the cash flow. The successful owner- manager will recognize his weakness and obtain relevant advice on a full or part-time basis from others.

Even then the owner will probably have to work much longer hours—at least until the business is well established—than the average salaried manager. Shopkeepers often have to stock-take after the last customer, has gone; farmers have to assess their needs for new machinery, fertiliser, seeds, and calculate the cost, after their 'working day' has ended.

Succession issues, i.e. what happens when the owner retires or dies, are also a cause for concern. Unless the business is to be sold as a going concern, future managers must be developed. It is sometimes said that a farmer should have sons or, if not, pretty daughters!

Partnerships

Partnerships are found mainly in the professions, e.g. doctors, dentists, lawyers, accountants. The partnership overcomes some of the problems faced by the one man business. First, capital is provided by all of the partners, who can be from two to twenty in number (except in the case of accountants, solicitors, members of a recognised stock exchange, patent agents, surveyors, land agents, valuers and estate agents). As providers of capital the partners share the financial risk.

Second, and probably more important, the partnership allows the spreading of the workload and the ability to draw on additional expertise; for example a legal partnership will try to ensure that at least one partner is expert in each of the major branches of the law.

The partners' salary and share of profits will be distributed on an agreed basis. In the event of insolvency, however, all of the partners are liable to contribute to the payment of the partnership's debts, and this means that great attention must be paid to the management of the business, including the choice and number of partners.

Limited Companies

The term 'limited' refers to the fact that the owners' liability is limited to the capital subscribed in the company. In contrast, partners can be obliged to use their private resources to pay the partnership's debts.

There are several types of companies:

1. *Registered companies.* The most popular type, these companies are registered in accordance with the Companies Acts.

2. *Chartered companies.* These are charitable bodies and other institutions that are granted a royal charter.
3. *Statutory companies.* These companies are formed under a specific act of parliament.

Registered companies are by far the most important of the three types. They can be further divided into private companies (over 97% of the total) and public companies (not to be confused with public enterprises) which are much more important in terms of their aggregate size.

The main reason for the small size of the average private company is that the maximum number of shareholders is limited by law to 50 (excluding employees). There is no limit to the number of shareholders in public companies. Moreover the securities of the larger public companies are quoted on the stock exchange, where they can be traded freely. This encourages small shareholders to buy shares, and companies such as ACC and Reliance have many thousand shareholders. (However, an increasing proportion of shares is held by institutions such as insurance companies and pension funds, who are now the major shareholders in most large companies).

Public companies operate in a wide range of industries: manufacturing, construction, retailing etc. The biggest usually operate in several industries and in a large number of countries. This means that their revenue is very substantial. In fact, the turnover of General Motors, U.S.A. is greater than the national income of many countries.

The management of these large companies or groups of companies is a very complex task, and a common way of making that task more manageable is to split the group into individual units (which may be companies or divisions) each of which is responsible for earning a profit. The main tasks of the Central Board of Directors is to monitor the performance of the subsidiaries and to take strategic decisions, e.g. whether to supply export markets from domestic plants or whether to build plants overseas.

Assistance to Small Companies

In our discussion of the one-man business we referred to the financial and managerial problems that might be faced by small companies. In recent years, attempts have been made to provide more assistance to small businesses, including, of course, one man businesses.

The government has adopted many measures to such as seed capital scheme, Re-finance Scheme etc. which are out of scope of this encyclopaedia. The government has also attempted to help small businesses by providing advice e.g. through the NSCI, by giving tax concessions, and by exempting small firms from the provision of some legislation.

Collective Organizations

This final set of organizations straddles the private and public sectors, although in most instances the membership is to be found mainly in private sector organizations. The main aims of collective organizations are first to link members in a (professional, trade or other) group capable of exercising collective pressure, and second, to provide information, technical advice, training and other facilities that an individual member might not be able to afford on his own.

Here we are *mainly* concerned with collective organizations that represent business organizations or their members (e.g. employees) in their dealings with other organizations and with government. There has been a considerable increase in the number and size of such collective organizations in recent years, for several reasons:

1. The tendency of governments to be more consultative in their approach to the private sector;

2. The growth and increased influence of public sector organizations at local level, calling for corresponding organized pressure from the private sector; and

3. The need for greater technical advice and expertise, not within the financial resources of individual members.

Also, increased influence on the part of one collective organization may lead to the establishment or growth of an organization able to exert countervailing pressure. The collective institutions that we are concerned with in this chapter can be classified as follows:

Business Groups. The largest business group, the Confederation of Indian Industry, is the management equivalent of the TUC, in that it advises and consults with the government on a wide range of issues affecting employers. Firms in particular industries have formed employers' associations to negotiate with trade unions on wages, conditions of employment etc. These or other associations may also make representations to government concerning the level of imports, energy prices etc.

Chambers of Commerce and Chambers of Trade are particularly concerned with local issues. They deal with local and regional authorities with regard, for example, to planning applications or the provision of local road or sewage facilities. However, this local focus may involve activities over a wide geographical areas, e.g. some chambers arrange visits to export markets and entertain representatives of overseas companies which might build factories in the area.

Labour Groups. The main objectives of unions are the protection and improvement of their members' positions, although they also enjoy a wider political interest. Unions may be organized on a 'craft' basis, an industry basis or a more general basis. Most unions have officials on the shop floor (shop stewards) who are responsible for day-to-day negotiations with management (often involving the resolution of grievances relating to the individual factory or office). There are generally local and district committees, co-ordinated by a national executive which usually has a paid secretariat. The executive deals with matters of policy.

Most unions are affiliated to the Trade Union Congress, a body representing nearly 50 per cent of the whole workforce of the country.

Professional Groups. These bodies control entry qualifications, lay down codes of conduct, provide advice and act as a pressure group for their members' interests. Because of their expertise professional groups are often consulted by government on relevant matters, e.g. one would expect the government to consult the Indian Medical Association on matters affecting the operation of the Health Service, the Institute of Chartered Accountants of India on financial matters, or the Indian Institute of Management on matters affecting managers in all types of organizations.

PUBLIC SECTOR ORGANIZATIONS

The public sector comprises many different types of organization, and these can be classified in several ways, two of which are considered here:

First, one can make a distinction between the trading and non-trading sectors. The trading sector consists of organizations which supply goods and services at prices designed to cover their costs. This sector, which mainly comprises the nationalized industries, accounts for around 10 per cent of the total employed labour force. The non-trading sector has organizations which provide goods and services free or at highly subsidized prices, or which are simply engaged in administrative activities. This sector accounts for over 15 per cent of the employed labour force, especially important areas of employment being health and personal social services, education and the armed forces.

An alternative classification follows what might be called the constitutional approach. It takes as its starting point the fact that all organizations in the public sector derive their authority from the Monarchy via Parliament. Parliament, as the supreme legislative authority, makes policy, largely by passing Bills introduced by the government. The government then has the responsibility for executing or implementing policy. It may decide that the implementation should be undertaken by central government departments, local authorities, nationalized industries, national service organizations or other government agencies.

The Nationalized Industries

The nationalized industries account for around one tenth of national income (GDP), almost one eighth of total employment and about one fifth of fixed investment (machinery, buildings etc.). Their assets are owned by the government, as representative of the public. Each industry is sponsored by a central government department, most often the Department of Industry, and the chairman of the board of directors is appointed by the government. However, the employees are *not* civil servants. The nationalized industries obtain the bulk of their revenue by the sale of products at commercial prices.

Evidently the state has a major stake in the industrial base of the country. The principle underlying nationalization was that while Parliament should have the right to monitor the progress of the industries, e.g. by questioning ministers from sponsoring departments, the industries would be free from ministerial interference on a day-to-day basis. In fact, ministers and civil servants have intervened in the industries' activities to a much greater extent than originally envisaged. (This is probably partly due to the heavy reliance of many of the industries on public finance in one form or another).

Here we shall not attempt to discuss the merits of government intervention, (the identification and measurement of the related costs and benefits is extremely difficult). The main point we make here is that government intervention, and a mix of commercial and non-commercial objectives, adds to the difficulties faced by managers in the nationalized industries. It also means that senior managers spend a great deal of time consulting with their counterparts in the civil service, and so have less time to devote to the process of forward planning than senior managers in private sector organizations.

One area in which governments have frequently intervened is the prices set by the nationalized industries. At times, the government has refused to allow the industries to increase prices as much as they wished. Subsequently, as financial losses have been incurred, controls have been lifted and prices have risen at a faster rate than in the private sector. This erratic pattern of price changes creates problems for the purchasers of the industries' products and adds to management's difficulties.

Central Government Departments

The Central Government plays an increasing role in the day-to-day lives of the citizens of most developed countries. Total government spending often amounts to nearly fifty per cent of the Gross National Product. Despite recent attempts by the present and past Governments to limit government involvement in the day- to-day operation of organizations (both large and small, public and private), the tide of central government influence shows little sign of retreating.

Although managers and organizations frequently seek more freedom to run their own affairs, they also demand government intervention; protection from cheap imports, or subsidies in difficult economic times, or government orders (as in the defence industry) to protect jobs. At the same time there are increasing demands for more social and welfare facilities, for minimum standards of health and safety in factories (the current asbestos scare is a case in point), for better job protection and minimum standards of training. These and many other demands lead to an expansion of government influence and involvement.

Departments Responsible for Macro-Economic Policy. Macro-economic policy is designed to influence the behaviour of the economy as a whole, e.g. the rate of inflation, the level of employment and unemployment. The Treasury is responsible for all aspects of macro-economic policy and its central role is recognized by the fact that the Prime Minister is its formal head, although the Chancellor of the Exchequer acts as its head on a day-to-day basis.

The basis of the Treasury's power is its responsibility for the raising of finance and government expenditure. (The Board of Inland Revenue and the Customs and Excise Departments, which also play an important role in the raising of finance, are both headed by Treasury Ministers).

The Treasury's responsibility for controlling expenditure frequently brings it into conflict with other departments which are anxious to maintain or increase their spending. This conflict becomes most acute when the government plans reductions in spending, as in the early 1980s.

The relationship between central government departments depends on the political strategies of the day. With the government's reliance on monetary policies and the abandonment of prices and incomes policies, the influence and importance of the Treasury increased. The desire to operate strict spending limits on Local Government and the Health Service (to quote just two examples) led to bitter in-fighting between the central departments involved and the Treasury, and these conflicts were mirrored in Cabinet between the various Ministers on the one hand and the Chancellor on the other.

At the same time relationships between and within central departments were upset by pressures, from the Prime Minister in particular, to cut the number of civil servants and to shake up the civil service hierarchy.

Departments Responsible for Micro-Economic Policy. Several departments are concerned with micro-economic policy, i.e. policy relating to particular markets, industries or sectors of the economy.

The Department of Industry is responsible for general industrial policy including overseeing the activities of the National Enterprise Board and government support for research and development, and for the industrial component of regional policy, including financial assistance to industry under the Act. Although major decisions are taken at the Department's headquarters in the capital, it has a regional network based on eight regional offices in the country. These offices represent the Department in its dealings with industry, local authorities and other organizations. They are also responsible for administering assistance to industry in Assisted Areas.

The Department of Trade has four main areas of concern. First, it is responsible for commercial and economic policies that affect the nation's international position. It promotes exports and overseas commercial interests, and negotiates on tariffs and other barriers to international trade. Second, it is responsible for competition policy (monopolies and mergers, restrictive practices) and consumer affairs (consumer protection and information, consumer safety, consumer credit, trading standards, product liability and advertising). Third, the Department is the sponsor for the shipping and civil aviation industries, and is responsible for several nationalized industries. Finally, the Department has general responsibility for the basic legal framework which regulates industrial and commercial enterprises, and administers a number of statutes governing company affairs and insolvency.

Departments Responsible for Social Policy. It is not always easy to make a distinction between economic and social policy and some departments are concerned with both. But social policy is the main concern of two departments. The responsibilities of the Ministry of Health and Social Security range from overseeing the operation of the National Health Service to the payment of social security benefits, such as child benefit and retirement pensions. These responsibilities are carried out through an extensive network of regional and local offices.

The Department of Education and Science is concerned with all aspects of education except the universities, which are funded by the Treasury via the University Grants Commission. Educational facilities are provided in conjunction with the local authorities, for whom education is the major item of expenditure.

Departments Responsible for Law, Order and External Affairs. The Home Office is responsible for maintaining internal law and order and the administration of justice. It fulfils these responsibilities via the police, prison, probation, after-care and, perhaps surprisingly, the fire service. The external security is in the hands of the Ministry of Defence, which is responsible for all the armed services.

The Structure of Central Government Departments. Differences in responsibilities mean that each department has its own organization and management structure. As we have seen, some departments are highly centralized while others have an extensive network of local offices; some departments operate in one country only, others in numerous countries within India and overseas.

THE RELATIONSHIP BETWEEN CENTRAL AND LOCAL GOVERNMENT

Relationships between central and local government have given rise to a series of conflicts, the most important relating to the financing of local government expenditure and to the allocation of responsibility for the implementation of policy.

In order to understand the debate between central and local government, it is necessary to say a little about the place in the economy of the government sector as a whole. There has been a long-term trend, which has continued in the post-war period, for the government sector to absorb an increasing share of the nation's resources. Government spending has risen as a proportion of total expenditure, and this has required an increase in the proportion of income taken by various forms of taxation. Corresponding to this increase in spending has been an increase in the share of employment accounted for by the government. People's views concerning the appropriate size of the government sector are influenced by political as well as economic considerations.

The Financing of Local Government

It has become increasingly difficult to finance local government expenditure from local sources of revenue. In 1990 rates accounted for only 28 per cent of the local authorities' receipts as compared to the 46 per cent received in the form of government grants. (The remainder comprised rent, interest, borrowing etc.).

Although the detailed spending decisions are made by the local authorities, they have to operate within broad parameters established centrally. For example, the basic structure of the education service is determined by the Ministry of Education and Science, and the system for administering law and order by the Home Ministry.

The heavy involvement of the central government, both in the provision of finance and influencing the broad pattern of expenditure, has led to the suggestion that it should take full responsibility for some of the services currently provided by the local authorities, e.g. education, which accounts for almost a third of their total spending and 43 per cent of spending on goods and services. Such a change would also make it easier for central government to control spending on those services and therefore public spending as a whole.

On the other hand, it has been proposed that alternative forms of local finance should be developed so as to reduce the local authorities' dependence on central government. A stronger link between spending and payment would, it is claimed, increase interest in local political affairs and hence strengthen democracy.

Responsibility for the Implementation of Policy

No government of the country can afford in the long term to have its policies thwarted at local level by local government, and yet the very fact that local government is run by locally elected officials means that conflict has been inevitable. In many respects, this situation has been made worse by the trend in recent years for the local government elections to return control of councils to politicians from a different party to that in control of central government. This has meant clashes on various items of policy between central government and local authorities of a different political viewpoint.

This conflict in policy formulation and implementation is not new and will no doubt continue as long as local government exists in its present form. How long this will be is open to debate and it is interesting to note that the Congress, the champions of democracy and freedom, mounted a concentrated attack on local democracy and accountability.

TECHNOLOGY AND ORGANISATION

Large-scale organisations have evolved to achieve goals which are beyond the capacities of the individual or the small group. They make possible the application of many and diverse skills and resources to complex systems of producing goods and services. Large-scale organizations, therefore, are particularly adapted to complicated *technologies*, that is, to those sets of man- machine activities which together produce a desired good or service.

As scientific knowledge has led to increasingly complicated technologies, large-scale organizations have multiplied; they have become necessary in new fields, and they have changed their characteristics. Medical care affords a striking illustration, for in this area the technology has been revolutionized within a generation. From reliance on a few simple home remedies, passed from generation to generation, and ultimate resource to a general practitioner with standard prescriptions for standard symptoms, health-care practice in Western cultures has moved to a much more specialized, more highly divided technology. The diagnostic equipment and procedures used by the physician are no longer simply constructed and exercised, and prescriptions are no longer blended from a small list of basic powders and essences easily stocked by any local pharmacist. The "simple" treatment of a virus infection, for example, now relies on a whole series of large-scale organizations which perform research, produce pharmaceuticals, and ship, store, and prepare medications. Certain conditions which once required confinement of the patient to the home with nursing by other (amateur) members of the family now call for confinement in the hospital, where a battery of technical specialists, nurses, and dietitians can contribute specialized skills toward therapy.

The list of examples is endless, illustrating the point that the elaboration of technology usually means that activities which formerly were considered single units of effort are dissected and split into multiple units of effort, each of them specialized and highly developed. With this "elongation" of the technology comes increasing complexity of the social organization designed to operate it.

In the following sections we will explore some of the ways in which technology, as a variable, may impinge on organization and on administration. We will develop the general proposition that the type of technology available and suitable to particular types of goals sets limits on the types of structures appropriate for organizations and that the functional emphasis, the problems of greatest concern, and the processes of administration will vary as a result. For this exploratory effort, we will focus on four types of organizations: the mining enterprise, the manufacturing organization, the hospital, and the university. While these clearly do not exhaust the major types of organizations, they have sufficiently different goals and technologies to serve as illuminating examples. The discussion necessarily will be general; we are seeking central tendencies. Each class of organization displays variations. This is particularly true in the field of manufacturing, and to make the discussion manageable we will conceive of a factory mass-producing a single line of products widely distributed to consumers. Moreover, references to technology will be based on present technology.

We will compare these types of organizations with respect to three broad functional areas of administration: the setting of objectives, or policy formulation; the management of resources (including people, authority structure, money, and materials); and execution.

Determination of Objectives

Whatever the motives of its members—accumulating wealth, achieving fame, exercising power, and so on—an enterprise must in the long run produce something useful or acceptable to others in order to merit support. The determination of what the enterprise will seek to produce we will refer to as the determination of objectives or goals or, alternatively, as policy formulation.

The manufacturing enterprise may have difficulty in determining what particular demands of what potential customers it will attempt to satisfy, and this is especially true in dynamic and highly competitive markets. Unless the product is extremely costly, however, or costs vary greatly with variations in volume, the manufacturing enterprise may test its decision through pilot operations. In any event the acceptance of the product is rather quickly and accurately reflected in sales figures or ultimately in profit figures, and reappraisal of decisions regarding objectives can therefore be rapid. If reappraisal leads to a redefinition of objectives, capital goods including machinery and raw materials can often be adapted to the new purpose or be sold, so that the manufacturing enterprise may be able to convert effectively from one objective to another, the technology may be relatively flexible. Finally, policy determination in the manufacturing enterprise is largely a matter for top administrators.

The mining operation is less flexible. It possesses highly specialized equipment and property rights which for the most part cannot be converted to other major objectives. The objectives of the mine may be adjusted to the extent that it may offer new sizes, grades, packaging, or delivery arrangements and hence may cater to a new market, but those responsible for the mining enterprise would find it difficult to get it out of mining and into a different industry—or even to shift from the mining of coal to the mining of a different mineral. The scope of alternative objectives thus appears to be less for those enterprises with heavy, specialized capital investments.

In both the university and the hospital the general or abstract purpose of the enterprise is relatively fixed. But in both cases there is wide latitude for interpretation of the general into more specific objectives. Because knowledge is so specialized the members of the university must decide what it will teach, and as new areas of knowledge develop or split off, they must decide anew. Here the product is intangible, and reappraisal of the policy decision is difficult and drawn out. Furthermore, because of the heterogeneity of university objectives and departments, top administrative officers can reappraise decisions only in gross or general terms; professional members specialized in the particular subject can claim greater qualification to judge. The university president is also highly dependent on that professional staff to interpret and implement a few educational policy. Hence, in a real sense, power to determine or veto objectives in the university is widely diffused.

The hospital, likewise, is highly dependent in the matter of objectives on the decisions of its professional medical members, who are the obvious authorities on health matters and who in the final analysis must implement the policy they believe in. Any shift in emphasis, for example, from treatment of the ill to maintenance of health can become effective only through the persuasion and conviction of professional members.

Thus in both the university and the hospital the general goal of the organization specifies an area of activity instead of a specific activity and therefore is subject to wide differences in specific interpretations. Since the technology employed by both types of organizations is relatively flexible as compared to that of the factory or the mine, goals may be revised or adjusted more easily to the technological resources available.

It appears, therefore, that the following variables are of particular importance as conditions affecting policy formulation:

(1) **Degree of concreteness of the goal** as expressed in the product. This is a matter of tangibility and is verbally expressed by such questions as the precision with which the product can be described, the specificity with which it can be identified, and the extent to which it can be measured and evaluated.

(2) **Adaptability of the technology** associated with the goal. Here the question is the extent to which the appropriate machines, knowledge, skills, and raw materials can be used for other products.

While these definitions have not been operationalized, they seem to be adequate for our exploratory purposes, and we can advance the following hypotheses regarding these two variables and their relationships to policy formulation:

(1) If the product is concrete, such as mined material, and the technology unadaptable, the major concerns over policy will be the possibility that the environment may reject or dispense with the product. This is happening now in the case of the tuberculosis hospital, for example.

(2) If the product is concrete or tangible and the technology adaptable, the major concerns over policy will be when to shift to new products and which of the possible alternative uses of the technology present the most favorable opportunities. For exam-

ple, should the watch manufacturer shift to cosmetic jewelry, to armament mechanisms, or to still another product calling for the machinery and skills at his disposal?

(3) If the product is abstract and the technology adaptable, the organization again has great adaptability to its environment, and the major policy-formulation problem will be achieving agreement on goals and on the application of technologies in pursuit of them. The modern university, for example, seems torn between emphasis on applied and on traditional studies.

(4) If the product is abstract but the technology unadaptable, environmental redefinition of goals presents a serious threat to the organization, since the technology can be adapted to redefined goals only within limits. The administrative problem here is to "educate" or influence relevant parts of the environment to accept those products which are possible with existing technology.

MANAGEMENT OF RESOURCES

Every enterprise has problems of acquiring and employing people, finances, materials, and authority. The difficulties of management are not necessarily equal in each of these four resource areas, however, and the amount of attention given to each probably varies from enterprise to enterprise as well as within one enterprise at different stages of its development. Likewise, the content of those activities which serve to manage any one resource varies as the following will elaborate.

Management of Manpower

The factory and the mine, as enterprises operating on physical objectives, have relatively few problems of personnel selection below the management level, since the operational activities are either standardized or are settled by experience, and the training of operators is not overly difficult. There may be a high degree of functional differentiation in the factory, but this differentiation tends to be based on the machine rather than on the operator; operation of a complicated machine may be so simplified and repetitive that individuals are relatively interchangeable. Hierarchical distinctions tend to be shaded or gradual, with normal skill and experience qualifying the operator for advancement. Vacancies, therefore, can be filled from below. Since machinery is so important, a major personnel-management problem is to ensure safety in its operation.

Because many members of the general population are potentially qualified as members of the factory or the mine and because training to entrance-level standards is quick, expansion of activities may be undertaken on relatively short notice. Long-range forecasting of personnel needs may be an important factor in factory location, but "personnel-development" or training programs can be confined largely to preparation for future executive or supervisory positions. The large percentage of operative personnel, coupled with an open hierarchy, provides the factory enterprise with opportunity to screen members on the job and hence to locate future supervisory or executive talents. This is less likely in the mine, where the division between those working above and below ground is rather sharp, and mobility between these categories is low. In the mine, moreover, flexibility of daily operations is necessary because of the lack of control over the natural environment from which the material is taken. This front-line flexibility requires the exercise of judgment, and hence experience is a major basis for functional and hierarchical differentiation.

Both the hospital and the university must rely heavily on professionally trained people. In the case of the hospital, moreover, the situation is complicated by the fact that some of the key professionals are not employees of the hospital, in the sense of being on the payroll. They are not, therefore, recruited as employees. This is true also for many supporting activities which are performed by a voluntary "staff." Functional differentiation is extreme in both the hospital and the university, and the intensity of training required for each special area is so great that interchangeability is virtually unknown. There is sharp differentiation between student, clerical, and professional ranks in the university, as well as little opportunity within a given university for a member to move from one level to another. Similar distinctions exist between patient, nurse, and doctor levels in the hospital. The length and cost of medical training mean that for practical purposes members cannot move from one category to a higher category; experience and seniority have nothing to do with a nurse's becoming a doctor.

The long periods of training required for professional competence in universities and hospitals mean that recruitment of professionals is not easy. On-the-job training may enhance the member's value within his specialty, but it is not a major means of obtaining replacements for vacancies in upper-level jobs. Moreover, while professional recognition or licensing presumably guarantees a minimum level of competence, there are many shades of ability above that minimum which are not easily judged until the individual member has already been established in the enterprise.

Thus in the modern factory and mine the technology relies largely on mechanical facilities supported by "know-how" which grows out of familiarity with the mechanical operation. But in the hospital and university, even complicated mechanical devices play second fiddle to professional expertise which is wrapped up in the human being and which grows out of long exposure to academic and abstract systems of thought. These differences are reflected in recruitment, allocation, and training of personnel.

Management of Authority Structure

In the factory, authority may be highly centralized or, conversely, the discretion of individual operators may be severely circumscribed, since activities are relatively routine and engineering standards such as quality controls can be used extensively. Particularly where various subassembly products feed into a final assembly line, central direction of the speed of operations and of the size, quality, or color mix is essential. The factory also has problems in maintaining a recognized position of authority for the supervisor, since experience tends to be a major basis for supervisory selection and the "boss" was formerly "one of us."

The mine, too is predominantly staffed by "blue-collar" members, but the lack of standardization of the environment, together with distance and communication difficulties, requires a more decentralized day-to-day operation, with greater discretion lodged in the mine team and the supervisor. Constant danger, coupled with discomfort and darkness, makes members of the mining team somewhat reluctant to accept authoritative communications from executives above ground, and the mining enterprise probably would run into severe resistance if it attempted to set up and enforce rigid, disciplinary communications. Instead, authority or the exercise of discretion tends to be based on familiarity with the problem, and hence it is lodged in the most experienced member of the work team.

In the university, traditionally dominated by professional persons, authority on educational matters must be highly decentralized, since knowledge rather than title of seniority is recognized as the basis for authority—as reflected in "academic freedom"—and knowledge is highly specialized. Discretion in academic activities is controlled less by university executives than by professional peers of the faculty member. Student members of the university are more subject to centralized authority, but this is limited by a tradition that faculty members determine academic or educational policies, and anything which affects the student can be construed as an educational matter.

The authority structure of the modern hospital is an even more complicated matter. Since treatment of patients is not easily standardized, judgment must be exercised frequently by those with greatest knowledge of the case. The professional physician has the greatest knowledge about the ailment or disease, but on the other hand the nurse who is with the patient much more often may believe she has more knowledge of the patient. The social distance between physician and nurse is great, however, and the exercise of authority by the physician tends to be resented by the nurse (or vice versa) unless a strong informal organization bridges the two ranks. The bridging of this gap may be helped by the fact that both the nurse and the doctor know that the nurse cannot really threaten the doctor's position either in the hospital or in the larger community.

Thus it appears that in the mine and the factory, which rely heavily on mechanical aspects of the technology, authority is allocated primarily as control over the mechanical operation and takes the form of authority over people to the extent that behavior must be disciplined to the requirements of the mechanical operation. In the hospital and university, however, the heavy reliance on human (professional) abilities means that authority is exercised primarily with reference to people. Lacking the mechanical referent to bolster authoritative behavior, the university and hospital must depend to a much greater extent upon agreement or consensus, backed up by professional ethics and standards.

Materials Management

The factory is concerned with acquiring and changing things, and there is emphasis, therefore, on moving inventory and on plant and machinery. Achieving volume and quality at low cost usually requires routinization of operations, and this in turn requires standardization of raw materials. Because a steady flow of standardized raw materials is so important to the factory and often constitutes a rather high portion of costs, purchasing, inventory, and transportation procedures attract a large amount of attention in day-to-day operations. The emphasis on precision scheduling and on predictability of production means that equipment failure may seriously cripple an entire operation, and preventive maintenance receives much time and thought. Control over use of materials can be approached in the factory through measurement of spoilage or waste. Since standardization is high, deviation can be measured readily. Hence responsibility for materials management can be widely diffused in the factory.

In the mining enterprise, rights to deposits replace plant as a major concern, and preventive maintenance and steps to control the sources of the mineral against flooding, cave-ins, and so on are particularly important. These can be standardized only in a rough way, and therefore judgment must be exercised frequently. Furthermore, maximum "winning" of the material must be balanced against risk to personnel and to the remaining deposits. Machinery is cumber-some and difficult to move, hence effective placement is important. Purchasing is not the major matter in the mine that it is in the factory, but shipping is extremely important, since storage facilities can be depleted rapidly by the bulky product, and breakdown of transportation facilities can lead to shutdown of operations. Materials management in the mine is by and large a matter for supervisory and executive personnel rather than for operators.

Both the hospital and the university have important interests in plant, since both deal with people (who are "bulky") and both must provide space and facilities for a variety of human needs, including sleeping, eating and recreation. Management frequently involves decisions as to the allocation of activities to various parts of the physical plant as shifts occur in technological procedures or in work loads.

Since in the university symbolic materials are major aids to the student and instructor, the collection, storage, and issuance of books requires constant attention. These materials, moreover, are far from standardized and are highly specialized, so that judgment regarding new materials must be exercised constantly and must be made frequently by the instructor concerned. Again, because symbolic materials are easily lost, stolen, or damaged, rigorous procedures must be established to maintain inventories.

The hospital has additional complications, since many of its expendable materials are highly specialized, easily confused, and perishable and since the hospital must be prepared for any of a variety of possible emergencies. Improper storage or errors in labeling medicines can be extremely costly, and the hospital often must rely on the health team to exercise care and discretion in these matters. Professional standards, reinforced by dread of being the cause of human suffering or loss of life, facilitate this decentralization of responsibility. Nevertheless the hospital provides a number of security routines, including the keeping of complete accounts of the disposal of certain materials and restriction on the identity of persons who can withdraw or use them.

Money Management

During periods of economic stability, at least, the manufacturing firm may be able to estimate its money needs rather accurately. Since its inventories and other assets are largely tangible, it can obtain needed money by frank exchange of the product for cash, by pledging assets as collateral, or by sale of an interest in the firm. Hence frequently the question of acquisition of money becomes one of seeking the most favorable terms, and large errors in such decisions can be detected relatively rapidly. During growth periods, however, investment matters may become more complicated, involving broader and less easily established alternatives and considerable risk. Expenditure of available money can be allocated within the manufacturing enterprise on the basis of expected return on yield and can be controlled by budgetary and accounting procedures, since standardization and predictability are relatively great. While neither allocation nor control are foolproof, such procedures are effective in the factory, and operating members can be held responsible for costs.

The mining enterprise can estimate its needs for money less precisely, since the cost of mining coal or ore is never perfectly known in advance, and disaster or geological fault may abruptly increase costs. Acquisition of money is again more difficult, reserves are less easily pledged as collateral than are the easily accessible inventories of the manufacturing firm. Allocation of available money may be budgeted on the basis of periodic estimates, but the technological requirements for flexibility may require frequent change of these programs. Formal control over the expenditure of money remains rather centralized, since the miner tends to be more safety conscious than cost conscious; and because mining operations call for judgment by the mining team, economic use of costly resources is not easily ensured.

For the university the determination of need is not difficult on the face of it, since enrollments and other costs can be fairly well forecast. But the intangibility of the product means that whether enough money has been raised is always a moot question. Acquisition, especially for the privately financed university, is a constant problem because those who most directly benefit from university activities usually are not able to pay the total costs for their training, and it is difficult to demonstrate graphically to potential contributors the indirect benefits they receive from the university's activities. Financial support rests largely on appeal, not trade.

Allocation of money is a time-consuming activity in the university. It cannot be accomplished by a few central officers because the various departments of a university are so specialized that there are few standards for evaluating the strength of their claims to scarce money. Control of expenditures through budgeting and accounting practices is relatively easy, although it tends to be accomplished only through administrative policing, since professional members of the university tend to place knowledge values above cost values.

Monetary needs of the hospital can be determined reasonably well; although work loads may vary widely from day to day or week to week, general trends can be predicted and irregularities averaged out. Acquisition of needed funds, however, presents another and more important problem, for the hospital in our culture is expected to render service on the basis of health needs rather than on ability to pay, and recovery of expenses often has been a drawn-out procedure. As far as operating costs are concerned, hospitalization insurance is relieving this problem, but capital funds still are difficult to acquire. Allocation of funds may depend partly on budget procedures, but changes in work loads or new technological developments may require frequent revision. Control over the use of funds is accomplished largely by centralized handling of purchasing, but professional norms of service sometimes conflict with cost-reduction norms, and professional personnel tend to feel that cost drives interfere with their activities. Control over expenditure of items which eventually are translated into monetary terms is therefore somewhat difficult. Waste and spoilage are not easily checked.

IMPLICATIONS OF CHANGE FOR RESOURCE MANAGEMENT

From the foregoing discussion, it appears that an important variable distinguishing various types of organization is the extent to which the technology is lodged in human as contrasted with nonhuman resources. For the sake of simplicity we will refer to this variable as the *ratio of mechanization to professionalization*. Reflecting this variable against the *adaptability of the technology*, discussed earlier, it is possible to hypothesize the following:

(1) If the technology of an organization has a high ratio of mechanization and is readily adaptable, the major resource problem involved in a change of product is likely to center around properly standardized raw materials.

(2) If the technology of an organization has a high ratio of mechanization but is not adaptable, the problem will be to avoid technological obsolescence; major resource concerns will involve materials and money and the maintenance of fluidity by amassing financial reserves.

(3) If the technology has a low ratio of mechanization but the human abilities are easily refocused on new products, the major problems are likely to be those involved in execution, to be discussed below.

(4) If the technology has a low ratio of mechanization and at the same time is not easily adapted to other goals, personnel-management problems are likely to come to the fore, with emphasis on replacing and retraining members of the organization.

EXECUTION

The problem of welding an enterprise into an integrated whole varies with the amount and kinds of differentiation of its parts and with the kinds of relationships which the technological process requires; that is, different kinds of heterogeneity call for different ways of homogenizing. The technology appropriate to a particular purpose not only determines in an important way the extent and type of differentiation but also determines the amount of coordination and cooperation required and the locus of responsibility for these.

The manufacturing enterprise, for example, may have major need for sequential interdependence, with each work team or section depending on others only for the timely and satisfactory completion of certain prior operations. Coordination required by this type of interdependence can be achieved largely by work scheduling and controls over the flow of materials and the quality of operations. In the factory, then, coordination between individual members of the work team may be the responsibility of an on-the-spot supervisor, but the linking together of various functional activities can be achieved largely by executives at relatively centralized points in the enterprise.

Mining involves separation or removal of minerals from their environment, and mining operations are therefore subject to unpredictable environmental changes—water seepage, geological faults, cave-ins, gas pockets, and so forth. Routinization is not easily achieved, and even with mechanized equipment environmental changes may make schedules inapplicable. The judgment of the minor is therefore indispensable, and the communication difficulties introduced by the above-ground and below-ground dichotomy increase the importance of the miner's reliability. Because day-to-day activities are somewhat unpredictable, relationships among members of the mining team can be specified only abstractly; specific relationships must be worked out on the spot, spatial requirements present close constant supervision, and coordination therefore is highly dependent on the informal organization.

Routinization of many aspects of hospital activity is essential, both to prevent dangerous omissions or oversights and to provide some predictability as the basis for carrying on when crises occur.

On the other hand, each medical case is considered unique, and hence considerable flexibility (based on professional judgment) is required. To a much greater extent than in the factory, the hospital has need for collateral coordination, with the nurse, doctor, laboratory technician, dietitian, and so on integrating their activities simultaneously around the needs of the patient. In these cases central executives may act to facilitate coordination, but in the final analysis it must come largely through the cooperative efforts of operating individuals. Moreover, while there is ordinarily a certain rhythm in the amount and type of attention required during each twenty-four-hour period, the patient is an around-the-clock charge and requires periodic attention. Hence communication between shifts is vital, and there is considerable attention given to accurate posting of elaborate records. Nevertheless the specialized and complicated nature of medical technology means that records and charts cannot convey everything of importance, and informal organization of the therapy team is essential.

In the university routinization of a superficial sort is easily achieved. Hours of class meetings, systems of examinations and grading, and so forth usually are standardized. But in teaching matters routinization is not easily achieved because the imparting of knowledge remains a matter of judgment. The ability of the instructor to inspire and motivate the student cannot be centralized, and the integration of extracurricular activities can be centralized only partially. The instructor is free to maintain that he and only he can determine what his students should know and how they should proceed to acquire that knowledge about his special area of competence. Routinization tends, therefore, to be by discipline or topic rather than university-wide, and standardization is accomplished more by professional codes and standards than by administrative directive. Traditionally there is little interdependence between faculty members; although it is recognized that each deals with only "part" of the student, the integration of these part activities has been up to the student or is accomplished through informal interaction among faculty members and students. Faculty members typically are "not interested" in administrative matters except to escape interference by administrators, but the faculty may involve itself in many matters outside the classroom under the guise of "educational policy", since the development of the "whole" student is believed to result from his total experience in the university setting.

Under the more standardized conditions of the manufacturing firm, and to a lesser extent the mine, coordination can be planned and controlled relatively effectively from the centre. In the less standardized, more professional fields, this is less likely to be the case—but at the same time more types of supporting activities usually are required. In the hospital and university these include feeding, housing, providing recreation, and providing opportunities for spiritual or religious expression, and so on.

Thus while responsibility for the integration of primary operations is relatively diffuse in professional-type enterprises, central executives tend to have a greater variety of activities and departments to integrate. Generally, it would seem, the greater the differentiation of an enterprise into identifiable parts, the greater is the need for fitting those parts together. Add to this the fact that human beings set themselves apart from one another on bases other than those officially arranged by administrators—on such bases as sex, age, ethnic origin, religion, style of living, political views, professional or union affiliations, and so on, and one perceives that the heterogeneity of the modern enterprise can be amazing.

Every criterion for differentiation of functions or hierarchy presents a possible or potential basis for cleavage and conflict—for the withholding of cooperation. Hence the more functional or hierarchical distinctions there are within the enterprise, the greater the problems of integration. Since systems low in mechanization of the technology and high in professionalization tend to be more clearly differentiated in this respect, it is in this kind of system that coordination problems are greatest.

Conclusions

The foregoing paragraphs have attempted to illustrate some of the differences that various goals—and appropriate technologies—can make for organization and administration. At one level of analysis, all large organizations have similar problems, but at a more detailed level of analysis, these problems become variables.

It has been seen that the following three variables are important enough to deserve extended research; (1) abstractness of the goal, as expressed in the product, (2) adaptability of the technology, and (3) ratio of mechanization to professionalization of the technology. We may perhaps underscore our argument that the general relationships between technology, organization, and administration provide important areas for study by advancing a final set of more general propositions:

(1) An organization overly identified with a particular technology may lose its opportunity to produce a particular product as more effective technologies are adopted by other organizations pursuing the same goal. This proposition simply applies the concept of "trained incapacity" to the organizational level rather than the personal level.

(2) As a technology becomes more specialized, it appears that the organization's flexibility in shifting from one goal to another is curtailed. The corporation desiring to withdraw from a given industry, for example, no longer rearranges its resources once applied to that industry, but rather sells a division or subsidiary as a unit to another corporation.

(3) As a technology becomes more complicated, entry of a new organization into a field becomes more difficult. Entrance seems to occur usually in the case of (a) an existing organization with tremendous resources, shifting part of those into a new field, or (b) the formation of a new enterprise at a time when a new technology is appearing; by avoiding problems of relearning and reequipping itself, the new organization may be able to exploit a new technology more advantageously than an established organization.

(4) As a technology becomes elongated, any particular organization will tend to have less control over the total technological process, to be more dependent on other organizations for prior or subsequent operations in the total process (for resources and so on). This, again, tends to reduce flexibility in deciding goals and managing resources. The increased dependence on specialists, for example, means greater reliance on pretraining of personnel by organizations specializing in that training, such as universities and institutes.

(5) The organization adapting to new technology—as most are doing constantly—will be faced with "new" resource- management problems which established procedures and strategies will

not always handle satisfactorily. Hence improvisation and constant learning will be characteristic of such organizations.

(6) Technological development, by requiring more specialization of personnel and equipment, adds to the heterogeneity of an organization. Related skills and knowledge formerly lodged in one person or one group are split. While such divisive developments undoubtedly allow for greater precision within an area of activity, they also intensify the need for, and concern over, integration of the several activities.

(7) Increasing technological complication is accompanied by the proliferation of professional and technical societies and associations, each with its unique values and code of ethics. Hence there is more likelihood for organizational members to owe loyalty or allegiance to a profession as well as to the organization, greater opportunity for the demands of the organization to conflict with those of the profession, and at the same time a greater opportunity for the individual employee to enforce demands on the organization by invoking sanctions from the profession. Finally, the proliferation of specialization provides additional bases for organizational members to differentiate among themselves and hence for cleavage to develop.

3

CORPORATE COMMUNICATIONS

COMMUNICATIONS in everyday life is referred to as such things as stating opinions, asking questions, issuing warnings and so forth. These everyday activities are, of course, part of the process of communication within organizations and are considered later in this and the following chapters. But first, we discuss two other closely linked aspects of communication that are part of the organizational setting: communication systems and communication channels.

COMMUNICATION SYSTEMS

A distinction can be made between internal and external communication systems. These follow:

Internal Systems

Communication systems link the various structural parts or units of the organization together. A very important element in this linkage is that between management and the various units for which it is responsible. Some of them are shown in Figure 1.

From management's point of view communication fulfills three main purposes:

(i) *To inform employees of management objectives and strategies.*

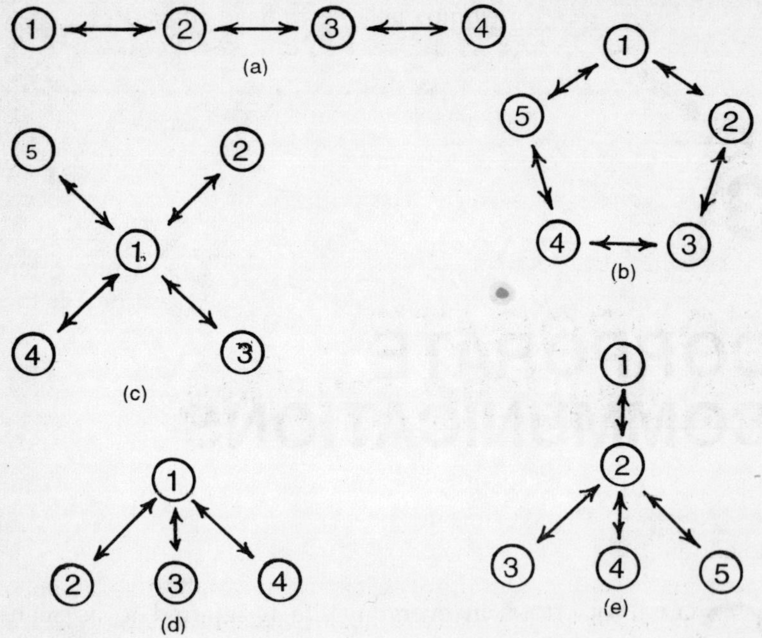

Fig. 1. Various communication Systems

In these days of ever increasing competition, only the more efficient organizations survive and prosper. One of the key aspects of efficiency is that every member of the organization should work towards the same objectives. This is possible only if these objectives are clearly defined by management and communicated throughout the organization.

(ii) *To enable these objectives to be attained with the expenditure of the minimum time and effort.*

(a) **Link or Chain.** This is a slow but effective method of communicating, with information being passed up and down the chain by each participant in turn.

(b) **Circular.** This allows the individuals to choose a variety of communication systems, within the overall circle. This type of communication system can give rise to duplication and time wasting as messages are passed to and fro from the various participants within the organization structure.

(c) **Star-shaped.** An effective method of communicating which places a lot of power in the hands of the person in position 1, and which would only operate in a very centralized organizational system.

(d) **Direct.** In this system all the power is with the holder of position 1.

(e) **Bureaucratic** (or hierarchical). In this type of structure, often used in such organizations as local government, position 1 is the Chief Officer post, position 2 the Deputy Chief Officer post and 3, 4 and 5 Assistant Chief Officer or Section Head posts. This system can have the disadvantage of isolating the Chief Officer, who has to rely on the Deputy, or can lead to the Deputy being by-passed by the Chief Officer, who makes direct contact with those in positions 3, 4 and 5.

This follows from the previous point, but it also implies that management should be open to communications from other members of the organization i.e. honest two-way communication. However, much thought is given to defining objectives and formulating policies, management cannot hope to identify in detail how these policies should be implemented. On the one hand unanticipated problems may arise, on the other hand better methods of operation may be discovered. The communication system should allow information on these matters to flow. This is the aim of so-called suggestion schemes in many organizations.

Once the best methods of operation have been identified and the required procedures established, management must ensure that these procedures are followed.

It can be seen that the monitoring of performance is central to the control system. The results of this monitoring are communicated to management. If management finds performance is up to standard it takes no action. On the other hand, if it finds that performance is unsatisfactory it will take steps to improve the performance; this may also involve setting new standards and work methods and so the process begins again. This improvement may also take the form of, for example, a reduction in cost, an increase in output, a smoother flow of work; points which are discussed in other chapters.

There are many ways of monitoring and modifying performance. In some instances these involve detailed scrutiny by individuals. For example, when a new worker is learning to operate a machine, he may in the initial stages be watched by a supervisor who tells him whenever he does something wrong. In other instances instructions are given via machines. A well-known example is the bar traffic light. When a vehicle hits the bar, or sensor, its presence is recorded by the control box. The control box in turn transmits information—a green light—to the driver of the vehicle, and other information—a red light—to drivers of vehicles travelling in a contrary direction.

In this instance the modification of performance or behaviour—stopping at a red light, going through a green—remains the responsibility of the individual. In other instances, a machine both monitors and modifies performance. A simple example is a thermostat which turns a valve which then controls the heating in order to maintain a constant temperature. A more complex example of monitoring by machine is the stock control system such as the one introduced by Mothercare, the retailer of baby, infant and children's goods. Sales made at all Mothercare branches are recorded by a central computer, which then calculates what goods remain in stock. When stock levels fall to a pre-determined level the computer prints out orders for despatch to the manufacturer.

The use of machines reduces the frequency and extent of intervention by individuals. But however much managers delegate to machines, they continue to receive information on performance and retain the ultimate responsibility and right of control.

Internal communication systems also link different functional areas of the organization. For example, marketing strategies are communicated to the sales force, the results of sales drives are fed to the production department so that the required output can be produced and orders fulfilled, the production department liaises with the distribution department to ensure that vehicles are available when required.

A good communication enables people to perform well and that this benefits the organization. But good performance is also of direct benefit to the individual in that it increases his or her job satisfaction, can influence earning capacity and may improve an individual's chance of promotion.

Good communication also helps to improve the social element which has been shown to be an important aspect of work. Having information about what is happening in the organization often, although not always, helps to reduce suspicion and conflict and thus contributes to a happier working environment.

External Systems

'No man is an island.' Nor is any organization. The business organization has to be aware of the behavior and attitudes of the consumers, or potential consumers, of the goods and services it provides. It must also remain alert to the activities of competitors. This implies constant feedback from the market place and this may require the organization to set up its own external communication network. As part of this it can make use of other networks, such as the statistics provided by various government departments, information appearing in the press and on television, etc.

The non-business organization, such as a central or local government department, has to take account of the opinions and attitudes of the general public as clients, tax payers or electors, and of the views of their elected representatives.

In addition, the external communication system of both business and non-business organizations can be used to convey information about the organization. This information can include advertising, lobbying, making representations to government departments and presenting financial results to shareholders.

COMMUNICATION CHANNELS

Just as water flows through a channel from one point to another, so information flows through communication channels. A further analogy can be deduced: water channels are sometimes the result of a formal planning process—as when a canal is built to link two towns—and sometimes accidental as when a river bursts its banks. So too, formal channels of communication are deliberately established whereas informal channels develop spontaneously.

Formal Channels

There is a close link between formal channels of communication and communication systems. In fact, we can see the system established by management as comprising a variety of formal channels. These channels might include negotiations between industrial relations officers and trade union representatives on issues of pay and conditions of work. When agreement is reached the results will be communicated to the wages office which will in turn transmit the actual money wages to the employees. When we consider later the method of communication used in formal channels, we shall see that there is a strong emphasis on written communication.

Informal Channels

No matter how well developed formal channels of communication may be, informal channels will also spring up. The 'office grape- vine,' 'typing pool gossip,' 'broad room leaks' and 'cabinet leaks' are to be found in many organizations.

These informal channels can be so effective that on occasions they may be used by management in preference to formal channels. A strategically made 'leak' can smooth the path for a future change in policy that it would be premature to announce formally. For example, consider a bus company which decided that, because of a shortage of male drivers, it will be necessary to conduct a recruitment drive aimed at women. If it was felt that some male drivers would not take kindly to the idea, their attitude could be improved by making it known that delays and cancelled services were causing the public to be hostile towards existing staff.

The use of informal channels can also increase the flexibility of the organization. If it was subsequently decided that improved recruitment of male drivers meant that it was not necessary to try to recruit females, no further action need be taken. Whereas if a policy decision had been formally announced, this would subsequently have to be retracted, with a possible loss of credibility on the part of management.

In some circumstances information travels more rapidly through informal then formal channels, since the latter may involve calling meetings, preparing agenda etc. Furthermore informal channels may be more effective. Employees may believe the 'real facts of the situation', as related by Doris the tea lady or George the chauffeur who just happened to hear two executives talking, then an official statement or memo. This is most likely to happen when employees perceive the communication system and style as secretive, or inadequate in some other way, and this may indicate that improvements in the system are required.

Information received through informal channels may result in a great deal of stress and anxiety being generated within an organization and this may eventually force management to make a formal communication earlier than they had planned. For example, in times of economic recession rumours abound concerning redundancies, cutbacks, closures, etc. These rumours—even if completely unfounded—can lead to poor morale, a lack of co-operation among the workforce and lower standards of performance. To clear the air, management may feel obligate to provide more regular detailed information on orders received, production plans, etc. In other words the formal communication arrangements are determined by the informal ones.

When information is fed through formal channels management can be fairly certain as to who will receive that information. Informal channels are much less predictable and this unpredictability can give rise to serious problems. Some employees will receive this information before others and this may give them a considerable advantage. For example, if a factory is likely to close and there are few alternative jobs in the locality, prior knowledge of the closure will enable those in possession of the information to snap up these jobs before the employment market becomes flooded following the formal announcement of closure.

Quite often those in junior and middle management are the last to know in these situations. Senior management is, of course, aware because they are involved in the decision. People like typists and the executive canteen staff are often the first to hear by chance in the course of their work; their informal grape-vine often extends to the shop floor and supervisory level, who are often relatives and friends. A middle manager may only find out when a shop steward knocks at his door and asked him to comment on the rumour about the firm closing down.

At a different level of the organization, people receiving unofficial or informal information about the financial performance of a company have been able to buy or sell the shares of the company. When this information becomes generally known and the share price changes, the person who has bought or sold earlier is able to realise a profit or avoid a loss. The unfairness of this situation has led to such 'insider trading' being declared illegal.

We can see then that informal communication channels, based in the main on personal relationships between individuals, can give rise to both desirable and undesirable consequences. Managers may sometimes encourage the development of such channels and indeed may use them themselves. But they must also remain aware of the dangers of misuse.

THE ART OF COMMUNICATING

So far we have considered communication mainly from the viewpoint of the organization as a whole. We have looked at the procedures that might be adopted by management, as a group, in order to ensure that the organization achieves its objectives.

Here we narrow the focus to consider how the individual can improve his communication ability. The discussion in this section can, in principle, be applied to all members of the organization and indeed to people who are not members of an organization. But in line with the main theme of the book, we draw most of our illustrations from situations in which the individual manager might find himself.

An emphasis may be made here that there is no single correct way to communicate; each situation must be treated on its merits. What follows, then, is a series of ground rules which experience suggests will contribute to a successful outcome in most situations.

Adequate Preparation

In formal meetings this may require the preparation of a check list, on paper or mentally, with thought being given to each point on the check list before the meeting begins. In other situations, preparation may comprise a few moments thought before speaking. But even this limited amount of preparation may make a tremendous difference. The result of a lack of preparation may be a bad start or aggressive words when a sense of calm and reassurances is required. This may make it impossible to put across the intended message no matter how much smooth talk follows. People expect managers to show qualities of leadership, control and calmness. This presumption that they will think before they act, rather than giving voice to their immediate impulses, is expected of managers at all levels. Moreover a smooth, polished performance will often reinforce the manager's status and standing among his colleagues.

Accuracy of the Communication

Adequate preparation implies making oneself familiar with the situation. The next step is to pass on one's knowledge as accurately as possible. This implies giving a straightforward answer to a question or admitting your ignorance if you do not know the answer. If anyone tries to cover up and the real acts of the situation eventually come to light, that person's credibility and future ability to communicate will be impaired. This is a particularly serious matter for managers who, because of their position of authority, are held responsible for what they say. If a manager says something, people assume they mean it.

Managers are sometimes asked to provide information which they think it would be premature to reveal. For example, if a company is negotiating for an important contract it may wish to keep this secret from competitors. In such situations, managers must retain the right not to divulge information. However, the good manager will 'come clean', he will make it known that he is exercising his right to control the timing of the release of information and will indicate why he believes release at that time would not be appropriate.

Simplicity

People can absorb only a limited amount of information at one time. This amount of intake is likely to be especially small during periods of stress or major change. Keeping the presentation and the facts simple, restricted to a small number of major issues or points, goes a long way to ensuring the comprehension of the communication.

Learning and Practising

Although some people are inherently less fluent than others, there is no one who cannot develop his natural ability. A manager's life is a constant learning process and it is in the communications arena that a manager has to learn as quickly as he can.

Learning is sometimes informal, as when a manager makes an error, recognizes that he has done so and takes steps to ensure that he does not repeat the mistake in the future. In other instances, learning is formalized, as when managers take part in mock interviews in a television studio. Managers and trade union leaders are often called upon to explain and defend their views on television and radio, and practice in this particular medium helps to ensure that their views are expressed as effectively as possible. In the institution in which the writers work, students who are about to seek work are given the opportunity to practise their communication skills. They take part in mock interviews, with a skilled interviewer playing the part of the employer. These are video-recorded and subsequently played back. In this way, the students can identify and rectify their faults or weaknesses in the way they present themselves.

Finally,- learning may be partly informal and partly formal. Communication is more effective when the speaker is aware of, and hence is able to take account of difficulties that might be faced by listeners. The effective communicator will learn from experience, but it is sometimes useful to supplement experience by examining communication problems in a formal, structured, manner. In this way, the communicator will be better prepared to cope with a problem that he has not previously encountered; even better, he may be able to ensure that the problem never arises.

COMMUNICATION PROBLEMS

Lack of Attention or Interest

This is particularly likely to occur if external circumstances are unfavourable e.g. if the listener has to sit through a long and boring speech, if he is tired at the end of a busy day, or if the crucial communication occurs in the middle of other items which are of no interest to the listover.

Inflexibility

Where the recipient has fixed ideas and the communication cuts across these ideas, the chances of its being accepted are slim. For example, if a person who has worked for the organization for twenty years and has been a very loyal employee, hears on the grape-vine that he is going to be made redundant along with other people, he may dismiss the rumour as pure gossip. On the other hand, a worker who believes that managers have not the slightest concern for the welfare of other employees may refuse to accept official assurances that the company is chasing orders in order to stave off redundancies.

The temptation to disbelieve information is particularly strong when good news is expected but the reverse occurs. For example, if sales have been booming, management may refuse at first to believe figures that show a downturn. Even if they believe this particular set of figures they may not take the appropriate action, such as reducing prices, preferring to treat the downturn as a chance occurrence or temporary aberration from the long-term trend. There are many examples of companies that have refused to heed warning signs such as falling sales and profits until bankruptcy was imminent.

Language Difficulties

When the source of the communication is a machine, the recipient may not fully understand the language used, which may involve combinations of sounds, colours, shapes, etc. A great deal of effort has been put into compiling computer languages which correspond as closely as possible to the language of everyday use. The aim is to enable people to communicate freely with computers either by writing and reading or, looking ahead, by talking and listening.

If communication is between individuals, understanding can be impeded by the use of technical jargon, accents and by difficulties in the interpretation of foreign languages. This problem is growing in importance as business becomes more technical and international and is very difficult to overcome.

Organizational Climate

A sudden change in organizational climate or management style can lead to a breakdown in communication. A change in senior management, a change of shop stewards, or the unionization of a previously non-unionized organization can all have a major impact on communication.

Source Credibility

If the person making the communication is not trusted the communication itself is less likely to be believed (see the earlier section on the accuracy of communication).

Management's Response to Communication Problems

As we said before, the more aware managers are of communication problems, the better equipped they will be to prevent such problems arising in their own organization. The prevention of such problems—including those which may partly be the fault of the listener—is management's responsibility.

Such problems are least likely to arise if managers create the right organizational climate and a management style appropriate to the situation. They should also reinforce each communication as soon as possible (actions speak louder than words), try to put themselves in the situation of those receiving the communication, and always provide for sufficient feedback.

This involves paying attention to all the aspects of communication considered earlier: communication systems, communication channels and the art of communication.

COMMUNICATIONS IN PRACTICE

Having demonstrated in the previous chapter the importance of good communication we now consider in detail three practical applications; writing a report; attending and chairing a meeting; giving a speech, talk or lecture.

Guidelines for Report Writing

Report writing is one of the most common communication activities undertaken by many employees, including managers. Reports are fundamental to the communication system within most organizations. Because they are formal, written and often available for wide circulation, it is worthwhile taking care over their content and presentation. Many an employee's promotion prospects have been enhanced by a particularly well-presented report at a crucial stage in his career.

In preparing a report the original writer has to bear in mind (a) what to say, i.e. the terms of reference and content; (b) how to say it, i.e. the style and phraseology; (c) who is going to read the report. These three issues are inter-related. For example, a highly technical report aimed at technically qualified readers can utilize technical jargon. On the other hand, if the report is aimed at non-technical readers the amount of technical jargon will be kept at minimum and indeed the on the whole a different approach will be adapted.

A report differs from other forms of communication by the fact that it is a permanent record of the author's thoughts, available for people to see over a long period of time. It can be referred to many times and, as many politicians have found to their cost, it can be embarrassing to be confronted by a report, written some time previously, showing a completely different viewpoint from that held at the present time.

For certain types of communication a report may be the only acceptable format. For instance, all companies are obliged by law to prepare an annual report, giving specified details of the past year's operations. The terms of reference of a report are often given to the writer by a senior manager, and in this respect the content is to some extent pre-determined. But it may be useful, before starting work on the report, to check the terms of reference to ensure that they cover all the relevant issues and to clarify the purpose of the finished document, since this will also influence the content and presentation. For instance, a report describing a new product might be phrased in one way if the objective is to provide information to the company's salesmen, or in a slightly different way if the objective is to persuade distributors to stock the product, and in yet another way if the report is to serve as the basis of a briefing for the company's advertising agency.

Being sure of the terms of reference helps the writer at the next stage, 'How to say it.' The style of a report is determined by a number of factors, such as the position, inside or outside the organization, of the people who will read it, the nature of the organization's communication channels, and finally the intended effect or impact of the report.

The readership also determines the format of the report's recommendations and conclusions. For instance, if the report is to be read by senior management, terms like 'recommend' or 'strongly advise' would be used. If the report has to be acted upon by more junior employees, a more direct approach would be used. It is far more difficult to write a report for a wide audience composed of people in different positions, with different educational backgrounds, ages and experience,than it is to aim at a more selective group. The danger in writing for a wide audience is that the writer may play it safe and use a soft type of terminology, which may be widely acceptable but which removes much of the 'fire' and reduces the impact of the finished document.

Assuming that the writer has clarified the situation with regard to the factors discussed above, then following the guidelines set out below will go a long way to ensuring that the report receives a sympathetic response.

Research Thoroughly. Make sure that any facts and figures quoted are correct; mistakes will discredit the whole report. Moreover, if it is felt that the mistakes are due to a lack of attention or, even worse, are deliberate, the credibility of the writer may be permanently damaged. Information can be obtained from a large number of sources: surveys, government statistics, files of clippings from newspapers and journals, personal research. In fact, one of the secrets of good report writing is often the ability to select the most salient pieces of information from the mass that is available.

Identify Sections and Headings. A report has a beginning, a middle section which usually examines the various alternatives or options and a final section with conclusions and recommendations. Each of these parts, especially the middle section, may be sub-divided. The various sections should be planned so that a busy reader can get the gist of the report by quickly skimming through it.

Write the First Draft 'as it comes'. All but the simplest reports normally require several drafts. This implies that the writer can allow the words to flow naturally in preparing the first draft, the niceties of style (discussed below) being attended to subsequently. This allows the real character of the writer to show in the report. If the writer can draw on his own experience this will help to show his personality in the report. However, he should include only those experiences that are appropriate, given his terms of reference.

Be Practical and Specific. Words have been described as 'ideas in print' and even though at first draft stage the writer can probably afford to disregard the finer stylistic points, he should try to ensure that the ideas are formulated in a logical, easily understandable style. Moreover, the ideas should be practicable since, if the report is accepted by senior management, the ideas will be put into practice.

It follows that the writer should attempt to be as specific as possible. He should state the terms of reference and objectives. He should examine each option in turn and he should clearly state his conclusions. A report should only be as long as is required to state what the writer wishes to say and to convince the reader of the necessary course of action.

Put Aside. If time allows, it is useful to put the first draft on one side for a few hours or perhaps even a few days. This allows the writer to give further thought to the issues without the distraction of writing. Furthermore, reading after an interval is more likely to show some matters in a different light and suggest the need for modification.

Re-draft, Modifying Content and Style. As suggested above that re-reading is likely to suggest a need for modification. If the report has been researched thoroughly in the first place, the content is unlikely to require much modification although the writer may feel it advisable to change the balance, playing down one point and giving more emphasis to another.

More modification to the style is likely to be needed and the point listed below should receive particular attention.

Engage the Attention of the Reader. A long introduction should be avoided so that the reader can get to the main point as quickly as possible. The opening paragraphs should be used to impress on the reader the importance of the issues to the organization as a whole and to the reader in particular. (However, superlatives should be used sparingly, both in this and other sections). The originator should also seek to put the reader in a frame of mind in which he is receptive to the conclusions to be presented later.

Varying the length of paragraphs and sentences also helps to retain the attention of the reader and reduces the risk of monotony. It also enables the writer to emphasize particular points.

The use of appropriate illustrations and examples can also be helpful in this context. Even the most technical reports can benefit from the use of illustrations, both visual and verbal. These should, of course, be chosen to match the readership.

Finally, it may be useful to consult guidebooks or manuals such as Roget's Thesaurus which can help with the choice of appropriate phrases.

Review. When these modifications have been made, the redrafted report should be reviewed, so that the writer can satisfy himself that the piece as a whole is acceptable. It may also be useful at this point to ask a colleague, who is familiar with the framework, to read the report and comment on readability, presentation, logic, accuracy, etc. If there are points on which the writer is not an expert, but on which he wishes to be doubly sure, he may wish to consult someone who is an expert.

Final Draft into Finished Document. The preparation of a further draft gives the opportunity to make any final modifications suggested by the review. Also at this stage the writer prepares the final instructions to the typist or whoever is responsible for the production of the finished article. Previous drafts might already have been typed and if the report is long, an automatic typewriter or word processor that can store and edit texts has its merits!

A long report may also require binding, and care should be taken that the first impression of the reader is favourable. A poor binding or dog-eared pages reduces the impact of the report.

Despatch. In some cases the writer will have been given instructions as to who is to receive the report. It may, for example, be only his immediate superiors. In these cirusmstances the only task is to ensure that it is despatched to these persons.

ATTENDING AND CHAIRING A MEETING

Most managers spend a considerable amount of time in meetings of one kind or another. In the public sector, meetings (and committee meetings in particular) are the cornerstone of the whole operation of managing, for example, a local authority. Because of the importance of meetings and their cost, especially in terms of managerial time, it is essential that they are properly planned and run so that they achieve their objectives as a communication medium without undue time wasting.

Advantages of Meetings as a Means of Communication

From the communications viewpoints, a meeting of several individuals, be it a committee meeting or a less formal meeting e.g. a weekly progress meeting, has several advantages.

1. It provides a means of instant communication with those present, minimizing the risk of errors in the communication chain.

2. Instant feedback, reactions, explanations, etc., can be given at one time to all interested parties.

3. A number of differing viewpoints can be put forward and tested.

4. Decisions will be shared. This has the advantage of obtaining commitment from all those present and makes future implementation much easier.

5. Young managers, trainees, outside researchers, can attend meetings in an observer's role. They can see the actual decision-making process in action and watch the various participants put their viewpoints, without being an interloper or an obstacle to the decision-making process.

6. Meetings can perform a variety of managerial functions: advisory, decision taking, forward planning, financial, etc. They are therefore a very flexible communication method.

7. Senior managers are provided with a forum in which to demonstrate their managerial skills; this is particularly true of the position of chairman of a meeting, about which more is said later.

Disadvantages of Meetings

1. Any method of communication that involves a number of people spending a period of time together will inevitably be costly, particularly if the participants are senior managers.

2. Meetings often require considerable additional communication time and effort, e.g. the preparation of agendas, minutes, research, etc.

3. Shared responsibility for the decisions taken may mean that no one individual can be responsible or relied upon to get things done; (although a good chairman will ensure that responsibility for the implementation of decisions is agreed).

4. A strong chairman will often get his or her way irrespective of the wishes of the meeting. An individual decision may be presented as a collective decision even though the majority do not really agree with it. This is a form of 'corporate dishonesty' and can be very bad for morale.

5. Friction between departments and individuals may come to the surface in meetings. This is not always a bad thing but it requires skilful chairmanship to overcome the problems and make progress towards an agreed solution.

The Importance of the Chairman

The skill of the chairman can determine whether a meeting is a success or failure. A manager's communication skills are tested to the full when he or she takes on the role of chairman and these general, as opposed to professional management, skills are not necessarily present in all managers. Consequently care must be exercised in the choice of chairman.

Ideally the chairman should possess the following skills:

1. The ability to manage a meeting to ensure it achieves its objectives.

2. The capability of smoothing over differences between individuals and departments and obtaining a consensus whenever possible

3. The skill of 'getting the feel' of the meeting.

4. Independence, combined with the ability to inject some sense of status into the position of chairman.

5. Being able to communicate the results of the meeting to outsiders, and having the ability to fight to get recommendations implemented.

Chairing a Meeting

As each meeting is, in one way or another, unique (e.g. the mood of the meeting may be different from the last meeting, there may be different people present), a chairman must have a flexible approach. He will set the tone of the meeting by his opening remarks, explaining the purpose, and outlining the agenda items. He should make sure that the overall objectives of the meeting are clearly understood and should pay attention, in particular, to the following points:

In *Preparing the agenda* the chairman should ensure that the items are placed in the correct order so that the main issues are considered before subsidiary ones. An experienced chairman knows that the strategic placing of items on the agenda can influence their success or failure. For example, early items often receive extensive discussion because time is not pressing. As the end of the meeting approaches, or as lunch or tea looms nearer, items may pass through almost 'on the nod' as people rush to get through the remaining items. A very controversial item placed early on the agenda can allow everyone to 'let off steam'; they may then be more prepared to be co-operative on later agenda items. The reverse could happen of course and the chairman should carefully weigh the benefits against the risks involved.

It is another function of the chairman to find out what issues other people may wish to raise and be prepared for them to be raised on the agenda or under 'any other business.' All relevant information relating to the agenda should be sent out to everyone concerned so that they can come to the meeting fully briefed.

The chairman has the following responsibilities in *running the meeting:*

(a) Keeping to the agenda unless there is a very good reason to do otherwise.

(b) Controlling time, i.e. keeping the participants' discussion to the points on the agenda and stopping people going off on issues or taking too much of the meeting's time at the expense of other issues.

(c) Steering the meeting to a decision and obtaining a commitment from a specific person or persons to implement that decision.

(d) Ensuring that all decisions and any major points of discussion are faithfully recorded. The chairman must check the minutes, ensure that they are a fair and reasonable record of the meeting's deliberations and distribute them to all interested parties.

DELIVERING A SPEECH

Those readers who are fortunate (or unfortunate) enough to spend time at lectures, speeches, or more social addresses, know the difficulty in trying to recall all the speaker said. In a one hour lecture, for example, the listening or attention pattern would be roughly as follows. For the first five minutes the audience is settling in and adjusting to the speaker. The next twenty to thirty minutes is the main period of fairly concentrated attention, this being followed by a period during which attention wanders as the listeners consider the speaker's mannerisms, the architecture of the lecture theatre, or the essay that must be completed that evening. The final five or ten minutes are normally fairly attentive as the audience gears itself to a final listening effort, secure in the knowledge that the end is in sight.

From this not untypical breakdown one can see that the speaker has the listener's undivided attention for only about half the scheduled hour. But the problem does not end there. Some of the information absorbed during this half hour will be forgotten before the listener leaves the room, and most of the remainder will be forgotten over the next few days. It is a rare individual who can recall five or six main points made in a speech or a lecture two weeks ago. This is no wonder that skilled, experienced lecturers often insist on their audience taking notes, or make use of copious handouts.

The less experienced person who is called upon to address meetings only occasionally, is likely to face similar problems, and he may be less well equipped to deal with them. But whatever a person's inherent ability as a lecturer or speaker, he can expect to improve his performance, i.e. the audience is more likely to absorb and retain what he has to say, if he pays careful attention to the following points.

Topic

In most cases, the broad area to be covered will be self-evident. The sales director addressing a sales convention will be expected to deal with past sales performance, factors affecting future sales, new products in the pipeline, future advertising campaigns, etc. The personnel officer, addressing a group of newly recruited management trainees, will no doubt describe the main features of the organization—number of employees, location of offices and factories, employee conditions, etc. and give an outline of the management training programme.

But the speaker will often have some discretion as to what areas he covers and he should choose only those areas in which he is an expert. If there are areas on which he feels his audience would like to have information, but on which he is not competent to speak, he should clearly identify these areas and indicate where his listeners could obtain the required information.

Audience

It follows from the previous points that the speaker must try to identify in advance the composition of his audience. It may not be sufficient for the managing director to know that he is to address a group of branch or departmental managers. He should know which branches or departments will be represented, so that he can deal with topics of particular interest to them.

If the audience is external to the organization it may be helpful to be informed about their political bias, their views on current economic issues and the aims and objectives of the professional bodies or societies to which they belong. Thus informed, the speaker is less likely to offend the audience with adverse consequences for the organization he represents.

Audio-Visual Aids

Audio-visual aids have two chief advantages. First, they enable information to be presented in such a way that it can be easily and quickly absorbed by the listeners. Second, when the speaker introduces, say a tape-slide sequence, the change in the method of presentation helps to avoid monotony or boredom and helps to maintain the listener's attention.

However, there are some risks attached to the use of audio-visual aids. One of the present writers remembers being asked to address a group of students in a school where he was assured a projector would be available. He planned his talk around a series of slides—most unwisely as it turned out, since the low-powered projector was completely inadequate given the bright sun pouring through the windows! Failures occur even in the best organized institutions, as shown by the blank screen that occasionally faces millions of viewers in the middle of a television news programme.

Notes

Few speakers feel confident enough to appear without any notes, but these may range from a few headings scribbled on the back of an envelope, to a transcript of the entire speech. The former has the advantage of giving scope for spontaneity. The latter ensures that no important point is missed out. The final choice will depend partly on the speaker's preferred style and party upon the nature of the address. An after-dinner speech, marking a colleague's retirement, is quite different from the chairman's address to the shareholder's Annual General Meeting.

Presentation

In some instances, such as the announcement of where redundancies are to fall, the content of the address will be of such interest that the audience will listen carefully however bad the presentation may be. But in most instances the presentation is important and the speaker should seek to attract and retain the audience's attention. It has been suggested that a teacher should tell his pupils what he is about to say, say it, and tell them that he has said it. Even with more mature audiences this is sound advice: a preview helps to gain attention and a summary helps to reinforce the message.

It also helps to retain the audience's attention if the speaker varies the tone, pitch and speed of his delivery. He should also avoid mannerisms, such as extreme gesticulations and constantly patrolling the platform, which distract attention from what he is saying. The language, e.g. technical and non-technical, should obviously be appropriate to the audience, and anecdotes and illustrations can help to enliven the presentation.

On a more personal note, the dress of the speaker can also play a major part in determining the audience's reaction to the content of the speech. Care should always be taken to ensure that this area of personal presentation is appropriate to the tone and setting of the event.

An experienced speaker is often able to judge his impact from the reactions of the audience and, if appropriate, to modify his presentation accordingly. If he feels that he has failed to put across an important point then he should re-state it in a different way. If he feels that audience participation would be useful, he might break off and invite questions.

INTERDEPENDENCE AND COORDINATION

Both the natural-system and rational models of complex organizations assume interdependence of organizational parts, the rational model being somewhat more specific about the location of interdependence and somewhat more circumscribed about the nature of the interdependence assumed.

To assume that an organization is composed of interdependent parts is not necessarily to say that each part is dependent on, and supports, every other part in any direct way. The X branch of an organization may not interact at all with the *Y* branch, and neither may have contact with the Z branch. Yet they may be interdependent in the sense that unless each performs adequately, the total organization is jeopardized; failure of any one can threaten the whole and thus the other parts. We can describe this situation as one in which each part renders a discrete contribution to the whole and each is supported by the whole. We will call this *pooled interdependence.*

Interdependence may also take a serial form, with the *A* plant producing parts which become inputs for the *B* assembly operation. Here both make contributions to and are sustained by the whole organization, and so there is a pooled aspect to their interdependence. But, in addition, direct interdependence can be pinpointed between them, and the order of that interdependence can be specified. *A* must act properly before *B* can act: and unless *B* acts, *A* cannot solve its output problem. We will refer to this as *sequential interdependence,* and note that it is not symmetrical.

A third form of interdependence can be labeled *reciprocal,* referring to the situation in which the outputs of each become inputs for the others. This is illustrated by the airline which contains both operations and maintenance units. The production of the maintenance unit is an input for operations, in the form of a serviceable aircraft; and the product (or by-product) of operations is an input for maintenance, in the form of an aircraft needing maintenance. Under conditions of reciprocal interdependence, each unit involved is penetrated by the other. There is, of course, a pooled aspect to this, and there is also a serial aspect since the aircraft in question is used by one, then by the other, and again by the first. But the distinguishing aspect is the reciprocity of the interdependence with each unit posing contingency for the other.

In the above illustrations—and in reality, we believe—the types of interdependence form a Guttman-type scale: all organizations have pooled interdependence; more complicated organizations have sequential as well as pooled; and the most complex have reciprocal, sequential, and pooled. Knowing that an organization contains reciprocal interdependence automatically tells us that it also contains sequential and pooled interdependence. Knowing that an organization contains sequential interdependence tells us that it also contains the pooled type. Knowing that an organization contains pooled interdependence, however, does not tell us whether it has the others.

In the order introduced, the three types of interdependence are increasingly difficult to coordinate because they contain increasing degrees of contingency. With pooled interdependence, action in each position can proceed without regard to action in other positions so long as the overall organization remains viable. With sequential interdependence, however, each position in the set must be readjusted if any one of them acts improperly or fails to meet expectations. There is always an element of potential contingency with sequential interdependence. With reciprocal interdependence, contingency is not merely potential, for the actions of each position in the set must be adjusted to the actions of one or more others in the set.

Because the three types of interdependence are, in the order indicated, more difficult to co-ordinate, we will say that they are most costly to coordinate, noting that measurement of such costs is far from perfect.

Coordination

In a situation of interdependence, concerted action come about through coordination; and if there are different types of interdependence, we would expect to find different devices for achieving coordination. The work of March and Simon is particularly useful for this purpose.

Under some conditions coordination may be achieved by *standardization*. This involves the establishment of routines or rules which constrain action of each unit or position into paths consistent with those taken by others in the interdependent relationship. An important assumption in coordination by standardization is that the set of rules be internally consistent, and this requires that the situations to which they apply be relatively stable, repetitive, and few enough to permit matching of situations with appropriate rules.

In the March and Simon formulation, *co-ordination by plan* involves the establishment of schedules for the interdependent units by which their actions may then be governed. Co-ordination by plan does not require the same high degree of stability and routinization that are required for co-ordination by standardization, and therefore is more appropriate for more dynamic situations, especially when a changing task environment impinges on the organization.

A third form can be called *coordination by mutual adjustment*, and involves the transmission of new information during the process of action. (In March and Simon terms, this is "co-ordination by feedback," but the term "feedback" has gathered a connotation of super/subordination which unduly restricts it for our purposes. Co-ordination by mutual adjustment may involve communication across hierarchical lines, but it cannot be assumed that it necessarily does.) The more variable and unpredictable the situation, March and Simon observe, the greater the reliance on coordination by mutual adjustment.

Now we can make two observations about interdependence and co-ordination which are crucial to our examination of structure:

(1) There are distinct parallels between the three types of interdependence and the three types of co-ordination. With pooled interdependence, co-ordination by standardization is appropriate; with sequential interdependence co-ordination by plan is appropriate; and with reciprocal interdependence, co-ordination by mutual adjustment is called for.

(2) The three types of co-ordination, in the order introduced above, place increasingly heavy burdens on communication and decision. Standardization requires less frequent decisions and a smaller volume of communication during a specific period of operations than does planning, and planning calls for less deci-

sion and communication activity than does mutual adjustment. There are very real costs involved in co-ordination.

Departmentalization

Luther Gulick, one of the pioneers of the administrative management school, observed that positions or components of organizations could be grouped, or separated, on four different bases: (1) common purpose or contribution to the larger organization, (2) common processes, (3) a particular clientele, or (4) a particular geographic area. These are, in brief, alternative ways of *homogenizing* positions or components. The difficulty with this scheme, and the difficulties real-life organizations have in choosing methods of grouping, lies in the fact that positions or components of complex organizations are not unidimensional. Homogenizing them on one dimension does not homogenize them on all dimensions. As Simon has noted, placing school health activities in the department of education relates those activities to other educational efforts, but prevent the assignment of school health activities to a health department where they would be related to other medical activities.

The fact is that complex organizations meet all four problems indicated by Gulick. Their components serve different purposes for the larger organization, they employ several processes, they frequently serve more than one clientele, and for the most part they are geographically extended. The question is not which criterion to use for grouping, but rather in which *priority* are the several criteria to be exercised. That priority, we suggest, is determined by the nature and location of interdependency, which is a function of both technology and task environment.

The question of the grouping of positions can be stated as a matter of arranging for some positions to be *tangent* to one another. Shall position *A* be placed tangent to position *B* or to position *H*? Should positions *A, B,* and *H* all be tangent to one another, or is it imperative that position *H* be placed tangent to *X*, which requires that it be removed from direct linkage with positions *A* and *B*?

We have argued that coordination by mutual adjustment is more costly, involving greater decision and communication burdens, than coordination by plan, which in turn is more costly than coordination by standardization. We would therefore expect first priority to be given to grouping in such a way as to minimize the more costly forms of coordination.

Organizations seek to place reciprocally interdependent positions tangent to one another, in a common group which is (a) local and (b) conditionally autonomous.

There is nothing startling about the fact that when technology calls for action by crews or teams, the necessary positions are grouped into crews or teams; this is commonplace at the grass roots, or lowest levels, of complex organizations. A more subtle aspect, however, is the localization of such groups. Because coordination by mutual adjustment is expensive, and its costs increase as the number of positions involved increases, we would expect organizations facing reciprocal interdependence to fashion the smallest possible groups.

Now if *A*, *B*, and *C* are reciprocally interdependent members of a team or crew and interact only among themselves, coordination is less troublesome than if one or more of the members were also reciprocally interdependent with *X*, or *Y*, or *Z*. Autonomy of the group as such facilitates coordination by mutual adjustment, but we must recognize that autonomy is modified; the fully autonomous unit would not be or remain a part of the organization. Thus we have used the term *conditionally autonomous*, and we would argue that organizations seek to group reciprocally interdependent positions into local units, autonomous within the constraints established by plans and standardization.

In the absence of reciprocal interdependence, organizations subject to rationality norms seek to place sequentially interdependent positions tangent to one another, in a common group which is (a) localized and (b) conditionally autonomous.

The costs of planning grow rapidly as the number of variables increases and as the lines of communication lengthen. The costs of planning are therefore minimized when done in small units rather than large ones, and we would expect organizations to lodge the planning chore in the smallest possible cluster of serially interdependent positions.

In the absence of reciprocal and sequential interdependence, organizations subject to norms of rationality seek to group positions homogeneously to facilitate coordination by standardization.

By definition a complex organization contains differentiation of parts, hence heterogeneity. But to the extent that technological requirements permit and environmental fluctuations can be warded off the grouping of positions performing similar processes permits coordination to be handled in the least costly manner. Homogeneity facilitates coordination because one set of rules applies to all positions in the group; and when changes in rules are necessary, one set of changes applies to all.

Hierarchy

Our argument can so far be summarized in the following form: The basic units are formed to handle reciprocal interdependence, if any. If there is none, then the basic units are shaped according to sequential interdependence, if any. If neither of the more complicated types of interdependence exists, the basic units are shaped according to common processes.

Problems arise, however, if the three types of interdependence form a Guttman-type scale, where all organizations have pooled interdependence; more complex organizations also have sequential interdependence, and the most complex have reciprocal interdependence in addition to the other two forms. If the basic groups are formed to deal satisfactorily with reciprocal interdependence, they still must deal with the other types. Moreover, it is not always possible to contain reciprocal interdependence within first-order groupings

When reciprocal interdependence cannot be confined to intragroup activities, organizations subject to rationality norms seek to link the groups involved into a second-order group, as localized and conditionally autonomous as possible.

On occasion, reciprocal interdependence is so extensive that to link all of the involved positions into one group would overtax communication mechanisms. When this occurs, organizations rank-order the interdependent positions in terms of the amount of contingency each poses for the others. Those with the greatest intercontingency form a group, and the resulting groups are then clustered into an overarching second-order group.

We have now introduced the first step in a *hierarchy*. It is unfortunate that this term has come to stand almost exclusively for degrees of highness or lowness, for this tends to hide the basic significance of hierarchy for complex organizations. Each level is not simply higher than the one below, but is a more inclusive *clustering,* or combination of interdependent groups, to handle those aspects of coordination which are beyond the scope of any of its components.

Chester Barnard noted that for every group in a complex organization there is one position which also "belongs" to another group, composed of representatives of other groups. It is our contention that the composition of each more inclusive group is determined by coordination requirements—by the locus of interdependence or contingency. The first rule for composition of this second order combination is to dispose of reciprocal interdependence not adequately handled by the initial grouping of positions.

After grouping units to minimize coordination by mutual adjustment, organizations under rationality norms seek to place sequentially interdependent groups tangent to one another, in a cluster which is localized and conditionally autonomous.

Again at the level of intergroup ties, as in the case of interposition ties, we are saying that after reciprocal interdependence has been solved by grouping, the criterion of sequential interdependence has been solved by grouping, the criterion of sequential interdependence is employed.

After grouping units to solve problems of reciprocal and sequential interdependence, organizations under norms of rationality seek to cluster groups into homogeneous units to facilitate coordination by standardization.

We would expect to find this criterion for higher-order clustering of groups only in relatively simple organizations. In the more complicated organizations, the criteria of reciprocal and sequential interdependence tend to exhaust the clustering possibilities before this third criterion can be exercised. In complex organizations, then, we would expect:

When higher-priority coordination requirements prevent the clustering of similar positions or groups, organizations seek to blanket homogeneous positions under rules which cut across group boundaries, and to blanket similar groups under rules which cross divisional lines.

We asserted that when dealing with coordination by mutual adjustment or by planning, organizations seek to localize interaction and to confine it to conditionally autonomous groups—to cluster positions and groups into the smallest possible inclusive units in order to minimize coordination costs. When coordinating via standardization, however, organizations seek to make rules pervasive in order to apply to the widest possible categories. Where grouping on the basis of common procedures is not feasible, organizations may still employ standardization by devising rules which apply to certain processes or categories of activity whenever and wherever these occur in the organization.

When organization employ standardization which cuts across multiple groupings, they also develop liaison positions linking the several groups and the rule-making agency.

We find a variety of "staff" positions in complex organizations, many of which are intended as linkages between operating groups and standard-formulating centres. Illustrative are personnel or industrial relations specialists at intermediate levels of the hierarchy who presumably advise specialists of other types when personnel or industrial relations actions are involved. Similarly, accountants or controllers at intermediate levels are presumably expert counselors to those levels on matters pertaining to the accounting for action. In both cases, of course, the staff specialists are as likely to be as responsive to the rule-formulating centres as to the level they advise.

These liaison or staff positions are appropriate when the interdependence is of the pooled type, requiring the formulation, interpretation, and application of rules for standardization. They are less effective for other types of interdependence, and complex organizations typically employ other devices to deal with interdependence which spills over or is not contained by the usual formal structure.

Organizations with sequential interdependence not contained by departmentalization rely on committees to accomplish the remaining coordination.

Organizations with reciprocal interdependence not contained by departmentalization rely on task-force or project groupings to accomplish the remaining coordination.

4

MANAGEMENT INFORMATION SYSTEMS

Management Information Systems are planned and organized approaches to supplying executives with intelligence aids that facilitate the managerial process. Table I contrasts the difference between conventional data processing and MIS. Increasingly, management information systems are designed to take advantage of modern tools and techniques. Fundamental to the concept is the tenet that information is a catalyst of management and is the ingredient that coalesces the managerial functions of planning, operating, decision making, and controlling.

Information is the symbolic representation of the real world (money, manpower, materials, machines, markets, etc.). Since decision-makers rely on information systems to supply them with intelligence that will influence the selection of particular means and ends, it is essential that the information system be an accurate representation of the real world. This underscores the need for a carefully designed and reliable operating information system: otherwise, a manager can be making decisions based on information that does not portray the real world.

Table 1

Data Processing and MIS Compared

	Routinized
Data Processing	Accounting-Oriented
	Historical
	Internal Focus
	Mechanistic
	Basic-Computations
	Non-Managerial Output
	Non-Routinized and Novel
Management Information System	Intelligence-Oriented
	Futuristic
	External, as well as Internal, Focus
	Behavioristic
	Complex Computations
	Managerial Output

The constantly increasing complexity of society, the growth in size of many organizations the expanding information demands, the short age of specialized human skills—these and other factors have increased the interest in a disciplined and analytical approach to the gathering, storage, processing, selection, and dissemination of information.

A fundamental consideration in the design and development of management information systems is determining which is the vital information needed for maintaining and extending the organization at desired levels of stability and growth. The selection of the key information requirements, from the universe of information available, prevents information underload or information overload. Thus, there follows the requisite that management itself must be deeply involved, along with technicians, in the overall specifications of management information systems.

The management information system should be viewed as essentially dynamic and subject to continual review and renewal. This viewpoint is required to avoid the situation of an information system which is out-of-phase with the environment and the current needs of managers. It need not necessarily be constrained by accounting conventions or legal requirements and governmental regulations: rather, the MIS is a flexible instrument which often is futuristic-oriented and combines external information with the organization's internal information.

A significant trend is that of organizational data bases. The data base is a carefully planned structure of basic data elements of the organization; the data are usually stored in a device that can be interfaced with a computer which permits various combinations of the data elements to be used. Also, the data base can be interrogated from some remote points (e.g. an executive's office), by use of a variety of data terminals (e.g. video displays, printers) connected, by communications lines, to the computer.

The data base has several important implications for MIS. First, it normally assumes that the fundamental data elements, vital to the organization, have been rigorously identified. Second, the data files are so defined and structured as to assure reliability and integration of all data elements. Third, the accessibility of a variety of data elements permits increased flexibility and responsiveness of the system for unique as well as recurring informational requirements. The data base should preferably be developed to provide for a certain open-endedness; that is, the specifications should provide for orderly growth and the capacity to absorb data elements overlooked in the original design.

Cost-effectiveness must be an important consideration in the design of the system. High quality data, large quantities of data, and rapidly available data involve higher costs for the management information system; however, the cost of the information must be balanced against the resulting reduction of uncertainty increased predictability of events, and more responsive managerial decision-making.

The MIS approach usually provides management with new information that previously was not envisioned, or which could not reasonably be obtained (cost- or time-wise) by conventional means. For example, the MIS may involve:

(1) Analysis of the organization's performance (by product line, geographical area; etc.) compared to the best information about competitors.

(2) Use of several economic forecasts or econometric models to determine the likely conditions the organization will find itself in forthcoming time periods.

(3) Use of input-output models to determine under- or over-exploited markets.

(4) Quicker signals about operational variations from desired plans, so that managerial corrections can be taken before extensive degradation has taken place.

The success of MIS is, of course, highly dependent on the availability of particularly competent executives and technicians who are versed in the organization's policies and procedures and the new managerial technologies of computer, systems analysis, management sciences, etc. While the MIS promises significant benefits in providing management with improved knowledge aids for decision-making, there is the need for relatively substantial commitments of time and money for its design, development, and maintenance, including its related computer, communications, and other equipment. The organization must use sound methods of appraising the MIS approach, and of determining which kind of MIS best suits the requirements and resources of the organization.

A CASE EXAMPLE

Texas Instruments Incorporated (TI) is a highly diversified, multinational corporation and a leader in today's "electronic revolution." This leadership position has resulted from 50 years of innovation and high technology developments.

TI Growth

The forerunner of today's Texas Instruments was established in 1930 as Geophysical Service. The company grew in two directions with two names: a parent company, the Coronado Corporation, was involved with oil production, and a subsidiary. Geophysical Service Inc., was involved with seismic exploration. With the onset of World War II, a new opportunity presented itself—magnetic airborne detection (MAD) systems which would locate enemy submarines. By taking advantage of this opportunity, the company entered a new field—military electronics.

In 1951, "Texas Instruments" became the company name: and in 1952 solid state technology in the form of the transistor opened the door for extraordinary growth and creativity. The invention of the integrated circuit in 1958 was a critical achievement that provided a base for future developments in electronics. In 1959, TI acquired Metals & Controls Corporation of Attleboro, Massachusetts, the company's only major merger. A key ingredient of TI's growth was the decision to expand manufacturing operations worldwide. Beginning with Bedford, England, in 1957. TI began operations in Europe. In 1968, TI began operations in the Far East with a plant in Tokyo. Today, TI employs more than 86,000 people and has a worldwide network of 50 major plants in 19 countries with worldwide sales and service offices.

The company has several major business groups which produce and market a wide spectrum of products from radar to hand-held calculators. In 1979, IT's net sales billed reached $3.2 billion. TI's goal for the late 1980s is $15 billion annual net sales billed.

According to J. Fred Bucy, TI President and Chief Operating Officer, at the 1980 Stockholder's Meeting, "One measure of TI'S leadership in technology in our patent position. TI holds more than 5,200 patents worldwide, but it is quality that counts more than the numbers... The ability of TI's innovators to think conceptually and bring concept to reality in the marketplace is TI's lifeblood." This philosophy is currently producing technological advances in semiconductor devices solid-state software, speech synthesis, microprocessors and mini-computers, software technology, thermal printing, defense electronics petroleum exploration, and in TI's solar energy system.

TI's growth, which has led to geographical dispersion of people and plant sites has presented major challenges and opportunities for TI management. One of the greatest challenges has been to provide the necessary flow of information and provide adequate communications between numerous multinational sites, considering the social, economic, and legal implications of doing business. The development of a rapid and reliable computer-communications network became vital to TI's continued growth.

TI Computing History

TI established its first data processing center in Dallas, Texas, in 1955, with the traditional programmers, key-punch equipment, and IBM hardware. Evolutions of centralized vs. decentralized concepts were tried. What started as a handful of EDP personnel and a few pieces of hardware located at the Corporate headquarters has mushroomed into a worldwide Information Systems and Services (IS&S) organization of approximately 2,000 people.

IS&S Organization

Information Systems and Services is chartered to provide computer systems and communications capability to TI worldwide. It is responsible for operating the Corporate Information Center (CIC), operating the data and voice communications network; defining, developing, and maintaining the computer-communications network, and providing distributed processing capability to TI world-wide users. It defines, develops, and operates application systems for TI's engineering, manufacturing, marketing, and control and administration activities.

Information Systems and Services personnel are now embedded in each of the TI business groups and staff functions to ensure that all TI organizations have management information systems and computer-communications network capabilities at all levels of the company. The create, make, market, and control functions of business are all linked through one of the most technologically advanced computer-communications networks and array of business and engineering application systems in use by the private sector today.

The management systems made possible by this worldwide network are key factors in continuing the company's productivity improvements. Engineers are pioneering interactive graphics to develop new engineering information data bases to aid their design work. Global production planning, manufacturing automation and control, and tracking material in-transit between sites are now realities. Every organization in TI uses standard on-line systems for financial planning and control, general ledger, and a worldwide personnel data base.

TI's Computer-Communications Network

TI currently has 300 remote job-entry terminals, over 8,500 inquiry terminals, and almost 200 distributed computers connected to the network. These terminals and distributed computers, interface with the general purpose computers in the Corporate Information Center (CIC), TI's Dallas-based central computer facility, and with the Scientific Computers located in Austin, Texas, which are used for seismic processing.

TI uses a significant number of distributed processors for interactive processing, having local data storage and terminal access to other distributed processors in the network and to the central computer facility. Programs and data are transferred to and from other processors in the network. Applications span engineering, manufacturing, marketing, control, and software development.

The Corporate Information Center is driven by six IBM 3033 computers. These computers have access to 376 disk drives and 80 tape drives. They operate in a loosely coupled multi-processor environment managed by JES3 software. In order to maintain the high degree of reliability essential for TI's requirements, all software and hardware systems are fully tested on an IBM 4341 computer in a virtual machine environment prior to being placed into production.

TI's international communications network circuits are satellite based. A 56 kilobit circuit between Dallas and Singapore serves the plant sites in Singapore, Malyasia, Taiwan, and Australia. A 19.2 kilobit connection between Dallas and Tokyo serves the four plant sites in Japan. Serving Europe, TI has three 50 kilobit lines with lower speed circuits used for voice communications and as emergency backup for the 50 kilobit links. Central America and South America are served with 9.6 kilobit links to El Salvador, Panama, and Brazil; and low-speed lines to Mexico and Argentina.

The communications network utilizes TI-developed Texas Instruments Communications Grid (TICOG) TI980/990 minicomputers, with TI-developed packet switching software to manage the data flow around the world. There are currently 32 TICOG's supporting this net-work.

This international network supports remote job-entry stations, distributed processors, and inquiry terminals. The network allows the multiplexing of these multiple devices and multiple functions such as Information Management System (IMS), Time Sharing Option (TSO), Job Entry System (JES), and distributed processor access over a single communications line. Alternate routing, used in cases of circuit outages, gives improved reliability to the communications network. By utilizing a continuous transmit/selective retransmit protocol, a 4 to 1 improvement in line utilization is realized over conventional protocols on these satellite links. Priority queuing for the interactive functions minimizes the impact of communications delays within the network.

This sophisticated network enables TI to process and store data in Dallas and at the various sites where distributed computers are located, from remote job entry and enquiry terminals at TI sites worldwide. In addition to processing an enormous volume of both batch and inquiry transactions each day, the network serves other requirements, such as electronic mailing and electronic filing.

Three Management Systems

TI's highly efficient computer-communications network has made possible the development of numerous systems which improve people effectiveness throughout the organization. Three such systems are: (1) MODPLAN, TI's planning and control system; (2) MSG, the company's electronic mailing system; and (3) TIOLR (TI On Line Reporting System), an electronic filing system. Office automation is a major thrust at TI, and these three systems used with the TI Office System word processor play a vital role in improving the productivity of managers, administrators, professionals, secretaries, and clerks throughout the company. The MODPLAN, MSG, and TIOLR systems are discussed in the following paragraphs to illustrate their impact on TI in solving the problems caused by geographic distances of multiple plant sites.

MODPLAN is used for the collection, manipulation, and interrogation of any numerical data which can be arranged by time periods, such as is commonly done in forecasting, planning, budgeting, reporting, and controlling activities. MODPLAN is composed of many diverse data bases which are three dimensional in terms of (1) line items, (2) time periods, and (3) organizational entities. There are currently 90 different data bases in MODPLAN using a total of 18,610 unique entities. MODPLAN is TI's standard financial planning and control tool. While the majority of the MODPLAN data bases deal with financial data, there are also many other applications such as product planning, manufacturing, overhead, and personnel analysis. In general, MODPLAN capabilities are flexible enough to be adapted to many numerical data-base applications and can provide both on-line inquiry and batch reporting.

The message system (MSG) permits video display or hard copy real-time communications to any point in TI's worldwide network. MSG is used for preparation, storage, distribution, and re-distribution of message text. The MSG system supports a broadcast capability allowing a message to be sent to multiple locations; security for storage, access, and distribution; and supports a direct interface to the public telex system. MSG permits messages to be inserted directly from other application systems for automatic distribution to predefined destinations, indicating such events as completion of processing cycles or the availability of computer produced reports. It also provides the capability for individual "electronic post office boxes" for private and timely review of personal messages. MSG is used by engineers, secretaries, managers, planners, controllers, even ships at sea.

TI's geophysical exploration business has a fleet of marine exploration vessels which communicate via MARISAT, a satellite communications link, to the TI computer communications network, and, thus, have access to the MSG electronic mailing system. Benefits to the manager and professional include the speed of communications and the privacy of the electronic mailbox. TI secretaries using TI Office System word processors connected to the computer-communications network can transmit message directly from the word processor while continuing to perform text editing on other documents. A key benefit of MSG is the synchronization of communication worldwide. A message can be sent to any or all points in the network where it can be reviewed in prime time which may not coincide with the sender's prime time. The recipient can then respond on a timely basis. The members of the TI Operating Committee, who report to the President of TI, each have secure terminals which can access this system; the President of TI has three terminals which he uses for communications—one at his office, one at home, and a dial-up portable terminal which he uses when travelling.

The number of MSG transactions increased from 10,000 per day at year end 1977 to an average of 25,000 per day at year end 1979, with a volume at this writing of about 30,000 per day, and an average of four recipients per message. During this period the cost per copy has decreased from eight cents to four cents.

TI'S system for electronic filing is referred to as TIOLR for TI On-Line Reporting. *The TIOLR system* is used for creating, storing, viewing, and retrieving information, and provides worldwide accessibility to this information from any inquiry or TI word processor terminal. Information stored on TIOLR is hierarchically structured by reports, generations, chapters, sections, and pages, and can be retrieved quickly. TI organizations use TIOLR to file standard policies and procedures, computer-generated reports electronic newspapers, reference information, systems documentation, standards, schedules, and other data.

The TI On-Line Reporting capability was introduced in 1977 and its usage has increased dramatically. Currently, there are approximately 12,000 TIOLR reports on-line. About 170,000 transactions per day access this information. Cost per transaction has been reduced from 3.9 cents to 2.7 cents over the past two years.

Benefits of electronic filing for the secretary are that it reduces copying and messengering time, and permits the word processor to create files on central computers, thus making the information created by word processors globally accessible to other users within the network. Thus, a document can be viewed on-line simultaneously at several TI plant sites. Benefits to the manager or professional include accessibility to worldwide information on a timely basis, and selective display of desired information without the need for paper reports.

IS&S Management Philosophy

Ensuring that the TI business group and staff activities have a rapid, reliable, and efficient network is an on-going effort. The Information Systems and Services list of priorities in ranked order are as follows: (1) providing the company with *accurate, secure* information; (2) ensuring *availability* of computer-communications service to all TI organizations; (3) giving TI organizations *efficient service* by improving response time and cost. From 1967 to 1979, IS&S reduced user charges to 40% of 1967 prices. But if one gives effect to the 120% increase in price levels in view of inflation over the same period, user charges have been reduced to 18% of what the 1967 price would be in 1979 dollars. IS&S introduces and implements new system and service capabilities only when data integrity, service availability, and system efficiency criteria have been achieved.

IS&S monitors operating systems performance closely to ensure that optimum service is provided to TI organizations on the worldwide computer-communications network Performance information, including downtime reason and length of time for all major services and response and turnaround time, are stored in data bases. Graphs are made weekly against goals and acceptable limits for major services. Tracking is done for mainframe computers, communications, distributed computers and key information systems. Rigorous tracking has been done since 1974. About 250 parameters are reviewed weekly by Information Systems and Services.

To ensure that IS&S meets TI systems and services requirements, an IS&S strategic planning organization has been implemented. It includes strategies for engineering systems, manufacturing systems, marketing systems control and administration systems, communications, distributed processing, central information services, and people/asset effectiveness. The strategic organization serves to centralize systems planning, design, and implementation for decentralized activities. Each TI business group has the same basic organizations—engineering, manufacturing, marketing and control and administrative activities; therefore, the strategic organization concept promotes standardization of systems and services and reduces duplication of effort across groups, thereby improving productivity.

Distributed Network Architecture

The distributed processing strategy makes possible the decentralization of the create, store, process and retrieval capabilities. The distributed processing-communications network is a four-level hierarchy of interconnected computer systems. Large central systems are referred to as Level I. At this writing, one center is operational in Dallas (the Corporate Information Center) and a second center is scheduled for Lewisville, Texas, in 1982.

At Level I, TI business are provided with standard worldwide application systems such as a personnel data base called Personnel File Management (PFM), MODPLAN, MSG, TIOLR, and many other systems used by all TI organizations.

At Level II, IBM 4341 computers are planned to support TI's major engineering marketing, and manufacturing requirements, and to process these and other systems at the local level. Level II computer are connected to Level I and thus can also access the standard worldwide systems.

Level III and Level IV computers are TI990 minicomputers supporting functions for order entry, work-in-process, financial, and other systems that require extensive real-time interaction. The Level III computers contain the TI990 Distributed Processing System (DPS) software packages. The DPS/990 system was released for use in TI this year. It makes available several capabilities for IS&S application systems using the TI990 computer family. DPS provides an efficient transaction processing environment for both COBOL and PASCAL languages; a communications link to the IS&S worldwide network; communications support for a variety of video and hard copy terminals; and the ability to transfer data files between Level I and Level III computers and between Level II and Level III computers.

Level IV systems are primarily individual work station computers supporting such functions as interactive design in the engineering areas, and word processing in the administrative and clerical areas of TI, or in manufacturing process control.

Using the network, TI business groups can collect, store, and process data at local sites, and/or communicate with other levels in the network heirarchy. Thus, a Level III computer at a plant in Tokyo can access production planning information stored on a Level II or III computer at TI's plant in Bedford, England. This enables TI to operate from multiple geographic sites as if it were based at one location. Through innovative products brought about by the electronic revolution, TI organizations are no longer remote, except for their geographic location. The latest information is immediately available and is as close as the nearest terminal.

Communications Technology

As a result of these new computer communications capabilities and new product technology, TI is already experiencing some revolutionary changes in the way that TI and the many TI customers and vendors conduct their day-to-day business. Here are some examples of the future impact of these capabilities:

Engineers will be using the power of the computer to design products by accessing design data bases at other sites worldwide.

Manufacturing planners will act in harmony with planners at other worldwide sites by interacting with common data bases.

Computer-driven manufacturing lines will produce and test new products.

Product engineering will be enhanced with the ability to inspect parts produced in one part of the world from a distant terminal through digitized images transmitted through the computer network.

Automated warehouses operated from computer consoles will provide products for shipment.

Inventory systems of these products will have worldwide visibility to other sites.

Sales and service offices around the globe will have immediate access to shipment schedules, market trends, statistics, and other pertinent information.

Managers will hold multiple-size electronic conferences without loss of productivity and expense associated with travel time. TIers making trips will be accompanied by portable terminals to enable them to access pertinent computer-stored data associated with their business.

Administrators will in some cases prepare their own memos and correspondence, access data, and electronically communicate through the network from their office via an Office System word processor.

Secretaries will be receiving electronic mail while creating text, sending electronic mail, electronically filing, or inputting data to a system from an Office System word processor connected to the network.

Home computing devices will enable TIers to access airline reservations, stock market exchanges, weather bureaus, library services, and other information at will, thus enabling them to be constantly informed.

Thus, while conquering geographical distances and multiplicity of plant sites, technology and innovation have provided the way of the future that will shape tomorrow's way of doing business. TI is uniquely positioned to "make it happen"—since most of the futuristic capabilities just described are already in place today in some part of TI.

5

CORPORATE ORGANISATIONAL FUNCTIONS

THE current rapid rate of change in the environment within which the organizations operate makes the functions of corporate management difficult. But even in such periods, circumstances and environments it is imperative for managers to look ahead, formulate plans, develop the organization, lead and direct and control the various activities of the corporation. It is with this purpose the present chapter is organised to cover the various functions of the corporate management. Before we delve into these functions let us have a look at the management levels.

Terms such as "top management," "middle management," and "supervisory management" are commonly used, but often there is no clear definition of them. Meanings attached to them sometimes differ from one company to another, so that care must be taken in interpreting discussions of management policy, compensation, and the like for various executive levels. And internally, while most managements seek to apply the same broad policies to all employees, the nature of tasks and measurements of performance change with increasing levels of responsibility, so that it is advantageous to classify jobs into well defined broad groups.

MANAGEMENT LEVELS

The following classification has been adopted by the Executive Compensation Service, American Management Associations:

Top Management

This is the policy-making group responsible for the over-all direction and success of all company activities. It is made up of the Board Chairman, President, Directors who are also officers, other officers, and key top management personnel. Positions other than the Chairman, President and often Executive Vice President, or General Manager are usually directly responsible for a major division or function of the business, but each also carries a responsibility for the performance of the business as a whole, participating in decisions of a company-wide nature and collaborating with others in the group in important matters affecting any or all phases of the company's operations.

Middle Management

This group is responsible for the execution and interpretation of policies throughout the organization, and for the successful operation of assigned divisions or departments. They have a high degree of responsibility for individual initiative and judgment, acting under policies and directives of top management. They have the responsibility for recommending new or revised policies and for establishing objectives of their assigned activities. They generally accomplish results through lower levels of supervision. Important staff functions may be assigned to this group.

Supervisory Management

This is the supervision directly responsible to the middle management group for final execution of policies by rank-and-file employees, and for attainment of objectives in assigned organizational units through practices and procedures approved and issued by top or middle management. It may include assistants to middle management positions and staff functions of a lesser nature than those in the two upper management groups.

Professional and administrative employees, exempt from the Federal Fair Labor Standards Act, may be included in any one of the three groups, depending on the importance of individual duties. For example, a consulting engineer could be a member of top management even though he is not responsible for the supervision of any company activity, provided he has the primary function of assisting other officers in important policy decisions. Likewise, engineers could be included in either the middle or supervisory group, depending upon the nature and importance of their duties. The term "management" is used for want of a more descriptive word, the purpose being to include in one of three broad groups all salaried positions that are exempt from Federal wage and hour regulations.

These definitions are further refined in some companies by reference to organization levels, job grade levels, or salary amounts, although this must be done with care and understanding because arbitrary limitations are not always applicable. For example, an assistant to the president is on the second level of an organization chart but the group in which the position would be included would depend on whether the duties are executive, administrative, or secretarial. Also, some companies use only two groupings for executive compensation purposes, combining the first two into one group.

THE PLANNING FUNCTION

All organizations, big or small, are faced by a number of questions. How can we best use our resources? What is the most favourable time for branching out in a new direction? Which way of meeting a particular objective should we choose of the several that are available? In formulating answers to such questions, managers are operating some form of planning system. Planning systems are tailored to the needs of individual organizations, and reflect differences in management style and in the number of managers involved. But most medium- and large-scale organizations (especially in the private sector) employ systems which embody the various steps or elements shown in Figure 1.

Although Figure 1 shows the planning process as a series of discrete steps, with one leading to another, it should be emphasized that in practice there may be overlap between two steps, and that a considerable amount of feedback may be built into the system. For example the organization's objectives will be heavily influenced by the opportunities that it perceives; similarly some of

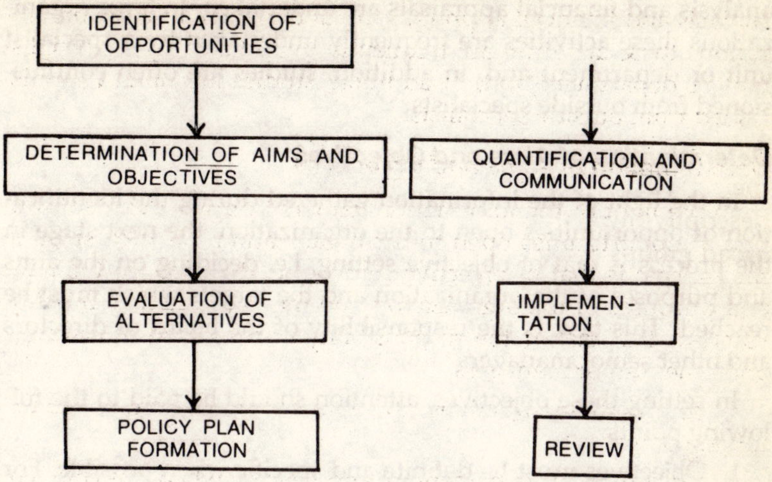

Fig. 1. The planning process

these opportunities may be identified only when alternatives are being evaluated.

We now examine each of the steps in detail, considering its position within the system as a whole, and the people within the organization who are most involved at each stage.

Identification of Opportunities

The board of directors and other senior managers are involved at this stage of the planning system. Most directors have responsibility for a specific area of the organization's activities, e.g. marketing director, personnel director. But many organizations employ, on a part-time basis, some directors who do not have specific responsibilities. Such non-executive directors often have wide industrial and commercial experience, and are well placed to draw attention to opportunities that the full-time members of the organization would not be aware of.

However, many other people are also likely to be involved in the identification of opportunities. Sometimes this will be a by-product of their main function, as when salesman report that the organization is not meeting all of its customer's current needs. In other instances the identification of opportunities is the person's or unit's primary concern, e.g. when market research, economic analysis and financial appraisals are undertaken. In large organizations these activities are frequently undertaken by a specialist unit or department and, in addition, studies are often commissioned from outside specialists.

Determination of Aims and Objectives

In the light of the information gathered during the identification of opportunities open to the organization, the next stage in the process is that of objective setting, i.e. deciding on the aims and purposes of the organization and the targets which must be reached. This task is the responsibility of the board of directors and other senior managers.

In setting these objectives, attention should be paid to the following points:

1. Objectives must be definite and specific when possible. For example, 'an expansion of output by 10 per cent' rather than 'to become bigger'.
2. It should be possible to translate objectives into policies and plans for execution, e.g. to achieve higher sales by heavier advertising and by spending more on research and development.
3. The timescale should be clear, and often have a series of short-term objectives which are part of, or steps towards, a longer-term objective, e.g. 6 months, 1 year, 5 years, 10 years.
4. The various objectives must be compatible; this requires that the constraints that one objective creates for others must be identified.
5. Flexibility and scope for the revision of objectives and policies must be maintained. For example, if economic conditions deteriorate it may be necessary to lower the planned rate of growth; alternatively new policies may have to be adopted if the initial objective is to be fulfilled.

Most organizations set objectives for some or all of the following areas:

1. Profitability;
2. Market standing and position;
3. Innovation;
4. Productivity;

5. Resources required;
6. Management performance and development;
7. Employee performance and attitude to the organization;
8. Public and social responsibility.

Another way of looking at organizations objectives is in terms of the relationship between the organization and the individual. If they are to be successful, organizations must meet the needs of the following four groups of people; (the numbers in brackets relate to the objectives listed above and indicate which objectives are particularly important with respect to each group):

(a) **Customers** (2,3). Goods and services are provided to meet the demands of customers. As consumers' tastes become more sophisticated, shoddy goods and poor service become less acceptable.

(b) **Employees** (4,5,6,7). The most obvious need of employees is for the money that enables them to meet their requirements as consumers. But other needs are also important, especially when choosing between one employer or occupation and another. The other needs include job security, job satisfaction, a socially acceptable working atmosphere and good working conditions. The satisfaction of these needs is becoming seen as the norm rather than the standard to be reached in the distant future.

(c) **Shareholders** (1). Organizations that have shareholders are expected to safeguard their investment and to provide a return that adequately compensates for the risks undertaken.

(d) **Community** (8). In addition to meeting the needs of these three specific groups, organisations are often deemed to have a more general responsibility to the community in general. All organizations must now reconcile their own objectives with those of the local community. These objectives range from providing employment by using local suppliers, to ensuring they do not pollute the environment. This responsibility involves maintaining contacts with local authorities, helping voluntary organizations, reacting to the views of local pressure groups, and encouraging managers and employees to contribute to local community needs (e.g. serving on governing bodies of schools).

Evaluation of Alternatives

The main purpose of this step is to consider how a given objective might best be met or how a given opportunity might best be exploited. At this stage a point mentioned in connection with the setting of objectives assumes importance again, namely that one objective may create a constraint for other objectives. To take an obvious example, there would be no point in reducing price in order to meet an objective of an increased sales volume, if this caused the firm to fall short of its profits objective. Consequently, alternatives have to be evaluated in the light of all the organization's objectives.

In many cases the question is whether the policy implemented hitherto should be continued or modified. Modification may be required because the initial policy proved to be mis-judged, because alternative policies have since emerged as possibilities, or because circumstances have changed.

The change in circumstances may arise in the external environment, e.g. it may be decided to modify the design of a truck so that it can be sold more cheaply to third world countries where demand is expanding. In other instances a change in policy may follow from a change in internal circumstances, e.g. a local authority may introduce a system of leasing rather than purchasing for its vehicles in the car pool in order to avoid the increased maintenance costs that would result from a wage award to mechanics.

The need to regularly evaluate alternative ways of achieving given objectives is generally most keenly felt by private sector organizations whose market is under constant threat from competitors. But the need also exists in the public sector, especially today when budget cut-backs require all managers to make the most efficient use of the resources under their control.

Although we have concentrated the discussion in this section on the evaluation of alternative ways of meeting objectives, we must remember the point made earlier, that this evaluation can lead to changes in those objectives. Consider the policies of the clearing banks. For the past few years, they have been considering how they could best meet the needs of their customers in order to counteract the increasing competition from foreign banks and other financial institutions such as the building societies. Several banks have changed their structure in such a way as to make a clearer distinction between those parts concerned with firms and other organizations on the one hand, and those concerned with personal business on the other. This clearer identification of a personal market is one of the reasons that has led the clearing banks to offer an increased range of services to this sector, the most notable recently being the huge expansion in loans for house purchase.

Formulation of Plans

We now reach the stage at which objectives are translated into detailed policies and plans. This is usually undertaken by an ad hoc team comprising personnel seconded from their usual operational roles. At this stage the broad implications for the various parts of the organization—divisions, departments or, in large groups, companies—are made clear. Targets for each manager are laid down, perhaps with an indication of the reasons for any changes from the current targets, and the available resources may be specified.

Quantification and Communication

We have noted that some degree of quantification and communication is involved at the policy/plan formulation stage. The reason for distinguishing this as a separate stage is to denote that a different group of personnel now became involved in the planning process. Accountants, engineers, work study officers, sales managers, and production managers all use their specialist skills to further quantify the plans, and to set departmental and individual work targets. These targets must then be communicated to the people concerned.

The principles underlying successful communication were outlined in the previous chapter. The plan must be well written, capable of being understood by all those who need to use it. (Some organizations have made the mistake of introducing massive corporate plans, comprising several volumes. While these are comprehensive, few managers read them). At one time it was thought desirable to present targets that were unattainable since this would make people try harder. It is now generally accepted that this is counter-productive, and that it is preferable to establish targets that are realistic in terms of both 'quantity' and time-scale; in this way people's commitment is more likely to be retained.

Implementation

The activities involved in implementing plans are discussed at length in later chapters, and there is therefore no need to discuss them here. It is sufficient to note that the more changes are made from current policies, the more problems in implementation will need to be overcome (unless, of course, the change are designed to remedy existing problems in implementation).

Review

Do the policies and plans work in practice? Line managers, supervisors, administrators and financial staff assemble data and compare performance with target, outcome with prediction (often utilizing computers). This information is then passed to senior managers for their consideration.

It is at this stage that the full benefits of having a proper management structure for planning are realized. If departmental managers make progress reports (implying a commitment on their part to the planning process), and if the top management structure ensures that these reports will be received, the system has a good chance of working. But any departmental jealousies, personal rivalries and power struggles are likely to inhibit the flow of information and cause the planning system, or total managerial system, to fail.

At the end of planning cycle, usually yearly to coincide with the annual budget, most organizations incorporate the results of the planning exercise in their annual report. Management must then ask whether, given the time and cost involved, the exercise has proved worthwhile. If the answer appears to be no, then the planning system should itself be evaluated and an attempt made to remedy deficiencies.

Corporate Planning

We have discussed the steps taken in the policy/plan formulation process. Some organizations, particularly those in the public sector, have developed this process to a high degree of sophistication and introduced a system of total or corporate planning to cover all the activities of their organization.

Corporate planning may be regarded as the planning process at its most sophisticated stage of development. Corporate planning makes use of the total information and communication resources of an organization, relates these to the decision-making processes and introduces a systematic approach to planning and management for all the resources of an organization. It implies the willingness of some managers and departments to subjugate their own particular plans to the overall requirement for the organization. To achieve this a central unit to control and monitor the developing situation is often essential.

There are a number of reasons for introducing a corporate planning system.

1. Many organizations need to think out their objectives and identify gaps that exist between their current supply of goods and services and what the market actually wants.

2. The larger the organization, the more likely there is to be a competing need for scarce resources. To achieve maximum benefit this implies the need for central planning and control as opposed to planning by individual departments or managers.

3. The pace of change is quickening and organizations have to adapt and react to changes corporately, rather than on an individual departmental basis.

4. Modern computer-based information systems provide an overall, as well as departmental, viewpoint and this aids overall planning to a degree that was impossible several years ago.

One of the major decisions senior management have to face when introducing a corporate planning system is, who is to gather the information and formulate the corporate plan. In many organizations corporate planning will involve changes in the existing management and organizational structures (e.g. in the public sector, changes in the committee structure, alterations to the membership of the management team). In some cases the answers to this preparation and control problem have been resolved by having a large central planning unit which gathers the information, formulates plans and then monitors the total process. In other cases, planners may be seconded to work with individual departments or managers, and a small central unit merely acts as a coordinator to the planning process.

Whichever system is chosen, corporate planning involves time and money, particularly the time of senior managers. It is essential therefore that a 'quick pay off' for all this time and effort is realized. If members of the organization have to wait several months or even two or three years before they reap any of the benefits of the corporate planning system, then they are likely to revert to their own individual, unco-ordinated planning systems.

Corporate planning can be very effective when operated properly. But it does involve time and effort in the setting up process, an acceptance of change and a realization by managers that the corporate need may be more important than their own individual needs and ambitions. Many organizations are now counting the heavy costs of corporate planning systems in the light of rapid changes in their operational environment, and comparing these costs with the benefits of a total approach against an unco-ordinated and individualist approach. This dilemma has faced managers and organizations for many years and is likely to continue to do so for the foreseeable future.

Management by Objectives

In the 1960s a technique of planning by objective setting on a total organizational and individual basis was developed, in the main by J. Humble of Urwick Orr and Partners. The system was called Management by objectives (MBO). This system was used to assess managerial performance, but it was in the area of planning that the system made its greatest impact.

The system rested on the setting of

1. Quantifiable objectives i.e. How Much?
2. Qualitative objectives i.e. How well?
3. Verifiable objectives i.e. With what result?

It was hoped that involving staff in the setting of their own objectives, in consultation with their managers, would lead to better and more committed performance by individuals, i.e. agreed plans and objectives = agreed performance.

The system was developed in the growth era of the 1960s and adopted by numerous organizations. However, in the recession-riddled 1970s the system fell into disrepute. Many organizations questioned whether the time and money involved in setting up the system really paid off when the pace of change quickened and the future was no uncertain. For example, during the three day working week era, 1973/74, organizations were re-assessing their objectives on an almost daily basis.

The supporters of MBO claim the following advantages for this system of planning and appraisal:

1. It results in better management as it clarifies and commits managers to agreed objectives.

2. The organizational structure is questioned and as a result anomalies and problems sorted out.

3. The system increases commitment on a total organizational basis to the organization's objectives.

4. Effective controls over departments and individuals are developed.

5. The discussions at all levels of the organization lead to better overall objectives and plans as everyone makes an input to the total process, not just senior managers or specialist planners.

Various problems in applying the system have been experienced, including:

1. Failure by senior management in many organizations to spend sufficient time teaching the philosophy of the system and selling it properly.

2. Failure to give proper guidelines to the setters of objectives.

3. Setting too optimistic objectives that in practice were difficult to meet.

4. The objectives and goals had too short a time scale.

5. Setting up an inflexible system that could not adapt to rapid changes within and from outside the organization.

6. The system sometimes proved unable to accommodate rapid environmental changes.

ORGANIZING

Any grouping or collection of people who are trying to work together to achieve a given objective, be it a number of soldiers trying to win a battle or a number of building operatives and craftsmen trying to build a house, work more effectively and quickly and have more chance of achieving their objective, if they are organized correctly.

Without organizations, modern day life would quickly degenerate into near chaos. We depend on organizations to bring our food to the local supermarket, to supply petrol to the pumps at the local garage, to educate our children and to look after us when we are sick. We are part of an organization in our working lives, while at home the family, that oldest organization of all, has stood the test of time and change the still survives, loved and cherished by most of us.

Organizations and organizing are so much part and parcel of our lives that we accept the concept of organizing without a second thought. Organizing means utilizing whatever resources are available—people, time, money, equipment, services etc.—to achieve objectives. For some people this may not mean such more than organizing their time throughout the day. Managers, however, control substantial resources, and they have to learn how to organize employees and organizations.

For managers the organizing function is made more difficult by the fact that much of their time is spent organizing people, and people change, daily, hourly, even by the minute. Managers are therefore constantly making adjustments to their organizations to cater for such things as the sickness of a key employee, an unexpected resignation, or the shortage of some key component because of a strike in supplier's factory. Organizations are also social units; help and advice are provided to the members of the group, worries are shared, and the chances of success are improved when people from different backgrounds, ages and skills work in unison towards an agreed objective.

It is this basic need for human contact, to relate to other people and to have a greater chance of achieving success in any activity, that gives rise to the desire to organize and be organized. We may all be 'loners' occasionally, but we only reach our full potential as part of an organization, however small. Management is about maximizing potential and management is therefore about organizing.

Principles of Organization

Spans of Control. There will always be a limit to the number of people a manager can effectively control. Some management expert feel that six to eight people is the maximum; others have suggested a smaller number. The appropriate span of control will depend on a variety of factors. First, are the subordinates qualified to make decisions without having to constantly refer upwards to the manager? Have they the skills and experience required to take the right course of action and see it through? Second, is the manager concerned prepared to delegate authority to his subordinates? Is this desirable for the manager's own career progression, or is it possible he might delegate himself out of a job? Third, a manager can supervise more people if the organization has a well-defined planning function and agreed set of objectives, than if the objectives are vague or not widely understood. (On the other hand when, in a period of rapid change, decisions of a vital nature have to be taken on an almost daily basis, managers may become involved in the detailed running of the organization in order to keep control of all aspects of the situation, thus reducing the effective span of control.)

Similarly, where an organization has well developed, tried and tested communication systems that feed information quickly, to and from senior management, each manager is able to control a larger number of people. Indeed this may be the primary benefit of the modern communications and information systems.

Finally, some organizations, particularly those in the public sector, depend a great deal on personal contact to operate effectively. These types of organizations will inevitably have small spans of control and involve many levels of subordinates and co-ordinates, the hallmark of a bureaucratic type of organization.

Unity of objectives

Whatever the organization structure finally decided upon, all parts of the organization should work towards common objectives. In these days of international competition and scarce resources no manager can afford the luxury of parts of the organization 'doing their own thing'. This is particularly true of labour-intensive organizations in the public sector and the service industries in the private sector, where the human resource plays such a key (and very expensive) role.

As noted above, people are more likely to pursue the organization's objectives rather than their personal interests if these objectives are clearly defined and widely understood. Unfortunately, experience shows that in public sector organizations 'politics' often leads to objectives being blurred or constantly changed, with consequential loss of efficiency.

Delegation

As noted during our discussion of the span of control, delegation implies that a senior manager gives discretion to a subordinate. Successful delegation requires that attention should be given to the following factors. *First*, adequate authority must be given to the subordinate to carry out the task. If a junior manager is given the job of running the mailroom, it should be made clear that he has authority over the mailroom staff and can specify the timing of the collection and delivery of the mail.

In situations like this, specifying the limits of authority is often easy. It is much more difficult where a senior manager has only a vague idea of what he wants and gives only broad and general instructions to a subordinate. In this situation there is much more likely to be a dispute later on as to whether the junior manager has exceeded his authority. Consider the situation in which a senior manager asks a subordinate to prepare a report on the feasibility of a proposed new product. The manager feels that a satisfactory report could be prepared as the basis of internal discussions with the production manager, personnel director etc. But the subordinate feels it necessary to obtain information about competitors' products and therefore asks the market research department to undertake a survey. Two obvious sources of conflict arise. First, the market research staff may refuse to do what the junior manager requests. Second, if they do accept his authority and undertake the work, the senior manager may complain because of the costs involved.

Second, and following from the previous point, tasks being delegated must be properly assigned, i.e. the subordinate must understand what is involved, accept the delegated discretion and know that his position and authority are not duplicated elsewhere in the organization.

Finally, responsibility for the discretion delegated cannot be greater than the authority delegated, e.g. if a manager gives a subordinate the authority to sell certain items, that subordinate cannot be held responsible for high rates of breakages and customer complaints due to a bad design or faulty manufacturing.

Most successful managers are happy to delegate. They see it as being helpful to themselves and their organizations for a variety of reasons:

1. By delegating one can see which subordinates are likely to be 'high flyers', suitable for promotion, and which have reached the limit of their competence.

2. Delegation can provide a useful training tool, in that it enables managers to develop their potential. This may mean that junior managers are given discretion even though they do not perform as well as their seniors in the early stages. As they learn from experience and gain confidence, their performance is likely to improve, and senior managers are often pleasantly surprised at how successful subordinates can be, given time and encouragement in undertaking tasks previously thought to be the preserve of the senior manager or 'the boss'.

3. All managers and individuals do some things better than others. If a subordinate is particularly skilled in some tasks it makes sense for a senior manager who may see these tasks as a 'bit of a chore', to let the junior manager do it. The tasks are likely to be performed more effectively and the senior manager will be able to spend more time on tasks for which he is better fitted.

4. Where an organization is spread out geographically, e.g. with a headquarters and a number of area offices, it may be wise to delegate certain functions to junior managers in the area offices who are in closer touch with customers and the general public.

Whatever degree of discretion a senior manager eventually decides to give to his subordinates the general principle is clear cut. Senior managers should concentrate their time and effort on the major issues facing their organizations. Most senior managers are overworked, with more calls on their time than the working day allows for. Delegation of tasks to subordinates wherever possible makes good business and managerial sense. The tasks will often be done more cheaply, employee job satisfaction will be increased, and senior managers will be more effective.

Unity of Command

Where an individual has responsibility to one clearly defined superior, the less likely it is that he will receive conflicting instructions. He is also likely to obtain more job satisfaction and a greater sense of purpose and responsibility in carrying out instructions, than if he is responsible to two or more superiors. The bigger the organization, the more specialists it employs, the more difficult it is to observe this 'unity of command' principle, with consequent adverse effects on morale and efficiency. For example a personnel officer may be asked by the production manager to provide additional workers; to meet this instruction may conflict with recruitment and induction procedures laid down by the personnel manager.

ORGANISATIONAL STRUCTURES

As mentioned previously, formal organization structures are constantly modified by managers in response to a variety of pressures. Nevertheless it takes time for a new structure to become fully operational, for all the relevant parts of the formal organization to be re-organized, and for all the relationships to be modified.

The Informal Organization

Within every organization, alongside the formal organization structure there exists the informal structure. This is based on relationships between individuals and groups and as such is much more dynamic and less easily definable than the more rigid formal structure. The 'old boy network', the 'office grapevine'; a temporary liaison between two sections to gain a working advantage over a third, e.g. sales and marketing versus production, are all examples of informal relationships.

In many ways, these informal organizations, because they reflect the present, real world situation, rather than what managers think the situation is, are more powerful than the formal organizational links. If the two structures seriously diverge, it may become necessary to formalize at least some of the informal relationships; otherwise communication channels may break down and managers' freedom of action become curtailed. However, it is usually undesirable to try to suppress all informal relationships, since they can sometimes help to lubricate the formal machinery and make the organization a more interesting place in which to work.

Each organization has its own individual number of levels, determined by an amalgamation of all the issues discussed in this chapter. But most organizations contain certain levels within the hierarchical structure, with clearly defined functions. At the top there are a few senior managers making policy decisions. At the bottom there are a much larger number of employees carrying out the detailed work of the organization at the 'sharp end' so to speak. In the middle are the co-ordinators, planners and section heads controlling their particular functions, referring issues to senior management and receiving instructions back. The organizational hierarchies of typical public and private sector organizations are depicted in Figures 2 and 3.

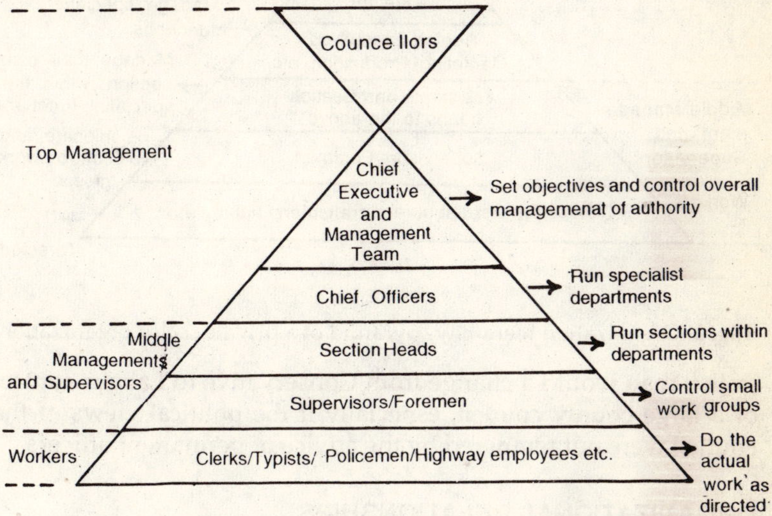

Fig. 2. Organization hierarchy/pyramid of a local authority

It will be seen that the hierarchy at the top of the public sector organization is more complex because of the political element involved. Ratepayers and politicians take a much keener interest in the running of a local authority and are much more likely to change their views—with consequent effects on the organization—than the shareholders of a private company. The bureaucratic organizational and management structure tends to operate so as to deaden and soften the impact of political change in order to aid the organization's survival and facilitate its management.

Private sector organizations reflect the impact of external changes more quickly and more fully, mainly because the implications of a change are less extreme. Although a loss of sales is a serious matter, it would usually lead to fewer changes in

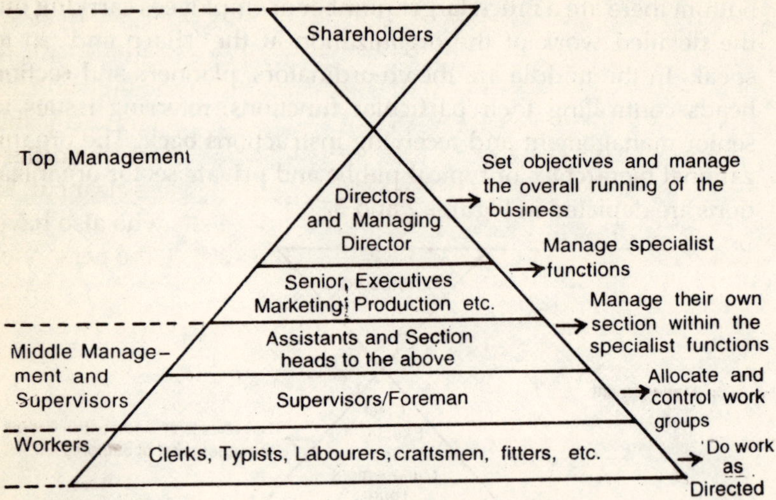

Fig. 3. Organization hierarchy/pyramid of a private sector organization

policy than would a change from Conservative to Labour control of a large county council, especially if the political views of the council were not tempered by the advice of permanent officers.

ORGANIZATIONAL RELATIONSHIPS

Whatever span of control is chosen, whatever the number of departments or groupings eventually decided upon, management has the choice of certain tried and tested organizational relationships within the organizational structure they finally decide upon.

Line Relationships

This refers to the direct working relationships between the vertical levels of an organization structure. This is the most common type of working relationships where authority flows from the departmental head to the deputy, to the section head and eventually to the person who actually does the job of work. The communication channels are clear, authority is agreed, and instructions and information flow down and up between the individuals concerned.

Staff Relationships

Most textbooks refer to a 'staff relationship as an advisory function in either a specialist or assistant type of position. This is true insofar as the personnel manager or a management services officer may be regarded as 'advisors' to the managers (e.g. the production manager). But in many large organizations the difference between the 'line' and 'staff' function is often less clear cut. In such organizations one often finds staff specialists who also have line responsibility over their own staff. For example the personnel manager or director would have a 'staff' relationship or advisory role to the managing director on personnel policy, but line responsibility over staff in the training, employment, recruitment and safety sections of his own personnel section.

The best guide to the reader in attempting to assess whether a position is 'line' or 'staff' is to remember that the ultimate test is based on the personal relationships, especially in terms of authority, between the individuals concerned and not by purely departmental or sectional activities.

In systems of 'corporate planning' or the 'management team' concept in local government, the two roles are often combined, e.g. the director of education will be acting as a 'line' manager when he comes to speak on educational matters to the other members of the management team, but will act in a 'staff' capacity or advisory role when, as a member of the corporate management team of authority, he criticizes some service aspect of the corporate plan or budget.

Functional Relationships

This relationship occurs where a line manager delegates to an individual or section the authority to carry out particular processes, policies, operations etc. The function can be delegated to either other 'line' managers or 'staff' advisors and specialists. This form of delegation is especially common in situations which require a grouping of people and activities to do a particular job, e.g. the move to a new office building, the installation of a new computer or the setting up of a new grievance procedure. Once the job is completed the functional authority often ends and the staff concerned return to their normal work.

Committee Relationships

We have already made reference to committees as a system of managing. Suffice it to say here that committees play a large part in organizational structures in both the public and private sectors. Indeed it is often said that they are part of way of life; if in doubt then set up a committee. Viewed as part of the organizing function, committees can either be formal, i.e. have written remit and authority to carry out a specific function, or informal or ad hoc, i.e. set up for some temporary purpose to act as a pressure release valve or as a 'sounding board' for management.

Working Parties

In recent years the increasing need for participation and specialist advice has led to the setting up, particularly in the public sector, of a variant of the committee system, i.e. the working party.

The aim of a working party is to co-ordinate the specialist knowledge of various interested parties to solve a particular problem. (The need to reconcile these differing viewpoints often throws a heavy burden on the chairman.) This means that the relationships in a working party differ slightly from those in a committee. In principle in a working party the members contribute from their own specialist viewpoint and not as equal participants able to criticize everyone and everything as in a committee. (In practice the members of a working party often behave as if they were members of a committee, as those readers who have served on working parties will know to their cost).

Matrix Relationships

This type of organizational relationship was pioneered by the Americans in their space programme in the 1960s. It combines many of the relationships we have discussed and involves staff having a dual responsibility. First, they have a responsibility to their immediate superior. Second, they have a relationship to the specialist working group and the project team of which they are members. The aim of this structure is to obtain the benefits of multi-discipline project teams at middle management level and below, whilst allowing line managers at senior level control of their specific responsibilities, even though these may be spread over several projects.

PROBLEMS OF ORGANIZING

Organizing the resources under their control is one of the most difficult functions managers have to undertake and, whatever the solution ultimately chosen, most managers will experience one, or a combination, of the following problems.

1. The plans laid down by senior management are translated into imprecise, unachievable objectives that have not gained the commitment of the employees concerned.

2. Working relationships within the organization are ill-defined, vague and exist only on an informal or very personal basis.

3. The degree of delegation is inadequate and inadequate authority is given to those to whom responsibility is delegated.

4. Communication systems are inadequate with the result that management does not really know what is going on or is unaware of the true feelings of the workforce.

5. A breakdown occurs in the chain of command, such as the mixing up of line and staff relationships, the granting of functional authority without responsibility, bad supervision.

6. A period of rapid change leads to constant re-organizations so that the whole structure is in a state of flux, and no one has time to adapt to and fully implement organizational changes.

Experienced managers will recognize the above symptoms and take steps to rectify the situation. In many cases the above issues are the results of 'people problems' and can only be solved by re-training and management development, or at the worst, removal of the individual concerned.

LEADING AND DIRECTING

There are various ways of structuring an organization in order to utilize resources effectively. But an organization's effectiveness also depends upon the leadership provided by its managers, whatever the structure adopted. Successful leadership means getting people to 'give of their best', often in adverse circumstances. In this chapter we examine the nature of this interpersonal relationship between managers and employees, and outline some of the theories that have been propounded to assist managers in their leadership role.

By the very nature of the management role and function, managers are responsible for people within their organization, for their work and for their working environment. In order to fulfil this responsibility managers must employ a range of communication and leadership skills. It is sometimes said that leaders are born and not made, and some people are undoubtedly better equipped with the skills than other people. But these skills can be developed and deployed more effectively through constant practice. In fact a careful study of 'natural leaders' usually reveals that they have very thoroughly practised the skills that now appear to come so naturally to them.

Motivation

Of these skills none is more important than the ability to motivate people. In order to motivate people, managers must understand what their needs are, what 'makes them tick'. We consider below the theories of motivation advanced by a number of writers, theories that have added to our understanding , and have helped to increase managers' efficiency. But we must emphasize that when seeking to apply any theory to his own organization, a manager must be sensitive to the current needs and attitudes of *his* colleagues. This is not as easy as it may sound. Each individual has a unique set of needs and attitudes; moreover these needs and attitudes change over time. A worker's attitude on a wet Monday morning after his car has suffered a puncture on the way to work will differ from that on a warm sunny Friday afternoon, with a long weekend ahead. A more widespread difference in attitudes will occur in times of economic recession as compared to an economic boom.

The challenge to the manager is to obtain a high level of commitment and good performance from the employees despite these changes in circumstances. In meeting this challenge managers utilize a range of motivators, which fall into two broad categories, 'rewards' e.g. holidays, company car, increased salarly, and 'punishments' e.g. demotion, redundancy, transfer to another section. The ability to identify the appropriate mix of rewards and punishments (carrot and stick) is one of the most important managerial skills. With this in mind let us see what light is thrown on this matter by other writers.

MANAGEMENT STYLE

'Style' is something all managers have to develop. The actual style chosen will depend on a variety of circumstances but will, in the main, be determined by how the manager perceives his role within the organization and his view of the employees for whom he is responsible.

Douglas McGregor is his book *The Human Side of Enterprise* (1960) highlighted the dilemma facing attitudes to employees. The 'theory *X*' manager assumes that:

1. His employees dislike work and will try to avoid it wherever possible.

2. Employees have therefore to be coerced, controlled, directed and threatened with punishment if they are to achieve the objectives set for them.

3. Most people dislike responsibility, have little ambition, and value security above all else.

The 'theory *Y*' type of manager, on the other hand, assumes that:

1. Physical and mental effort in work is as natural as play and rest.

2. If people are committed to objectives they will exercise self-direction and control, eliminating or reducing the need for threats and external control.

3. Commitment to objectives is a function of the rewards associated with their achievement.

4. Given proper working conditions people can learn to seek responsibility.

5. Imagination and creative thinking are widely, not narrowly, distributed among the population.

6. The intellectual potential of the average person in industrial life is only partially realized.

The theory *Y* assumptions are attractive to the participative and more democratic type of management required in most organizations today. But experience has shown that adopting theory *Y* assumptions is no more of a guarantee that a manager will be a personal success, than adopting theory X assumptions. There are many managers who are aggressive towards their colleagues and drive their subordinates hard, who nevertheless have achieved, and perform well in, senior management positions.

In practice an organization is unlikely to have managers who conform entirely to either of the models presented by McGregor, but the managers will combine, in one proportion or another, characteristics of each model. Moreover, the appropriate combination will differ as between organizations. In a company facing rapid technological change the theory *Y* style is likely to predominate, whereas the theory *X* style will be called for in a company in which most operations have become routinized and profits are being squeezed by vigorous competition from rivals. Furthermore, organizations may need to modify their management style in the light of changing circumstances. Although many changes in the post-war period have favoured the adoption of the theory *Y* approach, as noted above, theory *X* may be more appropriate in the current difficult economic circumstances, when decisions concerning redundancies etc., have to be made.

Leading and Directing

Blake and Mouton (1964) developed a two-tier framework for analysing managerial style. They used the dimensions 'concern for people' and 'concern for production' on a nine point scale or grid. They used their 'managerial grid' system in training programmes designed to develop the 'ideal managerial style'.

Whatever style is eventually followed, successful managers realize that there is no one single correct style. They will adapt their management style to the situation and the organizational environment, and pay particular attention to the human issues involved, including the need to deal with people on an individual as well as group basis; accept that people vary from time to time; see that employees obtain job satisfaction; try to get employee commitment to the organization's objectives. Managing is not an easy task, it has to be carried out in the bad times (such as a depression) as well as the good times (such as when the firm has gained an important export order). In the end all managers realize that whatever style is developed, it will have to accept the fact that in any organization 'people matter most of all'. That is why today's modern manager spends over half of his or her time on 'people problems'.

CONTROLLING

Senior managers are concerned with the establishment of control systems. Thereafter their involvement tends to be very limited, being confined to major decisions, relating, for example, to widespread changes in working practices that might be required if costs exceeded the target. Control is mainly exercised at lower points in the managerial hierarchy. At the level of first line supervisor, section head or departmental manager, the control process accounts for a major proportion of a manager's time and effort. In fact many first line supervisors spend nearly all their time controlling the workers in their section.

Whatever the level at which control is exercised, the process will involve a number of steps or stages:

Communicating of Plans to all Concerned. For control purposes it is usual to express the plans in terms of targets. At one time it was common practice to set targets that were virtually impossible to meet, the argument being that the more difficult the target the harder people would try to achieve it. More recently, research into motivation has suggested that this is most unlikely to be so; targets that are widely accepted as attainable are now seen as the best motivators. Moreover, an unobtainable target is certainly unsuitable as a basis for control. What is required for this purpose is a target that is expected to be achieved given satisfactory (not super-human) performance.

Many targets relate to the output that an individual or group is expected to produce. In manufacturing organizations output will often be expressed in terms of the quantity of goods. Output can also be measured quantitatively in some service organizations, e.g. a television engineer is expected to install a certain number of sets in a given time period. However, in those public sector organizations, which emphasize personal service, e.g. the social service departments of local authorities, the standard or level of service would appear to be a more appropriate measure. This is partly a qualitative matter and it is difficult to decide what standard should be expected from a department or organization of a given size.

If targets are to be meaningful to employees they must know their place in the organization and the limits to the authority. This may involve the preparation and distribution of job descriptions, organization charts etc.

Measuring Performance. The measuring rod should obviously be the same as that used in setting targets, e.g. the quantity of goods.

Comparing Actual with Planned Performance. The various techniques that can be used at this stage are discussed later in this chapter. We confine our attention here to more general considerations.

It is important to decide the most appropriate time period over which the comparison is made. The longer the period, i.e. the less often measurements are taken, the less will be the cost involved. Furthermore, a more reliable measure will be obtained if what is measured has an erratic or uneven pattern of behaviour. For example in setting targets for the number of calls made by salesmen an allowance has to be made for the distance between potential customers. Assume that it is known that a salesman travels on average 20 miles to reach each customer. There would be no point in measuring his performance on a daily basis if on some days he worked areas where his customers were 10 miles apart. It might be necessary to consider his call rate over a month to average out these differences.

On the other hand the longer the period of measurement, i.e. the bigger the gap between taking measurements, the more likely it is that there will be a delay in identifying deviations from targets and in correcting those deviations. Moreover, the magnitude of the corrections will have to be greater in order to get back onto target.

Frequent (short-period) measurements are most likely to be undertaken when the measurement procedures are automatic. Frequent measurement is also required when the process involves a potential safety hazard. Inadequate monitoring in meat-packing factories in South America has resulted in loss of life. Less serious, but still unfortunate, is the death of fish and the pollution of rivers that has resulted from a failure to monitor the performance of effluent-treatment plant in this country.

We referred above to the cost incurred in measurement. The most obvious cost is that part of the wage and salary bill accounted for by the time spent in measuring performance. But the psychological cost is also important; a system involving frequent measurement can be very demotivating.

Notifying Any Deviations

Any deviations of actual from planned performance must be notified to those responsible. This step should be taken as soon as the deviation is discovered so that corrective action can be taken as quickly as possible. Without a good communications system effective control is impossible.

One of the prime responsibilities of senior managers is to establish an adequate formal system of communications, with clearly defined channels of communication. Control information would normally be expected to flow through these channels. But it is also important to retain flexibility and to allow such information to be transmitted through informal channels if the established channels prove inadequate, e.g. if the unexpected absence from work of the officially designated recipient would cause corrective action to be delayed.

Identifying the Reasons for the Deviations

In some instances this stage precedes the previous one since it may become clear who is responsible for the deviation only after the reasons for the deviations have been identified.

Identification will probably be easiest when the reasons are internal to the organization. If output is less than planned it should be possible to discover from the company's records whether this was due to a labour dispute, a lack of components arising from poor production planning, the breakdown of machines etc. If, on the other hand, sales are less than planned it may be difficult to decide whether this is due to an inadequate performance by the sales force or to a fall in demand that has affected all suppliers.

Taking Corrective Action

The corrective action must be taken at the appropriate time. This will usually be as soon as possible after the reasons for the deviation have been identified. However, time should be allowed for adequate consultation with all individuals who will be affected by the corrective action.

Corrective action normally implies changing the current situation, e.g. if costs are too high steps must be taken to reduce them. But sometimes the horse has bolted by the time someone finds the stable door open. For instance, output might have been below target because of a strike at the supplier of a vital component. In these circumstances, the value of the control system is first that it enables the damage to profits caused by such an event to be estimated, and second that it demonstrates the need to prevent a recurrence, for example by dividing the orders for the component between two suppliers.

CONTROL TECHNIQUES

In exercising control in the areas mentioned above, managers use a combination of techniques. The final mix will depend on the type of organization, whether it is in the public or private sector, and the influence of external forces, e.g. government economic policies. These techniques are used to differentiate stages of the control process. For example, critical path and network analysis are used in translating objectives into plans while budgetary control systems are used in measuring performance and in comparing actual with planned performance. All the control techniques will include some or all of the following:

- corporate planning
- budgetary control systems
- value analysis
- operations research and other statistical techniques
- programme evaluation review techniques
- organization and methods and work study
- project evaluation
- management by objectives
- market and product research
- critical path and network analysis
- statistical control systems of stock and production requirements
- management audits
- management appraisal systems.

The most important consideration is that managers should feel confident that they are receiving the information on the organization's activities and environment that enables them to exercise effective control.

CONTROL AND ACCOUNTABILITY

Managers in the private sector are accountable to their Board and their shareholders. In the public sector accountability and ultimate control is much more diffused, involving full-time professional managers, elected or appointed lay officials and possibly the general public in their capacity as taxpayers, ratepayers and electors.

Consequently, the control process is much more involved in the public than the private sector. Account may have to be taken of the views of individual chief officers, the management team, the chairman and elected members of a committee, outside pressure groups and the ratepayers, before a major control decision is taken in local government. In such a situation managers have to be sensitive to the attitudes of a wide range of people, and have to constantly check that their communications network is adequate.

6

CORPORATE DECISION MAKING

SITUATIONS in which a decision must be made arise continually in our daily lives, in the organizations in which we work, and in the communities in which we live. Dealing with these decisions is a major part of the work of individuals at all levels in a modern organization. Some of the decision situations encountered occur repetitively and in essentially the same form on each occasion. These decisions can be approached effectively by following rules and patterns of behavior that have been established as a result of previous experience. Other decision situations encountered may be similar to situations that have been experienced in the past. However, a particular characteristic of the newly arising problem may make it different in some important aspect. Still other situations are new and unique in every respect. The intuition and judgment of persons who have had experience with similar types of problems is the most important resource available in an organization to deal with situations of these latter types.

THE NATURE OF DECISION PROCESS

The essence of decision making is in the formulation of alternative courses of action to meet the situation under consideration and in the choice between these alternatives after an evaluation of their effectiveness in achieving the decision maker's objectives. One of the most important components of the decision-making process is the gathering of information from which an appreciation of the decision situation can be made. If sufficient information can be gathered to obtain a complete specification of all of the alternatives and of their effectiveness in the situation under consideration, the decision making process is relatively straightforward. However, it may be impossible in practice to assemble all of the information and material that bears upon a given decision situation in view of the limited amounts of time and resources available for the task. Furthermore, it may not be possible in some cases to determine exactly what constitutes all of the relevant information, even if sufficient time and resources are available to collect it. An element of uncertainty then enters into the decision process, because of the lack of complete information. Under these circumstances, the decision maker may be unsure about the nature of the alternatives available and about the effectiveness of these alternatives in the achievement of his objectives. Uncertainty is one of the most pervasive characteristic of the decision situations encountered by modern management. It is also one of the factors causing the greatest difficulty in practical decision making.

In many decision situations, the responsibility for the choice between alternatives lies with one individual who makes the decision with respect to his or her own interests or those of the organization that he or she represents. In other cases, the decision must be taken by a number of individuals acting as members of a group, as in the management committee of an organization. Part of the decision process in such circumstances consists of a period of discussion, in which there may be some modification of the opinions of one or more of the group members. The process may lead to a consensus among those involved and to a mutually agreed evaluation of the alternatives in the decision situation under consideration. If this is the case, the agreed evaluation can be used as a basis for choice on behalf of the group as if it were a single decision maker.

A much more complex situation arises if the individuals concerned cannot arrive at an agreed position that represents the views of the group. This may occur when some or all of the individual members are pursuing different and conflicting objectives. In these circumstances, subgroups may form with differing opinions and evaluations of alternatives. The conflict between these opinions and evaluations may require a considerable period of interaction and negotiation between the subgroups before the decision situation under consideration can be resolved.

A similar condition arises in a decision situation in which a number of independent participants with conflicting interests are involved. For example, a proposal to build an airport or a power station may be opposed by citizen's groups and local government. It may, however, be supported by local contractors and the authority making the proposal. In situations of this sort, each of the participants envisages an outcome that is most preferred in relation to his or her own interests. For example, the citizen's groups may prefer that no facility be built because of the disruption that it would bring to their neighborhood. The contractors and the proposing authority may each prefer that the facility be built, but for somewhat different reasons. In situations in which the participant's initial preferences are different, the ultimate resolution takes place only after a period of interaction and negotiation between the participants. During this process, the views and preferences of some of the participants may change and a compromise may emerge. The passage of time often brings pressure on one or more of the participants to agree to an outcome that was not initially the most preferred. Nevertheless, all the participants may eventually accept this outcome in preference to a continuation of the confrontation. If the move towards a resolution of the decision situation does not occur and if the participants remain committed to the outcomes they preferred initially, a stalemate is reached which may take a considerable time to resolve.

The subject of decision making is concerned with a wide range of situations, each of which has a number of unique characteristics. The following is a disscussion of each of these situations and to demonstrate methods and techniques of decision making that may be helpful to those involved in the choice between alternatives. The first step is this discussion is to consider the background of a decision situation.

THE BACKGROUND TO A DECISION

It is interesting and helpful in the discussion of decision making to regard the organizations, individuals, and groups of individuals involved in terms of systems theory. In this theory, a system is envisaged as a set of elements or components that are bound together by some form of relationship. The behavior of the system is determined by the relationship between its elements. An organization is seen, for example, as a system that consists of a number of individuals, groups of individuals, or departments working together to achieve a set of common objectives. The behavior of the organization depends to a large extent on the behavior of its component parts and on the relationships between them.

Systems exist at a number of different levels. At a lower hierarchical level each of the elements of a system can be considered as a system in its own right. For example, the departments of an organization each exhibit all the characteristics of a complete system. At a higher level, the original organization might be regarded as only a element of an even more comprehensive system. Hierarchical arrangements of this nature are familiar in daily life. They appear in many forms of human activity. Generally speaking, there is no logical end to the process of dividing systems into elements. In practice, however, the process is usually carried no further than is necessary to serve the considerations at hand.

The Environment of a Decision Situation

Organizations and individuals that are involved in modern decision making operate in an environment and react to stimuli that impinge upon them in that environment. The external environment of an organization or of an individual may contain other organizations and individuals that compete for benefits from that environment. It may also contain elements that place constraints on the manner in which the participants in the environment can operate. These elements may be social, technological, natural, or quasi-natural. The social elements are those that refer to or result from relationships with other systems in the environment. They include commitments, laws, policies, guidelines, and other factors that arise in interactions between the systems in the environment. Technological elements are concerned with economic, physical, human, and organizational factors. Natural elements consist of events in which there is no discernible involvement by humans. Quasi-natural events result from the unintentional effects of one situation on the actions of individuals and organizations that are pursuing their own interests in other unrelated situations.

An organization has an internal as well as an external environment. The internal environment consists of all its component parts and of the set of social, technological, and natural elements that constitute the fabric of the organization. A particular decision situation may exist wholly within the external environment of an organization, wholly within its internal environment, or partially in the external and partially in the internal environments. The portions of the external and internal environments that relate to a particular decision situation constitute the environment of that decision situation.

The Objectives of an Organization

Individuals, organizations, and groups have ideals, objectives, and goals related to their functions, as expressed, for example, in their terms of reference or their charters under law. What is described as an objective by one person is often called an ideal or a goal by others. It may be helpful, therefore, to differentiate between ideal objectives and goals by means of the following definitions. These definitions are not unique and many might argue for a different distinction between the ideas conveyed by the words. However, for the purposes of this text, let us regard an *ideal* as something that is ultimately desirable but not necessarily ever attainable; an *objective* as something that is desired to attain, but not necessarily in a given time period; and a *goal* as an outcome to be obtained within a particular time period. For simplicity in what follows, the word "objective" will be used to cover the meaning of the three terms. The individual terms will be used only when it is necessary to emphasize the time period over which the desired condition is to be attained.

Covert and Overt Objectives

Statements of objectives prepared for organizations sometimes contain only those items that management is prepared to see published. Other objectives that management wants to keep confidential are not included in statements prepared for publication. This practice is understandable in the case of a business organization that does not wish to alert a possible competitor to its future activities. Under these circumstances, the statement that is published contains what may be called the *overt* objectives of the organization. There is in addition a supplementary list of *covert* objectives that remains in the minds of managers or in the company confidential files. In some cases, the overt and covert objectives may be mildly contradictory. They may even be in direct conflict with each other. Both types of objectives are important in establishing the background for decisions in the organization. Management policies and the decisions that spring from them are necessarily related to all of the objectives of the organization.

Multiple Objectives

Most modern organizations have many objectives. Some of these objectives may conflict with one another with respect to some activities of an organization. For example, a business enterprise may have an objective to attain a particular return on investment, but at the same time have objectives related to its social responsibility to the community in which it operates. Satisfying the social objectives of the organization may reduce to some extent the degree of achievement of the return on investment. Even if the sole objective of an organization were to maximize its return on investment, there might be some discussion and conflict over whether this maximization should take place over the short, medium, or long terms. Nonprofit organizations do not often have the same economic objectives as those that operate in a competitive business environment. Nevertheless, such organizations often have objectives related to their primary mission that are in conflict with others that refer to their secondary roles and missions. Individuals and groups also pursue many objectives. Achievement of one of these objectives often detracts temporarily from pursuit of one or more of the others.

It is necessary, therefore, to consider the range of objectives of the organization, individual, or group of individuals involved as a background to decision making. Furthermore, priorities must be established between the members of a set of multiple objectives. It may be possible to assess this priority in numerical form, so that a quantitative weighting factor can be applied to each of them. In many cases, however, it is not possible to express the priority between objectives in terms of a single number. In these circumstances, the objectives may be placed in a qualitative order of importance as a guide to those who may be involved in decision making.

It is particularly desirable in establishing priorities between objectives to distinguish between those that contribute to the achievement of short-term missions and those that relate to the maintenance of freedom of action in the longer term. It may be, for example, that the assignment of very high priority to the achievement of short-term objectives detracts from the longer-term strategic capability of an organization. It can be argued that all such considerations ultimately reduce to the single issue of the future survival of the organization, group or individual in a form acceptable to those involved. The relative priority assigned to the individual objectives in a multiple set may therefore be directly related to the perceptions of those engaged in the objective-setting activity with respect to this overriding consideration.

WELL STRUCTURED AND ILL STRUCTURED DECISIONS

A number of authors have made a distinction between two types of decision situations. Herbert A. Simon was among the first to do so when he referred to decisions that are "programmed" and those that are "non-programmed." He described programmed decisions as those that are met repetitively and that become routine as a result of many encounters with the same situation. These decisions are "programmable" because a specific procedure can be worked out by which they can be resolved. This procedure is based on experience in a number of situations of the same type. Once it has been established, all like situations can be treated by use of the standard procedure. The only innovative activity with respect to situations of this nature is a check that it is appropriate to employ the usual procedure for resolution.

Programmed decisions usually occur in the routine operational and administrative activities of an organization. They are found mostly at the middle and lower levels of management. The input data used in making a decision of this type is usually complete and well defined. Details of the procedures involved in resolving a programed decision are well known and are agreed upon by all who are concerned with the problem. Senior management is usually not involved with particular decisions of this kind. However, the results of a series of such decisions over a period of time may be of interest to senior managers. Sometimes many relatively straightforward programmed decisions can be linked together in a logical progression that forms the basis for resolution of a very complex problem. The use of mathematical models to provide the basis for decisions in scheduling the use of resources, distribution of products, inventory control, and handling of queues provides many examples of the use of a progression of programmable decisions in dealing with very complex situations. These examples are often comparable to the use of process control routines in industrial production.

By contrast, nonprogrammed decisions are not repetitive. They appear to be new and unique to the decision maker in one or more respects when they occur. No complete and well established procedure exists for dealing with nonprogrammed decisions, mainly because no direct experience has been obtained from previous encounters with a decision situation of exactly the same sort. In comparison to programmed decisions, the data available concerning a nonprogrammed decision is usually incomplete and ill defined. The means of dealing with situations of this nature are not unique nor are they usually agreed upon by all concerned. Different persons may have different perceptions of a particular situation and of the manner in which it should be handled. Nonprogrammable decisions are mostly found at the middle and senior levels of management and are often related to the policy making and planning activities of an organization.

The distinction between "programmed" and "nonprogrammed" decisions refers to the procedure that can be adopted in the process of resolution of the decision situation. Programmed decisions are seen as having a well defined and recognizable structure, so that new occurrences of a well known type of situation can be immediately placed in a category and processed routinely. Nonprogrammed decisions, on the other hand, are those for which no routine procedure or structure can be applied. Each nonprogrammable decision appears to those involved to have characteristics that do not fit into any of the structures that have been formulated for the routine treatment of decision situations. This emphasis on structure has resulted in the use of the terms "well structured" and "ill structured" (or "unstructured") to replace "programmed" and "nonprogrammed" in the recent technical literature. The fact that a complete and comprehensive specification can be written to describe the procedure for resolving a programmed or well structured decision situation has also suggested the terms "completely specified" to describe this sort of situation and "non-completely specified" to refer to non-programmed or ill structured decisions. None of these sets of terms describes the distinction between the two sorts of decision situations completely satisfactorily. However, authors have recently tended towards the use of well structured and ill structured to refer to this distinction and this practice will therefore be adopted in this text.

The use of two such terms to describe the distinction between decision situation may give the impression that only two types of decision situations are ever encountered. In practice, a continuum of situations exists, ranging from those that are well structured at one end of the spectrum to those that are ill structured at the other end. The decision situation in between have been called "partially structured" or "partially specified." An illustration of this spectrum of decisions and a brief description of the characteristics of each sort of decision is shown in Table 1.

Partially structured decision situation are those in which only a part can be well structured or completely specified. Typically, they consist of decision situations in which a great deal of data or a number of supplementary decisions can be processed according to a well structured routine. However, the final choice between alternatives is not as well structured. A number of matters that cannot be represented completely by a formal specification are involved in this final choice. It is therefore left to the decision maker to make the ultimate selection between alternatives on the basis of the data and supplementary factors that have been assembled, using judgment and experience in dealing with the ill structured parts of the decision. For example, consider the decision involved in filling a senior position in an organization. The individual who is to make the choice would probably agree to writing some broad specifications describing the staff member required and including necessary characteristics such as age, experience, and education. These specifications can be used to select from the personnel files all those who meet the general requirements for the job. The manager is thus relieved of the routine work of scanning all the personnel files. The final choice is made by the individual involved using the results of the well structured portion of the decision process, further information obtained during the interviews, and intuition and judgment gained from experience in similar situations in the past.

Table 1

Range of Decision Situations in an Organization

SPECTRUM OF DECISION SITUATIONS		
Well structured (Programmed or Completely Specified)	*Partially Structured*	*Ill-Structured (Nonprogrammed or Non-completely-Specified)*
1. Specification of decision procedure agreed in advance of resolution.	1. Only a part of decision process can be completely specified and structured.	1. Decision procedure cannot be completely structured in advance of resolution.
2. Little managerial involvement at time of each resolution.	2. Manager makes final resolution using results from structured portion and his experience and intuition.	2. Individuals resolve each situation on basis of experience, beliefs, and judgment.
3. Repeated resolutions with same data produce same result.	3. Two different managers may agree on certain relevant data but reach different conclusions.	3. Two different managers may reach different conclusions.

THE DECISION MAKING PROCESS

The nature of decision making has been studied intensively in recent years. The conclusions drawn from individual studies have been different in many respects. All agree, however, that decision making is a process involving a number of interwoven stages, rather than a single, isolated act. One of the first authors to describe the decision making process as a series of phases was John Dewey. Writing in 1910, he suggested that the process of problem solving could be thought of as consisting of three phases, namely, answering these questions: (1) What is the problem? (2) What are the alternatives? (3) Which alternative is best?

Stages in the Decision-making Process

Defining the Problem. It may seem strange, in the light of the introduction to the chapter, to begin with 'defining the problem'. If the problem arises because of a failure to fulfil plans, surely it will be obvious what the problem is? Unfortunately, this is by no means always the case. The issue that first comes to the manager's attention may only be a manifestation of a much bigger problem, and the manager must delve below the surface to discover whether this is so. Otherwise the wrong decision may be taken.

For example a firm may experience a cash flow problem because sales fall below the target. One way to overcome the problem might be to obtain a bank loan, and this solution might be satisfactory if the fall in sales is due to special circumstances, e.g. a spell of unusually cold weather, and is soon reversed. On the other hand the fall in sales may reflect a more permanent change, e.g. a loss of custom to a competitor who has recently introduced a new product. In these circumstances spending borrowed money might constitute 'throwing good money after bad', and a better alternative would be to try to re-allocate the firm's resources into the making of other products. It is clearly important that the cause of the decline in sales should be identified.

Let us take an example from the personnel area, an increase in employee absences on the grounds of sickness. If the manager simply reacts to the immediate issue, he might authorize the spending of more money on company medical facilities, or introduce more extensive medical checks for applicants. Before taking these steps, however, it would be sensible to ensure that the increased absences were not, in fact, symptoms of a deeper problem, e.g. a loss of job satisfaction because of changed working methods, or personal conflicts due to staff changes.

It follows that managers should ensure that they give adequate attention to all the elements that impinge on the area of decision. However, having done so, they should then decide which of the various issues are the most important. An experienced manager is able to isolate the critical factors and concentrate his attention on them.

Determine the Decision Process to be followed. Several important issues arise under this heading. First, who should take the decision? The person who first becomes aware of a problem (or at least of the symptom) may not be in a position, or have the authority, to provide the solution. For example, the sales manager may first become aware of a short-fall in sales, but this may be due to a failure on the part of the production department to provide the quality of products required by the customers. Even when the person who first identifies the problem is involved in the solution the organization's style of management may require that the decision be taken jointly with other managers.

In the public sector decisions are often made by committees of several individuals (see below). Even in organizations with a large amount of delegated responsibility, decisions are often shared between several managers or departments; only the really crucial issues are ultimately decided by one person and that is often someone very senior in the organization.

If a decision ultimately gives rise to a number of more minor decisions the responsibility for these minor decisions may be delegated to junior managers or even supervisors. For example, a decision may be taken at a senior level to introduce a work sharing scheme. In some of these schemes the actual design and production methods are pre-ordained, but it is left to the employees to allocate various functions amongst themselves so as to avoid boredom or undue fatigue.

Public sector organizations, especially those in the non-market sector, frequently take decisions on the basis of precedent, i.e. 'What did we do last time in a similar situation?' This may involve getting out the relevant files and going through all the previous correspondence and minutes relating to similar issues, and using these as the basis for the present decision. Alternatively, reference may be made to manuals in specifying the course of action to be taken.

There are two justifications for proceeding in this way. First, by 'routinizing' decisions it is possible to push responsibility to lower levels in the organization. Second, it ensures consistency in decision making, a factor that is particularly important in organizations implementing government policy, e.g. in paying social benefits to individuals or granting financial assistance to firms.

On the other hand such a system would not be appropriate in organizations using new technologies or in other innovatory situations. Previous 'case histories' are unlikely to exist and even if they did they might inhibit rather than encourage change.

Choosing the Time Scale. Two separate issues arises here: the time period within which the decision must be taken, and the period within which the decision's consequences will be felt. We have stressed the importance of carefully defining the problem and of considering all the relevant factors. However, there is often a trade-off between information and cost. The more information is sought the greater the cost involved, in terms of employees' time (which could otherwise be devoted to doing other things), and also, perhaps, in commissioning special studies. Moreover, delaying the decision may also increase the cost of implementing the solution, especially in inflationary conditions when costs rise over time. For example, if a firm has to buy new machinery to improve product quality, that machinery is likely to cost more next year or even next month than today. Consequently, it is often necessary to have a cut-off point, by which time the decision must be taken, even though it might be possible to obtain more information.

If the decision is a particularly difficult one to make or is likely to have wide-ranging effects that cannot be immediately ascertained, it may be better to make a temporary decision on the issue so as to postpone a final solution until the situation becomes clearer or until more favorable times, e.g. in the hope of an upturn in the market or lower interest rates. The building societies often operate in this way, delaying a change in their mortgage rate following a change in other interest rates. They make a temporary decision to leave the rate unchanged, knowing that subsequently they may have to change this decision.

The effects of some decisions are felt over a longer period of time than others. Changes in fiscal or monetary policy may take a long time to work their way through all sectors of the economy and their initial impact may be slight. This may be a good thing from a producer's point of view since sudden changes in economic conditions make it difficult to plan their operations efficiently. On the other hand it is obviously undesirable if the government is faced with a crisis requiring an immediate change in conditions.

The use of computer simulation techniques now allows managers to achieve, what a few years ago was almost impossible, a fairly accurate estimate of the total impact of a decision, over a given timescale, on all sections of their organization or in the case of government, on individual sector and the total economy.

This facility may also be available to critics of the decision maker. When the Government or the Chancellor announces a change in economic policy, the effects of the policy can be predicted by simulation using the Treasure economic model, which is now made available to the public, or other models, e.g. that of the London Business School. This allows the critics not only to comment on the chances of the outcome predicted by the Government coming to pass, but also to work out the assumptions on which policy is based, e.g. changes in wage rates. This has made government economic decision making much more of an 'open event' than in the past.

Managers have to weigh up their long and short-term objectives. These may sometimes conflict, e.g. a decision to cut the price of a product may keep the cash coming in and maintain production and employment for a few weeks. But in the long term such a price may be impossible to maintain. One of the advantages of planning is that it enables the effects of the decision on the total organization to be estimated and reduces the chance of taking decisions are not in accordance with the long-term objectives of the organization.

Gathering Information. Organizations generate a great deal of information in formulating and reviewing plans. Consequently, when a problem arises much of the information required for the solution may already be to hand. If for example, a decision has to be made concerning a change in the level of output, the managers involved ought to be able to 'call up', perhaps from a central computer file or from the records of individual departments, data showing the effect of the change on production costs, materials requirements, the number of workers needed, etc.

In current circumstances, when private sector firms are facing keen national and even keener international competition, when the public sector is being requested to give even greater value for money, information on costs is vital. The growth in importance of the accountancy profession in recent years mirrors the vital role financial information now plays in all managerial decisions. Increasing competition has also led to more information being gathered on a regular basis on the markets served by producers. This information relates to trends in demand and to the activities of competitors—prices, advertising, changes in product quality etc. Much of this data is quantitative but decisions are also made on mere 'qualitative' grounds, including people's past experience. There are still managers who have a distrust of figures ('There are lies, damn lies and statistics') and prefer to manage 'by the seat of their pants.' But a good manager will combine both these approaches in his decision-making process. He will use quantitative data, but will be aware of the potential deficiencies and will interpret the data in the light of his own experience.

If the necessary information is not available within the organization then it may be necessary to use outside resources. Specialist consultants in, say, the engineering or marketing areas can undertake surveys and provide information, and make recommendations for management to act upon. External statistics, particularly those produced by government agencies, can also help, and 'on line' computer systems and document and data transmission systems enable organizations to draw on statistics from all over the world, e.g. the use banks make of international financial data, stock market data etc.

Managers have to sure that the format in which information is gathered and presented is understandable, not only by themselves, but also by other people who may wish to check the basis of the decision at a later date. Managers have to be confident about the reliability of the information and of its source.

When all the available information has been examined managers must return to stage one and consider whether, in the light of this increased knowledge, the problem still appears to be the same as it did initially and whether the original aims of the decision are still valid.

Examining The Alternatives. Many decisions, especially in the control area, are in effect taken by computers, the role of the manager being confined to decisions relating to the introduction and design of the system. However, as noted in our discussion of planning, managers are seldom presented with information that leads to only one possible decision or course of action. (If this were so there would be no real need for managers, as people would merely act according to the dictates of the information). In choosing from the alternative courses of action the manager will be aware that he will have to live with the consequences of the decision. Indeed if the decision is a major one his future career may depend upon the outcome. Choosing the right alternative, far from being a matter of simply following the direction indicated by the statistics, becomes a very personal decision.

Implementation. Unless the manager is running a one man business every decision will require the assistance of someone else to carry it out. This means that to complete the decision-making process a manager must:

1. Ascertain who takes what action and at what time;

2. Ascertain the time each part of the decision will take to implement;

3. Decide on the methods of communicating the decision;

4. Consider what effect the decision is going to have on other people and take steps to counteract any adverse reactions;

5. Set up a system of information feedback so that he can modify his decision in the light of experience, if necessary.

A number of other models of the decision making process follow the same general approach as the proposed by Dewey. Perhaps the best known is that of Herbert A. Simon. His model consists of three stages that may be described as follows:

Intelligence. The internal and external environments of the decision maker are searched for conditions requiring a decision, and information is gathered about these conditions.

Design. The courses of action available to the decision maker are determined and analyzed as possible solutions to the decision problems that have been detected.

Choice. One of the available courses of action is selected for implementation on the basis of an evaluation of their effectiveness relative to the achievement of objectives.

In his later work, Simon added a fourth phase which he called *review.* This review phase consists of a process of assessment of past choices during which possible modifications to the approaches used are considered in preparation for further decision making activity. This fourth phase represents a revision of general decision making techniques rather than a part of the process applicable to any one situation.

A somewhat more detailed description of the decision making process has been provided by Eilon in an article that seeks to explore a number of aspects of the nature of decisions. Eilon's description of the decision process consists of eight steps that can be listed briefly as follows:

1. Information input
2. Analysis of the available information
3. Specification of measures of performance and cost
4. Creation of a model of the decision situation
5. Formulation of alternatives available to the decision maker
6. Predictions of outcomes of the alternatives
7. Specification of criteria of choice between alternatives
8. Resolution of the decision situation

Both Simon's and Eilon's models provide an initial framework for consideration of the decision process and an idea of the progression of steps that may be necessary before the decision situation can be resolved. In practice, the steps described may take place in a somewhat different order. Some may be undertaken implicitly and some concurrently. Furthermore, the actual decision process often consists of a series of iterations through some or all of the steps described, rather than a single run through a process consisting of a simple series of phases.

DEALING WITH WELL STRUCTURED SITUATIONS

A procedure for resolution of well structured decision problems can be constructed from a combination of the Simon and Eilon models of the decision process. Remembering that the objectives of the decision maker constitute the background to the decision process, the steps in this procedure can be described as follows:

Intelligence

(a) *Perception and formulation of the situation:* The identification of a decision situation and the definition of its main characteristics.

(b) *Construction of a model of the situation:* A model provides a vehicle for estimating the possible outcomes of a decision situation over a range of possible conditions.

(c) *Determination of such quantitative measures of costs and benefits as are appropriate to the situation under consideration:* Uniform measurement systems facilitate comparisons between the alternate ways of resolving the decision problem.

Design

(a) *Specification of available alternatives:* Possible courses of action are identified and clearly formulated.

Choice

(a) *Evaluation of the benefits and costs of the available alternative courses of action:* The effect of the implementation of each course of action is assessed in terms of the measures of costs and benefits specified earlier.

(b) *Establishment of a criterion for choice between courses of action:* Rules are established by which outcomes can be related to the objectives of the party making the choice.

(c) *Resolution of the decision situation:* A choice is made from among the available courses of action on the basis of an acceptable criterion.

As before, these steps need not necessarily be taken in the exact order shown. Also, in practice, the procedure may consist of a series of repetitions of all or some of the above steps before the decision situation is finally resolved. The individual steps can be described in more detail as follows:

Perception and Formulation of the Situation. This first step in the decision making procedure consists of (1) searching the environment of the organization concerned for conditions that call for a decision; (2) collecting as much information as appears necessary and as available time and resources allow on situations that are detected; (3) forming a perception of each situation on the basis of the information at hand; and (4) placing each situation in a category consistent with its perceived characteristics. Drucker has described four different conditions that the decision maker may detect at this stage:

1. An event that is truly one of a type that is met repetitively by the individual or organization concerned and that may be classified as well-structured after further investigation.

2. An event that is new to the particular organization or department in which the individual is working, but which is in fact well structured and met repetitively in other similar organizations or departments.

3. An event that appears to be unique, but that is in reality the first manifestation of a situation that can be well structured and which will be met repetitively in the future.

4. A truly unique event that is unlikely to occur again in the same form in the foreseeable future.

Correct initial identification of the observed conditions and accurate perception of the symptoms are essential to effective resolution of the decision situation. Treatment of a routine and repetitive situation as new and unique most always results in inefficiency and wasted effort. On the other hand, misperception of a new and unique problem as one that can be handled routinely is likely to cause even greater difficulty. There is no prescription for accurate diagnosis better than persistence and dogged determination to explain the observed phenomena. This persistence involves repeated inquiry as to whether the perception and formulation of the problem explain all the observed events. It is important to establish whether some event has been ignored or forgetten that is not compatible with the proposed formulation. If that is the case, a modification of the problem definition may be necessary.

Construction of a Model of the Situation. Perception and formulation of the decision situation is the basis for the construction of a model, giving full details of the factors involved and the relationships between them. This model is used to explore the effects of actions that might be taken to resolve the decision situations. In some of the more routine situations, it may be appropriate to describe the relationships between the factors in a situation by mathematical formulations. Such expressions provide a convenient method of description in a format for which rules of manipulation of the parameters involved have already been established. However, the attractiveness of mathematical models should not be a source of temptation to use them without considerable thought. In particular, many such models involve assumptions that are clearly stated in their formulation. The applicability of these assumptions to the decision situation at hand must be checked thoroughly before any such model is adopted.

John D.C. Little states in a recent article that a model of a decision situation should be "...simple, robust, easy to control, adaptive, as complete as possible and easy to communicate with." In addition, it should contain a complete statement of the constraints or boundary conditions existing in the situation. A solution to a decision situation that does not satisfy the existing constraints is, in fact, a solution to the wrong problem. Tannenbaum has listed five types of constraints that may exist in a typical decision situation:

- □ *Authoritative constraints*, which result from policies or directives within an organization.
- □ *Biological constraints*, which arise from the limitations of individuals who may be affected by the decision.
- □ *Physical constraints*, including such factors as geography, climate, physical resources, and characteristics of man made objects.
- □ *Technological constraints*, involved with the state of the art in relevant technological development.
- □ *Economic constraints*, concerned with the money or other resources available to implement the chosen alternative.

These constraints are the result of the social and technological elements of the environment described earlier in the text. One of these constraints, or a combination of them, may limit the number of alternatives available to the decision maker. Since the time frame of the decision situation normally extends into the future, it is necessary in many cases that the estimated future bahavior of the constraints and boundary conditions be included in the model.

Determination of Quantitative Measures of Costs and Benefits. The task of the decision maker is considerably easier if the results of each of the alternatives that must be considered can be expressed in terms of quantitative measures of costs and benefits. When maximization of monetary gain is the objective, there is little difficulty in choosing between two alternatives if one is estimated to produce more profit (measured in dollars) than the other. The search for quantitative measures that are true representations of the benefits and costs of the alternatives is therefore an important part of the decision making process. These measures must be directly related to the objectives that form the background to the decision situation under consideration.

Specification of Available Alternatives. The individual dealing with a decision situation must list the alternative courses of action that he considers to be available within the boundary conditions of the situation as it is perceived and formulated. The effect of constraints existing in the environment of the decision must be taken into account and the limitations on available alternatives that are caused by these constraints must also be studied. Care should be taken to list as many of the available alternatives as possible, including some that may not come immediately to mind. It is often useful to seek the opinions of persons with substantially different backgrounds and experience before being satisfied that the listing is as complete as possible.

Estimation of the Outcomes from Available Alternatives. Given a list of available alternatives and a model of the decision situation, it is possible in well structured situations to estimate the outcomes that would be expected from implementation of each of the alternatives in terms of the chosen measures of benefits and costs.

Establishment of a Criterion of Choice Between Outcomes. Having estimated the benefits and costs of the available alternatives, it is necessary to establish a criterion of choice between them. This criterion must be closely linked to the objectives that form the background to the decision situation. Maximization of benefits for a given cost or minimization of cost for a given benefit are criteria of choice often found in situations in which the economic welfare of an organization is the prime objective.

Resolution of the Decision Situation. Resolution of the decision situation is the final stage of the decision process. It consists of the choice of a course of action after completion of all the above steps. In many cases the process consists of a number of cycles through all or some of these steps. Once resolution has been achieved, implementation of the chosen alternative course of action can begin.

The above procedure provides a means of dealing with well structured decision situations. In fact, a typical characteristic of a well structured decision situation is that it can be resolved by the application of a logical sequence of steps such as that described above. It is interesting to note that in practice, there is no unique quality that determines that a decision situation is well structured. It is necessary only that the individuals, organizations, or groups involved in the decision situation agree that it be considered to be well structured. Such agreement is often based on expediency.

It is sometimes economic in time and resources to agree to a specification of a decision situation that is admittedly not perfect, but that is nevertheless adequate for the purposes at hand. For example, most payroll systems do not provide payments to employees that represent the exact amount due to them in a given time period. The amount paid is usually an approximation to this exact amount. The approximation is nevertheless acceptable to the employees who do not argue over minor discrepancies in the amount received. They have some faith that these deviations from their exact entitlement will be corrected in due course. In the same way, some models used to evaluate operational systems do not consist of an exact representation of those systems. These models often neglect characteristics that are judged to have only a minor effect on the operation of the system. They do, however, provide a representation that is regarded as accurate enough by the individuals who are involved in the decision situation under consideration.

Resolution of well structured decision situation by an agreed procedure has been called *impersonalistic* by Eilon. His reasoning is that adoption of an agreed procedure precludes the insertion of individual decision makers' beliefs, attitudes, and value judgments into the decision process once the agreement on the procedure has been reached. The outcome of the decision process under these circumstances is the same for all decision makers who use the procedure. It is interesting to note that the writing of an agreed specification for resolution of an operational or administrative process is a necessary step in preparing that process for computer support. The decision situations that we delegate completely to a computer are therefore necessarily well structured and the resolution of these situations is carried out by the computer in an impersonalistic and well structured fashion.

Use of an agreed procedure to resolve a well structured situation can be said to contribute to rational decision making. The notion of rationality is one of the most contentious in the technical literature of decision making. The dictionary definition of the word rational as "endowed with reason" is not adequate for our purposes. A broader concept of rationality is that a rational decision maker is one who, after consideration of alternatives, chooses that which is most preferred relative to stated objectives. To do otherwise can be called irrational. Choice of the most preferred alternative after application of a well structured and agreed procedure can therefore be regarded as rational. This view is supported by Diesing in his review of the role of rationality in society and of the many forms that it can take. However, later in his work he seeks to broaden the concept of rationality by applying it solely to the selection of a decision making procedure rather than to the choice between alternatives. The choice of a well defined stepwise procedure in the case of a well structured decision situation would in this way of thinking be regarded as rational and as leading to rational choice between alternatives. We will return to this subject later in the text as we ponder the question of what constitutes rational behavior in decision situations that are not well structured.

DECISION MAKING IN AN ILL-STRUCTURED SITUATION

Decision situations are classified as ill structured when conditions in their environment preclude the possibility of resolution using a routine procedure such as that described above. There are four main characteristics of ill structured situations, some or all of which may be present in practical circumstances. These characteristics are:

1. Lack of complete information regarding the decision situation and its environment.

2. Lack of quantitative measures that truly and completely describe the costs and benefits of the available alternatives.

3. The existence of multiple objectives on the part of the organization, individual, or group concerned.

4. The existence of more than one participant in the decision situation with power to influence the outcome.

Lack of Complete Information

Lack of complete information about a decision situation leads to uncertainty among those involved in its resolution with regard to many of its characteristics. This uncertainty has three main effects. First, it is usually impossible with incomplete information to construct a comprehensive model of the decision situation that includes all the relevant factors and the relationships between them. With an incomplete model of the situation, those involved may feel that some of the more important aspects of the situation are beyond their immediate comprehension. Furthermore, much of the information available may consist only of symptoms of a need for action (such as an increase in absenteeism in a factory or an increase in violent crime in a city) rather than being a detailed description and formulation of all the vital aspects of the situation. In these circumstances, a great deal of time and effort may need to be spent in identifying the nature of the situation under consideration. Without complete information, it cannot be certain at any time that a correct identification has been made.

Second, under conditions of limited information, different individuals involved in a decision situation may form different impressions of its characteristics. Each individual's perceptions of the situation are based on the information available viewed against his previous experience and factors relating to spheres of competence, judgment, and motivation.

It may be very difficult, therefore, for two or more individuals to agree to a specification and formulation of the problem. In these circumstances, it is unlikely that complete agreement can be reached between the individuals involved on such matters as alternative courses of action, quantitative measures of costs and benefits, and criteria for choice between alternatives.

Third, lack of complete information leads to uncertainty about the exact conditions in the environment of the decision situation. There may be a considerable period of time between the choice and the completion of the implementation of a course of action. There is a possibility therefore that conditions in the environment of the decision when the course of action has been implemented will have deviated from those that had been predicted. The effects of a course of action chosen in an attempt to resolve a decision situation may therefore be different from that estimated at the time of its selection. The longer the implementation time, the greater is the risk that the outcome of a course of action will be different from that estimated during the decision process.

Lack of Appropriate Quantitative Measures of Benefits and Costs

Choice between alternatives is considerably easier when the comparison between them can be made in terms of well understood benefits and costs. This condition, which is often found in well structured situations, allows the alternatives to be compared in like terms. In many situations, however, the assignment of purely quantitative measures to the benefits and costs of alternative courses of action is very difficult. This difficulty arises particularly in situations in which the health, happiness, and welfare of a segment of the population is affected. Measurement of these factors is not easily accomplished and there is a danger that vital aspects of benefits or costs will be neglected by an inappropriate choice of measures. The same problem arises in business decision situations also. For example, it is difficult to suggest a truly appropriate measure of the public image of a corporation or of the manner in which a company meets its social responsibilities.

There is a temptation in these circumstances to assign quantitative measures of benefits and costs even if they do not relate exactly to the factors involved in progress towards achievement of the objectives that from the background to the decision situation. This temptation arises from the simplification of the decision process if the choice between alternatives can be made in quantitative terms. However, this simplification may involve a considerable distortion of the decision situation. Conclusions reached after analysis of the distorted situation are frequently misleading when applied to the conditions that are actually facing the individuals involved. Unfortunately, such conclusions often have an aura of validity purely from having been derived by an apparently logical process. Individuals who are not familiar with the analysis and with the effects of the assumptions that have been made may therefore be seriously misled.

When the individuals have different perceptions of a decision situation and its characteristics, they may also have different views with respect to the measures of benefits and costs that should be employed in the decision process. This possible difference in views is a further reason why a completely agreed upon specification of the process of resolution of an ill structured decision situation cannot be obtained.

The Existence of Multiple Objectives

Most organizations, individuals, and groups have more than one objective. In such cases, adoption of a course of action that provides satisfactory achievement of one objective may result in less progress towards satisfying some or all of the others. There may be no means of selecting an alternative that is unequivocally best in these circumstances. The choice between alternatives is more easily handled if progress towards achievement of each of the objectives can be measured in the same well understood unit (such as dollars) and when the priority between objectives can be expressed in terms of numeric weighting factors. However, these conditions often do not exist in ill structured decision situations. Individuals involved in such a decision situation may disagree regarding the priority to be assigned to each of the objectives and on the manner of evaluating alternatives with respect to them. In such cases, the choice between alternatives is made using the intuition and judgment of experienced individuals rather than by the adoption of a well structured decision making routine.

The Existence of Many Participants

In many of the ill structured decision situations encountered today the power to bring about an outcome does not lie with a single decision maker. A basic characteristic of such situations is that two or more participants each have the capability to influence the outcome. These participants may have conflicting interests and intentions. They may each have in mind outcomes that they feel they can achieve and that they think will be most appropriate to the achievement of their objectives. However, no one participant has the power at the outset of the decision situation to bring about by unilateral action the outcome that he or she most prefers. Satisfactory resolution of a decision situation of this kind can be achieved only by agreement between participants that retain the power to influence the outcome. For example, in an industrial relations dispute, management cannot obtain the settlement that it wishes as long as the union has in mind an outcome that it considers to be more in its interests and as long as management has no means of forcing the union to accept its will.

The actual outcomes of situations of this nature are usually determined as a result of an open or implicit process of negotiation between the participants. The objective of each of the participants during this process of negotiation is to persuade the others to accept the outcome that he or she most prefers. Often, the outcome that emerges is not one that was originally seen as most preferred by any participant, but one that each is prepared to accept after the process of negotiation as preferable to a continuation of the confrontation. In industrial relations disputes, for example, the outcome of negotiations is often a compromise that is eventually accepted by both parties in order that the dispute can be resolved without further passage of time.

Complex decision situation such as those described above do not lend themselves to resolution by a routine procedure such as can be applied to well structured situations. A logical process of this sort may well be useful in determining an order of preference of a particular participant for possible outcomes of a decision situation. However, the actual outcome results from a process of negotiation between participants for which no well structured procedure has yet been devised. Even if a completely structured process of resolution of these complex situations could be devised, it would probably be unacceptable as a basis of resolution by participants with different interests, objectives, and perceptions of the situation in which they are involved.

THE RESOLUTION OF ILL STRUCTURED SITUATIONS

A pervasive feature of ill structured decision situation is the lack of complete information concerning their characteristics. There can therefore be no unique and undisputable formulation of such a decision situation and no unequivocal method of resolution that is acceptable to all. Individual decision makers form their perceptions of a decision situation and of the means by which it can be resolved on the basis of the information available to them at the time. In the absence of a well structured and agreed model of the process of resolution, the experience and intuition of those involved in a decision situation becomes a major factor in the choice between alternative courses of action and between outcomes. Under these circumstances, decision making is personalistic, as contrasted to the impersonal nature of the use of a well structured and logical procedure. Nevertheless, some aspects of the well structured procedure can be retained. The logical sequence of steps provides at least a guide to the considerations that are important in a first approach to a decision situation. The three-stage model of Simon (intelligence, design, and choice) is applicable to many ill structured situations in which a single decision maker is charged with the choice between alternatives.

Some modification of the original Simon model is necessary, however, in approaching decision situations in which there are two or more participants. This modification is required to take account of the process of negotiation between the participants that is essential to the determination of the outcome. The modification consists of a redefinition of the three phases of the decision making process, as follows:

Information Gathering. The internal and external environments of the organization are searched for incipient decision situations, information gathered about each situation that is detected, and alternative courses of action listed for each of them.

Analysis. Possible outcomes of a decision situation that may be brought about by a combination of courses of action taken by the participants are analyzed and placed in an order of preference. Tactics designed to bring about preferred outcomes are considered in this phase.

Interaction. Preferences and intentions are communicated explicitly or implicitly to other participants with the objective of persuading or coercing them to agree to a most-preferred outcome.

The question remains as to what constitutes rational behavior in the resolution of ill structured decision situations. The concept of rationality is relatively straightforward in well structured situations in which there is complete information, a single objective, the ability to evaluate benefits and costs in quantitative terms, and a single decision maker. In these circumstances, all possible alternatives can be envisaged and evaluated. Rational behaviour consists of choosing the alternative that is seen as best (or most preferred) in terms of a criterion related to the objective. Any other choice can be seen to be against the interests of the decision maker and can be called irrational.

The concept of rationality in ill structured situations is not as clear-cut. Lack of a simple decision making rule is possibly one reason why these situations have been called "wicked" as compared with the "tame" and more tractable well structured kind. Without complete information, any list of the alternatives available to the decision maker is necessarily incomplete. There is no guarantee that another course of action that is preferable to those considered would not be revealed if more information were available. In these circumstances no choice between alternatives can be said unequivocally to be the best and therefore to be uniquely rational. Furthermore, two individuals involved in the same decision situation might have different information and consequently different perceptions of that situation. In these circumstances, the two individuals might recommend different courses of action for resolution of the same decision situation, each claiming, however, that he had acted rationally in the choice between alternatives.

Some qualification of the concept of rationality is clearly needed in the case of ill structured decision situations. This qualification can be introduced in the following manner. Choice of the alternative or outcome that is most preferred relative to an objective under conditions of complete information is termed *objectively rational*. An objectively rational choice is unique and optimal under the conditions stated. A choice between alternatives when information is not complete and under other conditions found in ill structured decision situation is called *subjectively rational*. A subjectively rational choice is not unique. Two individuals may reach different conclusions and each be subjectively rational in the circumstances as they perceive them. Subjective rationality can be considered in some cases to be more related to the approach to the decision situation than to the actual choice between alternatives. A subjectively rational approach may be one that, in Diesing's words, "...yields adequate decisions for complex situations with some regularity."

A further extension of the idea of rationality is necessary when two or more participants are involved in an ill structured decision situation. In these circumstances, the outcome is often reached only after a process of negotiation between the participants. This outcome may be viewed as being *jointly rational*, insomuch that it permits resolution of the decision situation and is preferred by all participants to a continuation of the confrontation.

DECISION MAKING BY COMMITTEE

So far our comments on the decision-making process have been mainly concerned with individual management decision making, although the steps to be taken are common to all decisions. Readers who work in, or are familiar with, the public sector will know that committee or group, rather than individual, decision making is the norm. It may be useful to outline the advantages and disadvantages of this type of decision-making process.

Advantages of Committees as a Decision-making Medium

1. A committee allows differing viewpoints to be brought together in the same place and at the same time. Differences can be aired, alternatives hammered out, all the relevant information being available for all to see.

2. The committee, as every good politician realizes, is a good coordinating medium. Having all the relevant parties to the decision in one room is a far better and easier way of co-ordinating progress, than relying on memos or telephone calls. (This benefit is felt mainly by the manager who would otherwise have to write the memos or make the telephone calls. There are, however, corresponding costs, as pointed out below).

3. Individuals feel better motivated if they have been involved in making the decision and have personally followed the arguments and discussions over the alternatives. By involving everyone concerned, by obtaining a consensus, a committee can achieve a higher level of motivation than most other decision-making methods.

4. Committee procedure is useful for training purposes. Newcomers, e.g. management trainees, can 'sit in' on committees and gain experience at first hand. They see the personalities in action, learn about the power play and observe the operations of pressure groups.

5. Creativity, it is argued, is improved in a committee environment. People bounce ideas around and follow the various threads

of an argument. The clash of trained minds can spark off new ideas that may not occur to an individual sitting alone pondering a set of alternatives on a computer-print out.

6. The committee system provides work for a large number of people—committee clerks, typists, reprographics staff, information gatherers and disseminators. It is, perhaps, not surprising that the committee system is so popular in the public sector where 'size is might', where the bigger your committee, the more important a chief officer or a chairman you are. (Again there are corresponding costs, as noted below.)

Disadvantages of Committees as a Decision-taking Medium

1. People may hide behind committee decisions. No one person can be held responsible: 'It was the committee's decision, I was against it, but...'. This can lead to 'buck passing' and delays if further decisions are required or if the original decision proves to be wrong. The bureaucratic process thrives on the 'vagueness' of the committee system.

2. Committees take time. Time is money, and if one works out the costs of the committee system of a local authority, for instance, the result can be frightening. To the salaries of the committee members have to be added the costs of typing the minutes, printing the agendas etc.

3. Committees lead to compromise. In some circumstances the 'good old British compromise' can be beneficial. In other situations it lead to a 'second-best situation' and merely glosses over the real divisions between those involved. In effect the real decision is postponed.

DECISION MAKING AND ACCOUNTABILITY

As sources of information multiply, availability and access improve, and educational standards rise, several issues concerning decision making and accountability have received greater attention.

Use of Information

There is general public disquiet at present about 'hidden information' held on individuals on computer files compiled by government departments, the police, or various private sector organizations. This issue was examined by the Lindop Committee.

In Sweden the 1776 Freedom of the Press Act, re-affirmed in 1810 and 1949 gives every Swedish citizen free access to official documents. In practice even foreigners are not excluded and 'documents' include punch cards, computer tapes and memory banks. Norway and Denmark also allow access to documents providing a security risk is not involved and the searcher specifies the documents required. In America, there is much more freedom of information than in Great Britain and the trend to more open government is now well established (overseas that is, but not in this country).

Public Participation in Decision Making

Decisions taken, or about to be taken, by organization ranging from governments to multinational companies, are increasingly subject to public scrutiny and debate. The spread of television has been of paramount importance here, as noted in our discussion of communications. Although this may not, strictly speaking, amount to public participation in decision-making, the decision makers themselves are often influenced by the public debate.

The Factors Influencing Decisions

Extending public discussions almost inevitably means that decision makers take into account factors that otherwise they would not have done. A good example is the debate concerning the siting of a third London airport. There seems little doubt that the committees that have examined the issues have been influenced by the opinions expressed by the inhabitants of the various possible locations. Furthermore, when the government made the decision not to build another airport, at least for the time being, it was also influenced by public opinion.

CATEGORIES OF DECISION SITUATIONS

The division of decision situations into well- and ill-structured categories serves as a first step in identifying their characteristics. A more detailed differentiation is necessary, however, in discussing methods by which each of the various decision situations that are encountered by modern organizations and individuals can be approached. It has been conventional in the technical literature to divide decision situations into categories depending on whether they exist under conditions of certainty, risk, uncertainty, and competition. These conditions are defined as follows:

- *Certainty*—when all possible alternative courses of action are known and when there is only one consequence or outcome of each of these courses of action.
- *Risk*—when there is more than one possible consequence or outcome of each of the alternatives and the decision maker is assumed to know the probability of occurrence of these consequences or outcomes.
- *Uncertainty*—when neither the number of possible consequences or outcomes nor the probability of their occurrence is known to the decision maker.
- *Competition*—when an identified opponent to the decision maker exists, whose objectives, intentions, and choices may be in direct or indirect conflict to those of the decision maker.

These categories are derived to some extent from the types of mathematical approaches to decision making that have been devised in the past forty years. However, this classification has a number of deficiencies in the light of more recent work on the characteristics of decision situations. It does not, for example, take explicit account of the existence of multiple objectives or the lack of truly appropriate quantitative measures of benefits and costs, which are important features of many modern decision situations. Furthermore, the naming of the categories tends to give the impression that uncertainty and competition are mutually exclusive, whereas much of the complexity of many decision situations derives from a combination of these and other factors.

It has recently been suggested that the four characteristics that have a major effect on the process of resolution of a decision situation should be used to construct a new series of categories for the purpose of detailed study of these situations. These characteristics are:

1. whether or not uncertainty exists in the decision situating being considered;

2. whether or not the benefits and costs resulting from the implementation of available courses of action can be truly represented in quantitative terms;

3. whether a single objective is involved or whether multiple objectives must be taken into account;

4. whether the power to make the decision lies in the hands of one organization, individual, or group or whether many such participants have power to influence the outcome of the situation.

CONCLUSIONS

Decision situations encountered by modern organizations, individuals, and groups range from those that occur repetitively in essentially the same form to those that are new and unique. Repetitive decision situations can be approached by following rules and patterns of behavior that have been established as a result of previous experience. The approach to new and unique situations relies much more on the intuition and judgment of those involved.

The essence of decision making is the choice between alternatives. This choice is made against a background of the objectives of the decision maker and after as much information has been gathered as seems necessary and as time and available resources allow. Organizations, individuals, and groups involved in decision making can be regarded as systems operating in an external environment and having an internal environment of their own. The portions of these environments that relate to a particular decision situation constitute the environment of that situation. Decision makers may have more than one objective. Organizations are groups can be regarded as coalitions of components, each of which may have objectives that are to some extent in competition with those of the overall entity.

Decision situations can be divided into those that are "well structured" and those that are "ill structured." Well structured decision situations are those that have become well understood as a result of many encounters with situations of the same kind. Resolution of well structured decisions can usually be achieved by application of a standard procedure. In contrast, each ill structured decision situation that is encountered appears to have characteristics that make it not exactly like any other that has been met in the past. Some decision situations have only a part that can be regarded as well structured. These situations are called "partially structured."

Early descriptions of the decision making process divided it into three phases called *intelligence* (or search for information), *design* of alternatives, and *choice* between these alternatives. A step-by-step procedure can be devised from these three phases that can be applied to the resolution of well structured decision situations. Decision making using such a procedure has been called impersonalistic because none of the decision maker's beliefs, attitudes, and value judgments enter into the process, once the procedure has been established. Choice of the alternative that is seen as most preferred after application of such a procedure can be regarded as rational.

There are four conditions characteristic of ill-structured decision situations that preclude the possibility of resolution using an impersonalistic, step-by-step procedure:

1. Lack of complete information concerning the situation.

2. Lack of appropriate quantitative measures of benefits and costs.

3. The existence of multiple objectives.

4. The existence of many participants with power to influence the outcome of the decision situation.

Lack of complete information dictates that there cannot be a unique and indisputable formulation of an ill structured decision situation. Individual decision makers often have different perceptions of the situation and of the means of resolution. The decision process therefore becomes personalistic and resolution depends upon the intuition and judgment of those involved and on negotiation between them. These conditions require a modification of the three-phase decision process so that it consists of the following:

1. Information gathering (as before).

2. Analysis of possible outcomes, with each participant placing these outcomes in an order of preference and the design of tactics by each participant designed to bring about his or her most preferred outcome, and

3. Interaction between participants during which the actual outcome is determined by a process of negotiation.

The concept of rationality requires some modification in the light of conditions in ill structured decision situations. Choice of a most-preferred alternative under conditions of complete information can be called *objectively rational*. However, when information is not complete, decision makers can hope only to be *subjectively rational*. Two different individuals can recommend different alternative solutions to an ill structured decision situation and each can claim to be subjectively rational. Rationality, in such situations, is perhaps best applied to the choice of an approach to decision making. A rational approach might be regarded as one that yields adequate decisions for complex situations with some regularity. A further extension of the concept of rationality is needed when two or more participants are involved in a decision situation. In these circumstances, an outcome that is accepted by all participants can be regarded as *jointly rational*.

Until recently, approaches to resolution of decision situations have been considered in categories related to conditions of certainty, risk, uncertainty, and competition. However, this classification does not take explicit account of the features of many modern decision situations. A more comprehensive classification can be based on the following four characteristics:

1. Whether or not uncertainty exists in the decision situation.

2. Whether or not benefits and costs can be truly represented in quantitative terms.

3. Whether or not multiple objectives are involved.

4. Whether the power to influence the outcome lies with one or more than one participant.

7

CORPORATE DECISION SITUATIONS

WELL structured decisions situations are those that have become well understood as a result of many encounters with situations of the same kind. The experience gained in these many encounters leads to the construction of a standard procedure for dealing with situations of a particular type. Most well structured decision situations contain little or no uncertainty about their characteristics. Sometimes the minor uncertainty that exists in an otherwise well structured situation is neglected in the interests of obtaining a solution to a problem that is sufficiently close to reality for all practical puposes.

The decision situations described in this chapter can usually be formulated in terms of well understood measures of benefits and costs, such as profit from a production process or the cost of performing a service. The single participant involved in these decision situations has the sole objective of maximizing benefit for a given cost or of minimizing cost for a particular benefit.

Models that can be used to represent decision situations of this nature have been described in great detail in the technical literature. It is not the purpose in this chapter to repeat these technical expositions. Rather, the approach will be taken of describing the types of situations that are amendable to treatment by models of this sort and of discussing the results that can be obtained by this type of analysis. The objective is to provide a means of recognizing practical situations of the various types as they occur as well as the manner in which they can be treated.

OPTIMIZATION IN PRODUCTION PROCESS

Many operational decision situations arise in the management of production processes that have the following general characteristics:

- ☐ A product or a service is being produced to meet a demand.
- ☐ The product or service results from a mix of ingredients or resources.
- ☐ The product or service can be produced in a number of alternative ways each of which has a different profitability or efficiency.
- ☐ There are certain conditions or constraints usually concerned with the resources that effect the way the product or service can be produced.
- ☐ There is a desire to optimize a payoff or an "objective function" which usually concerns cost or profit.

Consider, for example, the following fertilizer-mix problem. A particular fertilizer has two main ingredients *A* and *B* in a 50/50 mix. It can be made by mixing the ingredients directly. However it can also be made from two other mixes that are already on hand. These mixes are a by-product from another operation. They contain the same ingredients but in proportions that are different from those required in the fertilizer. Mix 1 has two parts of ingredient *A* and one part of *B*. Mix 2 has one part of ingredient *A* and three parts of *B*. Furthermore, for each ton of mix 1 that is used, a saving of Rs. 50 is made over the use of pure ingredients. *A* saving of Rs. 100 is realized for each ton of mix 2 that is used. There are 70 tons of mix 1 available and 60 tons of mix 2 available for each 100 tons of the fertilizer that must be produced.

Situations of this type can be analyzed by use of the linear programming model. The first step in the analysis is to formulate the situation in terms of an objective function and some constraints. The objective function is a statement of the factor that we wish to maximize (for profit) or minimize (for cost). In the present case the objective is to maximize the saving that can be obtained by the use of the by-product mixes. From the above description of the situation, a saving of Rs. 50 per ton can be made by using mix 1 and Rs. 100 per ton by using mix 2. If X_1 and X_2 represent the number of tons of mix 1 and mix 2 used respectively, the total saving can be written as $50X_1+100X_2$. The objective function is therefore:

$$\text{Maximize} \qquad 50X_1 + 100X_2$$

There are, however, some restrictions or constraints on this maximization process. First, each 100 tons of the required fertilizer (which is 50% ingredient A and 50% ingredient *B*) cannot contain more than 50 tons of each ingredient derived from the by-product mixes. Taking into account the different contents of mix 1 and mix 2, these constraints can be written as:

Ingredient A $\qquad \frac{2}{3}X_1+\frac{1}{4}X_2 \leq 50$

Ingredient B $\qquad \frac{1}{3}X_1+\frac{3}{4}X_2 \leq 50$

In addition, only 70 tons of mix 1 and 60 tons of mix 2 are available. The constraints representing these availabilities can be written:

$$X_1 \leq 70 \qquad X_2 \leq 60$$

The whole situation can now be summarized as:

$$\begin{aligned} \text{Maximize} \quad & 50X_1 + 100X_2 \\ \text{Subject to} \quad & \tfrac{2}{3}X_1+\tfrac{1}{4}X_2 \leq 50 \\ & \tfrac{1}{3}X_1+\tfrac{3}{4}X_2 \leq 50 \\ & X_1 \leq 70 \\ & X_2 \leq 60 \\ & X_1, X_2 \geq 0 \end{aligned}$$

The latter two (non-negativity) constraints recognize the fact that negative amounts of the two mixes cannot be used.

The linear programming model provides a method of obtaining a solution to a formulation of the simple resource allocation problem described above. The solution in this case shows that maximum saving is made by using 60 tons of mix 1 and 40 tons of mix 2. No pure ingredients *A* or *B* are necessary. The 100 tons of fertilizer with the required 50/50 content can be made entirely from the by-product mixes. In the above case, a graphical solution is possible and that solution is described in Appendix A to this chapter. In most other circumstances, a graphical solution is not possible because the analysis involves more than two variables such as X_1 and X_2. In these cases, significant amounts of computation are necessary to obtain the desired results. Fortunately, however, simple and effective computer packaged routines are available for such work. Once the formulation of the situation is accomplished, the resolution of even the most complex problem can be done easily and cheaply using these computer packages.

A Product Mix Problem

As a further example of the application of the linear programming model to the optimization of production processes, suppose that a company has the option of using one or more of four types of production process to manufacture a product from certain materials. Suppose, further, that:

1. each unit of production by the four processes yields a net profit of 4, 5, 9, and 11 dollars respectively;

2. the resources from which the product is made consist of three materials *A, B,* and C of which there are 15, 120, and 100 units respectively available;

3. the four processes require different amounts of each of the three materials as shown in Table 1.

Table 1

Units of Materials Required in the Product Mix Problem

	Process 1	*Process 2*	*Process 3*	*Process 4*
Material A	1	1	1	1
Material B	7	5	3	2
Material C	3	5	10	15

Management wishes to know which of the processes or which combination of processes results in the maximum profit under the above conditions.

Formulation of the Product Mix Problem

Application of the linear programming model requires that the problem situation be formulated in a manner that specifies (1) the objective function; and (2) the constraints inherent in the situation. The formulation of the Product Mix problem is shown in Table 2. The objective function is an expression of the desire to maximize profit. Suppose that X_1, X_2, X_3, and X_4 are the numbers of units of product made by each of the processes respectively. Since the net profit obtained from each unit produced by using each of these processes is 4, 5, 9, and 11 dollars respectively, the total profit can be written as: $4X_1 + 5X_2 + 9X_3 + 11X_4$. The objective function is therefore the maximization of this expression, namely,

$$\text{Maximize} \quad 4X_1 + 5X_2 + 9X_3 + 11X_4$$

Table 2

Formulation of the Product-Mix Problem

Description	*Formulation*
Objective Function	
The total profit from production of product from each of the four processes should be maximized	Maximize $4X_1 + 5X_2 + 9X_3 + 11X_4$
Constraints	
The amount of Material *A* used cannot exceed 15 units	$1X_1 + 1X_2 + 1X_3 + 1X_4 \leq 15$
The amount of Material *B* used cannot exceed 120 units	$7X_1 + 5X_2 + 3X_3 + 2X_4 \leq 120$
The amount of Material C used cannot exceed 100 units	$3X_1 + 5X_2 + 10X_3 + 15X_4 \leq 100$
Other Conditions	
No negative amounts of product can be made by any process	$X_1, X_2, X_3, X_4 \geq 0$

The constraints in the situation arise from the amounts of materials available. Three materials are used so that there are three main constraints. These constraints express the necessary conditions that the total amount of material used in the production of the number of units by each process cannot exceed the amount of materials available. The three constraints can be written as:

Material *A*	$1X_1 + 1X_2 + 1X_3 + 1X_4 \leq 15$
Material *B*	$7X_1 + 5X_2 + 3X_3 + 2X_4 \leq 120$
Material C	$3X_1 + 5X_2 + 10X_3 + 15X_4 \leq 100$

The coefficients of X_1, X_2, X_3, and X_4 in the Material *A* constraint are written as 1 in order to maintain consistency of the format in which these conditions are expressed. One further condition requires that X_1, X_2, X_3, and X_4 must all be non-negative. This condition expresses the obvious fact that negative amounts of the product cannot be manufactured by any of the process.

Further examples of the formulation of situations using the linear programming model are given in the practical decision situations section at the end of this chapter.

Limitations on the Use of the Linear Programming Model

A number of conditions must be met in a problem situation before the linear programming model can be applied without reservation. These conditions refer to the nature of the relationships that are expressed in the formulation of the problem.

First, the linear programming model demands that the objective function and every constraint function be linear. This condition requires that the measure of effectiveness contained in the objective function and the measures of resource usage contained in the constraints must be strictly proportional to the level of each activity conducted individually. For example, in the Product Mix situation just described, it is necessary for truly appropriate application of the model that the amount of profit realized by the additional production of one unit by each of the processes be the same over the entire range of production levels considered. Similarly, the change in use of resources for increases or decreases in production level in each of the processes must be constant over the range of activity covered in the situation.

Clearly, these conditions are not always met in situations to which the linear programming model may seem to be applicable. In many practical situations, for example, the unit profitability or the amount of resources needed for additional production changes as the level of production changes. In these circumstances, either the objective function, or some of the constraint functions, or both may not be exactly linear. The linear model may not therefore be strictly appropriate. It may be justifiable in such cases to assume a condition of linearity as a first approximation to the practical situation. However, assumptions of this nature can lead to serious misrepresentations of the practical conditions and consequently to incorrect analytical results. The temptation to fit the practical situation to the model (rather than the way round) for reasons of analytical convenience should always be resisted.

Second, a form of nonlinearity arises if there are interactions between the activities in terms of profitability or the use of resources. For the linear model to be strictly applicable, the total measure of effectiveness represented in the objective function and the total resource usage represented in the constraints must equal the respective sums of these quantities resulting from the component activities being conducted independently. For example, in the Product-Mix situation, the profitability of production by process 1 must be unaffected by the level of production by processes 2, 3, or 4. Similarly, the use of resources in any one process must be unaffected by the level of production in any other process. These conditions are usually referred to as the requirement for *additivity* with respect to the objective function and the constraints.

Third, even if all the values of the parameters contained in the formulation of a practical solution are integers, the optimal solution obtained by the model may contain fractional values of some of them. However, it may not be possible in many practical situations for some of the parameters to take fractional values. For example, certain resources may be available only in integer amounts. Production process may need to operate only at nonfractional levels. It is tempting in these circumstances to round the results emanating from the analysis to the nearest integer values. However, there is no guarantee that the situation described after such rounding of results is close to optimal or even a feasible solution to the problem as formulated. Arrival at an optimal integer value solution may require considerably more analysis using more complex techniques. The requirement that fractional values of the variables be admissible in an analytical solution is usually referred to as the condition of *divisibility*.

It is rare that a practical situation meets all of the conditions necessary for unreserved application of the linear programming model. It may be possible, however, to obtain useful information from such an application in cases in which all the necessary conditions are not met. In such cases, it is wise to be aware of all the assumptions implicit in the use of the model, so that any reservations arising from these assumptions can be taken into account in the consideration of the analytical results.

Results in the Product Mix Situation

With the foregoing matters in mind, it is interesting to consider the nature of the results obtained in the analysis of the Product-Mix situation described earlier. The analysis of this situation can be done by hand calculation or by the use of a packaged computer program. In each case, the analytical procedure defines a set of values of X_1, X_2, X_3 and X_4 that determines levels of production in each of the four processes. The conditions under which the profit defined by the objective function is a maximum are as follows:

Number of Units Produced in Each Process

Process 1	$X_1 = 50/7$
Process 2	$X_2 = 0$
Process 3	$X_3 = 55/7$
Process 4	$X_4 = 9$

Amount of Available Resources Unused in the Optimal Feasible Solution

Material A	all used
Material B	325/7 units unused
Material C	all used

Profit Obtained from the Optimal Solution

Value of the objective function $4X_1 + 5X_2 + 9X_3 + 11X_4$ at the optimal feasible solution = 695/7

The analytical procedure yields two other useful results. The first of these results concerns *shadow costs*. In the above situation, a shadow cost is the cost of production of a unit by the processes from which no units are required in the optimal solution. It can be shown, for example, from the complete solution of the Product Mix situation, that if one unit were produced by process 2, the maximum profit would be decreased by 3/7. This information is useful in estimating the inefficiencies that might arise in the region of the optimal production situation if the number of units produced by certain processes were marginally changed.

A similar measure is available in the complete solution of a linear program concerning the resources that are used. This measure is called the *shadow price*. It is defined as the unit worth of each resource in the region of the optimal solution of the linear program. In the Product Mix situation, the solution shows that the profit level can be increased by 13/7 for each additional unit of material *A* and 5/7 for each additional unit of material *C* that is made available. This information is useful in deciding whether to bring in more material in order to increase the profitability of the production process. Shadow prices and shadow costs are usually presented in the output from computer- supported linear programming packages. They can be obtained also from hand calculated solutions to the linear programming model.

COMPLEMENTARY OPTIMIZATION PROBLEMS

Situations sometimes arise in which two participants take different but complementary views of the same circumstances. Consider, for example, the situation in which a farming cooperative plans to buy fertilizer in bulk for the following crop year. It is necessary that the fertilizer purchased contain four basic ingredients in the following amounts:

4014.4 units of ingredient 1
366.0 units of ingredient 2
648.5 units of ingredient 3
329.0 units of ingredient 4

The cooperative knows that it can purchase any amounts of three standard fertilizer mixes (F_1, F_2, F_3) at prices of Rs. 18.50, Rs. 24.00, and Rs. 38.50 per bulk loading. Each bulk load of the three mixes contains the number of units of the required basic ingredients shown in the following table.

Table 3

Units of Ingredients of Each Bulk Load of Fertilizer Mix

		Units of Ingredients			
		1	2	3	4
Mix	F_1	3.92	0.20	0.15	0.30
	F_2	1.30	0.65	0.12	0.44
	F_3	1.32	0.80	2.30	0.20

The cooperative wishes to know how much of each fertilizer mix it would need to buy to satisfy its needs for the required ingredients at minimum cost. This problem can be formulated as in the left hand side of Table 4. The optimal solution to the cooperative's problem is that it should buy.

950 bulk loads of mix F_1
0 bulk loads of mix F_2
220 bulk loads of mix F_3

The minimum cost of these purchases while still allowing the need for ingredients to be satisfied is Rs. 26,045.

However, an independent supplier has heard of the cooperative's situation. He proposes to deliver to the cooperative the basic ingredients from which the required fertilizer mixes could be prepared. The cooperative stipulates and the supplier agrees that the costs of the mixes under this arrangement should not exceed those already quoted Rs. 18.50, Rs. 24.00, and Rs. 38.50 per bulk loading respectively). The supplier would like to know the prices he should quote per unit of each ingredient so that the above cost of the three fertilizer mixes should not be exceeded but at the same time his total contract price should be the maximum possible under these conditions. The supplier's problem can be formulated as in the right hand side of Table 4. The optimum solution is that the supplier should charge

Rs. 2.50 per unit of ingredient 1
Rs. 21.00 per unit of ingredient 2
Rs. 7.00 per unit of ingredient 3
Rs. 11.50 per unit of ingredient 4

for a maximum total revenue under these conditions of Rs. 26,045.

Reference to Table 4 shows that there are a number of links between the cooperative's problem (which can be called the primal situation) and the supplier's problem (which can be called the dual situation). Each constraint in the primal situations corresponds to a variable (Y_1, Y_2, Y_3, Y_4) in the dual. Each variable (X_1, X_2, X_3) in the primal corresponds to a constraint in the dual. The right- hand-side values in the constraints of the primal are the coefficients of Y_1, Y_2 and Y_3 in the objective function of the dual, and vice versa. Minimization in the primal situation corresponds to maximization in the dual and vice versa. It is entirely arbitrary which of the two solutions is called the primal and which the dual (the dual of the dual is, in fact, the primal). The desire of the decision maker in the primal in the above example is to minimize costs while ensuring that certain needs for ingredients are met. The objective in the dual is to maximize benefits to the supplier

Table 4

Formulation of the Fertilizer Mix Problem and of its Dual

The Cooperative's Problem (Primal)

Minimize $18.5X_1 + 24.0X_2 + 38.5X_3$

Subject to:

$$3.92X_1 + 1.30X_2 + 1.32X_3 \geq 4014.4,$$
$$0.20X_1 + 0.65X_2 + 0.80X_1 \geq 366.0$$
$$0.15X_1 + 0.12X_2 + 2.30X_3 \geq 648.5$$
$$0.30X_1 + 0.44X_2 + 0.20X_3 \geq 329.0$$

where X_1,, X_2,, X_3 are the amounts of fertilizer mixes F_1, F_2, F_3 purchased.

Optimal Solution

$X_1 = 950$ units of F_1

$X_2 = 0$ units of F_2

$X_3 = 220$ units of F_3

Total Cost = Rs. 26,045

The Supplier's Problem (Dual)

Maximize $4014.4Y_1 + 366.0Y_2 + 648.5Y_3 + 329.0Y_4$

Subject to:

$$3.92Y_1 + 0.20Y_2 + 0.15Y_3 + 0.30Y_4 \geq 18.5$$
$$1.30Y_1 + 0.65Y_2 + 0.12Y_3 + 0.44Y_4 \leq 24.0$$
$$1.32Y_1 + 0.80Y_2 + 2.30Y_3 + 0.20Y_4 \leq 38.5$$

where Y_1, Y_2, Y_3, Y_4 are the prices quoted per unit of the four ingredients respectively.

Optimal Solution

Y_1 = Rs.2.50 per unit of ingredient 1

Y_2 = Rs.21.00 per unit of ingredient 2

Y_3 = Rs.7.00 per unit of ingredient 3

Y_4 = Rs.11.50 per unit of ingredient 4

Total revenue = Rs.26,045

without exceeding cost constraints imposed by the customer. The solution point in each problem is at the same figure, namely Rs. 26,045.

Many situations in which two participants are in opposing and competitive positions can be represented either by a primal formulation or by its dual. The choice of which form of representation is used for analysis is often a matter of analytical convenience. In particular, a case in which an objective function contains more than two variables but in which only two constraints are present can be solved graphically in the dual format. It is interesting to note that the strictly competitive situation in which two participants are involved in a two-person, zero-sum game can be formulated in the primal and the dual from the point of view of each of the participants

SITUATIONS IN WHICH THERE ARE SPECIFIC STAGES

A number of different types of situation arise that have the characteristic that they may be studied by reference to a series of stages or time periods. Consider, for example, the situation in which customers requiring a certain item are supplied from inventory. The inventory can be replenished from time to time from production or by ordering from a supplier. There are certain set-up (or ordering) and deliver costs which make it desirable to replenish the inventory by larger rather than smaller amounts. However, if production or reordering is done in larger quantities there is a greater chance of the inventory of the item being reduced to zero before replenishment. On the other hand, the costs of maintaining the inventory may be greater if it is replenished in larger rather than smaller quantities. Situations of this nature have been studied extensively in the technical literature. The objective in all the analytical approaches has been to minimize the cost of maintaining the inventory whilst at the same time meeting certain conditions with respect to the demand.

DISTRIBUTION PROBLEMS

Many operational situations are concerned with the distribution of a commodity (goods or materials) from a number of sources (production or storage points) to a number of destinations. Each source has a limited supply in a given time period and each destination has a limited requirement in that same period. The cost of transporting one unit of the commodity from a source to a destination is known. The objective is to meet the demands of the destinations within the supply restrictions of the sources in a manner which minimizes the total cost of transportation of the commodity between the sources and the destination points. The situation can be illustrated as in Table 5. The figures in parentheses in this table represent the cost of transportation between the respective destinations and sources. Such situations are often referred to as transportation or distribution problems.

Problems of this nature can be treated by application of the linear programming model as long as the conditions specified earlier for the use of this model are satisfied. In addition, it is necessary that the total supply be equal to the total demand as it is in Table 5. However, if the supply is greater than the demand, the problem can be "balanced" and the model applied by the creation of a "dummy" destination to which the excess supply is transported at zero unit cost. If the demand is greater than the supply, a dummy source is used in much the same way.

Table 5

A Typical Distribution Situation

		Destinations				
		1	2	3	4	*Supply*
	1	(25)	(23)	(8)	(25)	15
Sources	2	(40)	(40)	(45)	(7)	12
	3	(9)	(14)	(28)	(27)	40
	4	(5)	(7)	(31)	(30)	25
Demand		7	30	20	35	92

North-West Corner Rule

Use of the linear programming model provides a method of determining a minimum total transportation cost in such situations. However, a number of simple techniques exist by which feasible, but not necessarily optimum, distribution arrangements can be determined. The best known of these techniques is called the North-West Corner Rule. Using this rule, the analyst starts at the top left of the table (as in Table 6) and inserts the maximum supply or demand figure allowed by the requirement of the destination or the capacity of the source. The analyst then moves to the space below or to the right and once again inserts the maximum figure allowed by the characteristics of the problem. The movement is continued until supply is exhausted or demand is satisfied, after which a right-angled turn is made and the process is continued. The completed process is shown in Table 6. The numbers in this table following the format of 7(25) indicate 7 units distributed at a cost of 25 for each unit. It is easy to confirm that the total cost of the distribution plan determined in this manner is 2559. This distribution is at least feasible in that demands are met within the supply restrictions. However, it is not necessarily optimal. In this particular case it is far from the minimum cost distribution mode.

Least Cost Rule

Other heuristic rules often give much improved (but not necessarily near-optimal) distribution plans. For example, in the above case, the Least Cost Rule can be applied with advantage. In using this rule, the greatest possible amount of the commodity is shipped by the lowest-cost route and then the greatest possible amount by the next cheapest route and so on until all demands are met within the supply restrictions.

Table 6

Use of the North-West Corner Rule

		Destinations				
		1	*2*	*3*	*4*	*Supply*
	1	7(25)	8(23)			15
	2		12(40)			12
Sources	3		10(14)	20(28)	10(27)	40
	4				25(30)	25
Demands		7	30	20	35	

Application of this rule provides the distribution plan shown in Table 7. The total cost for this plan is 1294, a figure considerably below that obtained by the North-West Corner Rule.

It is interesting to note that the optimum distribution is as shown in Table 8. This distribution obtained by use of the linear programming model has a minimum cost of 1273,21 units of cost below that obtained by the Least Cost Rule.

Table 7

Use of the Least-Cost Rule

		Destinations				
		1	*2*	*3*	*4*	*Supply*
Sources	1			15(8)		15
	2				12(7)	12
	3		12(14)	5(28)	23(27)	40
	4	7(5)	18(7)			25
Demands		7	30	20	35	92

Table 8

Optimal Distribution Plan

		Destinations				
		1	*2*	*3*	*4*	*Supply*
Sources	1			15(8)		15
	2				12(7)	12
	3	7(9)	5(14)	5(28)	23(27)	40
	4		25(7)			25
Demands		7	30	20	35	92

MAXIMAL FLOW SITUATIONS

Maximal flow situations are closely related to shortest route problems and to the linear programming model. They arise when the supply of commodity (oil, gas, or electric power, for example) can be obtained by means of a number of alternative routes through a network consisting of connections between certain modes. Flow through each component of the network is limited to a certain maximum level. The flow may be possible in both directions, but the maximum flow in any component may not be the same for each direction.

Suppose, for example, that a mining company intends to build a new smelting facility. The company will need a large amount of electric power at the facility. It has asked the electric supply company to estimate the maximum current flow that could be expected to the facility from the existing grid. It is assumed that the supplying station can generate sufficient power to satisfy the maximal flow characteristics of any route through the network.

The situation can be stated in a form suitable for treatment by the linear programming model as follows:

Objective function: Maximize total current flow through the network = (I)

Constraints:

1. The total flow in components 1 → 2 and 1 → 3 (in- flow to the network) must be equal to I.

2. The total flow components 4 → 7, 5 → 7, and 6 → 7 (outflow from the network) must be equal to I.

3. The amount of flow into each node must equal the amount of flow out of that node.

4. The capacity constraints of each component cannot be exceeded.

CRITICAL PATH SITUATIONS

Critical path situations are typically in which specific activities necessary to complete a project must be scheduled so as to minimize the time between the beginning and end of the project. Suppose for example that a building project requires work by various contractors. Each job has an estimated during. Some jobs can be carried out simultaneously while some cannot be started until others have been finished. The relationships between eight jobs (A to H) comprising the total project can be stated as in Table 10. The dotted lines in this diagram (for example between node 6 and node 5) represent "dummy" activities that have been inserted to express a particular precedence relationship between some of the other activities. Note for example that G cannot start before D,E, and F are finished, so that a dummy activity with duration zero is necessary between node 6 and node 5.

The architect in charge of the project would like to know the minimum time necessary to complete the project. He would also like to know which of the jobs has a duration that is critical to the completion of the project in that minimum time. The analysis of a situation of this nature is conducted in terms of two factors: (1) the earliest starting time, (ES) of an activity; and (2) the latest finishing time of the activity (LF).

Table 10

Jobs in a Critical Path Situation

Job (Activity)	*Immediate Predecessor*	*Estimated Duration*
A	—	2
B	—	8
C	—	6
D	A	14
E	B	6
F	B, C	9
G	D, E, F	7
H	F	4
Termination	G, H	—

The first of these times is the earliest possible starting time taking into account any work that must be completed prior to starting the activity. The second time is the latest finishing time of the activity without extending the overall duration of the project. If, for any activity, the earliest starting time plus the duration of the activity is equal to the latest finishing time. this activity is called *critical.* A critical activity is one for which no increase in duration and no delay in starting is possible without increasing the overall project duration. An activity that is not critical is said to have *slack.* The amount of slack may be defined as the total of the delay in starting and extension of the duration that is possible before the activity becomes critical. In the analysis, the earliest starting time for each activity is found by determining the maximum of the sum of the earliest starting time and the duration for each of the predecessor activities. The latest finishing time for each activity is found by determining the minimum of the sum of the latest finishing times of the following activities minus their durations.

INVENTORY MANAGEMENT

Inventories contain a stock of items held against future needs. If terms that are sold or used could be replaced immediately, there would be no need for substantial inventories. Because it usually takes time to order and replace such items, stocks must be held to avoid disappointing customers or to prevent processes dependent on these items being delayed. Maintenance of an inventory requires capital that might otherwise be put to other productive uses. The cost of providing this capital must therefore be balanced against the arising costs if an item were temporarily out of stock.

Complex inventory replenishment situations are best treated by the dynamic programming model as discussed earlier in this chapter. There is, however, a simple formula that can be used in situations in which certain assumptions can be said to apply. This formula determines the optimum reorder quantity as a function of the rate of depletion of an inventory, the cost of reordering, the costs of holding items in inventory, and the cost of any shortage.

Consider the situation of a retail drugstore that sells 1000 packages of disposable diapers each week. Demand is very predictable. The store can at no time be without stock. The company replenishes its inventory by making a trip to the manufacturer's plant. The cost of each such trip is Rs. 900. Goods not immediately sold are held in the stores until sold. The total cost of holding unsold goods is 5 cents per package per week. Application of the above formula shows that the optimal reorder policy would be to pick up 6000 packages per trip to the manufacturer. With a demand of 1000 packages per week, the trip would need to be undertaken every six weeks on the average.

Suppose now that the store is prepared to risk being sold out of the diapers for one quarter of the time and that the cost of such shortage in 15 cents per package per week. The optimal delivery policy given by the first of the two formulae above is to obtain 6928 (or 7000) packages per delivery every seven weeks.

Calculations of this nature can be used by managers as a guide to decision making rather than as an unbreakable rule. Duckworth argues that the use of the popular square root economic order quantity rule almost certainly results in an inflated level of stock being carried in circumstances in which no shortages are allowed. The basis of his argument is that the marginal rate of return on capital employed in inventory replenishment near the optimum reorder quantity is very close to the marginal cost of capital. Therefore, an organization without unlimited resources could find other uses for capital with a much greater return than that obtained by keeping high levels of inventory. The EOQ formula should therefore be used with care and with a constant reference to the practical decision situation in which any choices will be applied.

8

PROCESSES OF ORGANIZATIONAL DECISION

DESPITE the apparent importance of decision-making for theories of administration and the considerable attention the topic has attained recently present models and knowledge of decision-making have generated few hypotheses about administration, and they have not been adequately linked with organizational models.

A major deficiency in most decisions models has been observed that they are economically logical models seeking to describe maximization processes. These *econo-logical* models have utility as criteria against which to reflect behavior, but they have contributed little toward the explanation or prediction of behavior.

Simon has achieved a major break-through with his "satisficing" model. This is much more than the mere substitution of one word or one concept for another, for Simon's model is a *psycho-logical* model designed to describe and predict behavior.

This psychological model of decision-making is essentially one dealing with individual human beings. It applies equally to purposive choices of a personal or an organization nature. Its generalizability is, however, both a source of power and of limitation, for it does not deal explicitly with the particular phenomena which surround the making of decisions in organizational contexts.

As a companion to the psychological model, therefore, we wish to develop *sociological* models. We believe they will point to important decision-making behavior which has been observed in organizations but which is neither described nor predicted by econological or psychological mode's.

We will attempt to show (1) that there are several types of decisions to be made in and on behalf of collective enterprises, (2) that each type of decision calls for a different strategy or approach, (3) that there are several varieties of organizational structures which facilitate these several strategies, and (4) that the resulting behavior defines variations in decision processes. It has been our purpose to construct models which are neither culture-bound nor discipline-bound, containing no evaluative or normative elements.

FUNCTIONAL DEFINITIONS

"Choice" from among alternatives seems to be the end- point of decision-making, but the term "decision" will not be confined simply to ultimate choice. Rather, "decision" will refer to those activities which contribute to choice, including recognizing or delimiting and evaluating alternatives as well as the final selection. Thus an individual may have responsibility for making a final choice on behalf of an organization, but if others help him delimit or evaluate alternatives we will not describe that individual as *the* decider.

The term "decision" here should also be understood to refer to organizational decisions. Personal decisions, i.e., choices presumed by an individual to have consequences only for himself, are excluded. Likewise, unconscious choices or habits are not within the scope of this encyclopaedia.

The term "decision unit" will be used to refer to that individual or group within an organization which has power, responsibility, or authority to choose, on a particular issue, for the organization. To illustrate, in jurisprudence, "the court" may be the appropriate organization, but the power to decide certain issues is assigned to a single presiding judge as the decision unit; other issues are assigned to a jury as the decision unit; still others are assigned to a panel of justices as the decision unit.

DECISION ISSUES

The notion of differing types of issues calling for decisions is not new. More than a decade ago Simon distinguished ethical from factual decisions but no one seems to have extended his analysis. More recently there has been considerable discussion of decision-making under the differential conditions of certainty, risk, and uncertainty. Dorwin Canwright has suggested distinguishing among judgment, preference-ranking, and "actual decision-making" (which he defines as commitment to action). There have, however, been few attempts to build typologies of issues or decisions.

A typology of issues will enable the sorting out of (a) those aspects of decision situations which *conform* decision units from (b) those actions which decision units may take in such situations.

The main elements of decision—found both in the econological and psychological models available—seem to be three: (1) alternative courses of action, (2) differential consequences of the several alternatives (means), and (3) evaluation of the potential outcomes on some scale of desirability (ends).

We will work with two of those three variables, dropping "alternative courses of action", since by definition a unit called upon to decide is aware of at least one pair of alternatives. Before working with the remaining two variables, however, we redefine them slightly in order to achieve greater generalizability.

The notion of "consequences of alternative courses of action" assumes only a concern with present and future, not with past actions. Yet it seems reasonable, for example, to conceive of the trial jury as a decision unit which works backward from one present fact, e.g., a corpus delicti, to choose one of several possible past actions which may account for the present fact. This sequence may also characterize certain decisions in scientific research and in audits or inspections. The notion of *causation*, as applied to several alternatives, seems to us to subsume both questions of present and future states and questions of past actions which may explain present states.

We would also like to avoid some of the possible implications of such terms as desirability scale, which is inanimate, and to substitute for them some term with more explicit behavioral overtones. For this purpose we will speak of *preferences about outcomes*. In conceiving of our major variables as *causation* and *preferences*, we have gained a certain flexibility without losing the value of previous work on economic models. The means-ends approach falls within our scheme, but we have the added advantage of being able to include other approaches too.

Since we are dealing with organizations, it cannot be taken for granted that causation will be "known" as soon as a decision issue appears, nor can it be assumed that the organization is certain of its preferences regarding the several alternatives apparent. Often the organization's decision unit cannot simply choose, but must act to determine what its knowledge or beliefs are regarding cause-and-effect relationships, and what its preferences are about the postulated effects.

Now, if the two variables *causation* and *preferences* are reflected against the additional question of whether there is *agreement* or *consensus within the decision unit* about those two matters, it is possible to construct a four-fold typology of decision issues.

		Preferences about Possible Outcomes: Agreement	Preferences about Possible Outcomes: Disagreement
Beliefs about Causation	Agreement →	Computation	Compromise
	Disagreement →	Judgment	Inspiration

The labels in the four cells—computation, judgment, compromise, and inspiration—are descriptive of four *strategies* which we believe are appropriate for the four types of decision issues. In the following section we will elaborate on those strategies, and connect them with certain types of social structures. For the time being we will deal only with "pure" cases.

Decision by Computation

Where there is agreement regarding both causation and preference, i.e., where a preference hierarchy is understood and where knowledge is available or believed to be available, decision- making is a technical or mechanical matter. In its extreme form, this situation requires no genuine choice, since the problem-solution appears as common sense.

But in many instances, the appropriate techniques for equating cause-effect knowledge with known preferences are quite complicated. The data may be so voluminous for example, that only an electronic calculator can make sense of them. Likewise, the particular sequences of action involved in the techniques may be hard to master and difficult to carry out, so that only the highly trained specialist can arrive at an appropriate choice. In either event, the strategy for decision is straightforward analysis, and we term this decision by computation.

A Structure for Computation. Assuming for the moment complete freedom to build an organization which will face *only* computation issues, and that our guiding norms are economy of effort and efficiency of performance, what kind of organization shall we build?

This will be an organization of specialists, one for each kind of computation problem we can anticipate, and we want to introduce four constraints or rules to: (1) prohibit our specialists from making decisions in issues lying outside their spheres of expert competence, (2) bind each specialist to the organization's preference scale, (3) route all pertinent information to each specialist, and (4) route every issue to the appropriate specialist.

The organization which we have just built contains the heart of what Max Weber described as the "pure type" of bureaucracy. This bureaucratic model is clearly expressed in the "formal" or "official" structure of the great majority of business firms, governmental agencies, and military units. For each of these, presumably, preferences can be stated with some clarity. Members are appointed to positions only so long as they embrace those preferences. Moreover, bureaucracy is formulated on the assumption that rules or procedures can be established for classes of cases or problems, and that the events which will call for organizational decisions are repetitive or serial events for which expert competence can be developed. Candidates for these positions are expected to hold licenses or degrees indicating successful completion of training for the specialized positions or to pass tests.

Decision by Majority Judgment

Where causation is uncertain or disputed, although preferences are clearly known and shared, decision-making takes on new difficulties. Lacking in acceptable "proof" of the merits of alternatives, the organization must rely on judgment. Triangulation illustrates this simply and clearly. Each member of the three-man team is presumed competent by virtue of his training and his equipment to make a judgment, but because none has indisputable and complete evidence, none is permitted to make the decision alone, and no member may outvote or override the judgment made by other members. But triangulation is a special case of the more general problem—special because each judge focuses on the same empirical phenomenon from his own special vantage point. More frequent, perhaps, is the case where there is not only differential perception but also differential interpretation, and this is most clearly illustrated by the voting situation in which the collective judgment determines the decision. This strategy of organizational decision is referred to as one of majority judgment.

A Structure for Majority Judgment. What kind of organization shall we build as an ideal one to handle only judgmental problems? This is to be an organization of wise and knowing men, operating according to constraints or rules which: (1) require fidelity to the group's preference hierarchy, (2) require all members to participate in each decision, (3) route pertinent information about causation to each member, (4) give each member equal influence over the final choice, and (5) designate as ultimate choice that alternative favored by the largest group of judges—the majority.

What we have just described may be labelled, for lack of a better term a *collegium*. This concept has been used in ecclesiastical literature to refer to a self-governing voluntary group, with authority vested in the members. Whatever this type of organization is labelled, the social science literature does not seem to contain formal models of it, as it does for bureaucracy.

Nevertheless, this type of organization is described in case studies of "voluntary associations" and in the constitutions and by-laws of many organizations, including many American universities and trade unions. All of these not only take steps to "get out the vote," but incorporate into their by-laws provisions requiring a quorum for the transaction of official business. Direct elections of governmental officials approximate the collegial situation, with each literate citizen-of-age presumed to have equal competence and influence at the polls.

Decision by Compromise

On occasion there may be agreement by all parties as to the expected consequences or causes of available alternatives, but lack of consensus over preferences toward such "facts." Neither computation nor collective judgment is "appropriate" for this type of issue, for the blunt fact is that if one preference is satisfied, another is denied. An organization facing his situation may fall apart through schism, civil war, or disinterest, unless some common item or point can be found on the several extant preference scales. It can be illustrated by imagining an organization composed of two factions. For faction A, the preference scale runs 1, 2, and 3, while for faction B, the scale is 4, 5, and 6. In this case, in order for either faction to obtain at least an acceptable solution the other must be denied all satisfaction, and this presages the end of the organization. If the preference scales run 1, 2, and 3, in that order, and 3, 4, and 5, both factions can attain a modicum of satisfaction by choosing 3. The appropriate strategy where causation is conceded but preferences are in dispute thus appears to be one which will arrive at the common preference. This strategy is known as decision by compromise.

A Structure for Compromise. Now the task is to construct an ideal organization to handle compromise types of issues economically and efficiently.

Whereas computation problems call for the smallest possible decision unit, and collective judgment for the widest possible participation, compromise seems to require a decision unit of intermediate size. What we want is a structure to facilitate bargaining, and since this involves detailed and subtle exploration of the several factional preference scales, the decision unit must be small enough to permit sustained and often delicate interchange. On the other hand, there is the requirement that all factions—or certainly all important factions—be involved in the decision. This leads, to the *representative body* as the appropriate structure.

For this purpose, we will build rules or constraints into our organization to: (1) require that each faction hold as its *top* priority preference the desire to reach agreement, i.e., to continue the association, (2) ensure that each faction be represented in the decision unit, (3) give each faction veto power, and (4) give each faction all pertinent, available information about causation.

Decision by Inspiration

The fourth and in above typology the final type of issue is one in which there is disagreement both as to causation and as to preferences. This is, of course, a most dangerous situation for any group to be in; certainly by definition and probably in fact the group in this situation is nearing disintegration. While this situation seems to be far removed from the usual discussions of decision-making, we believe it has empirical as well as theoretical relevance.

The most likely action in this situation is the decision not to face the issue. Organizations which appear to be slow to seize opportunities or to respond to environmental events may, on close inspection, be organizations which contain disagreement as to both preferences and causation. To the extent that the organization in this predicament can avoid an issue, it may at least maintain itself as an organization. If it is forced to choose, however, the organization is likely to dissolve—unless some innovation can be introduced.

Anthropologists have recorded on numerous occasions institutionalized means of gaining inspiration by referring "insoluble" problems to supernatural forces, and it is no secret that responsible public officials in "less superstitious" nations call on Divine Guidance when they must make momentous decisions for which there is not precedent and the consequences are highly uncertain. A related device is for the group to rely on a *charismatic* leader.

As Weber pointed out, the charismatic leader is thought by his followers to have solutions or at least the wisdom to find them. Frequently he offers a new set of ideals or preferences which rally unity out of diversity, by shifting attention. Pointing to a real or fancied threat from outside is one ancient device for this.

A Structure for Inspiration. It is difficult to conceive of an ideal structure for decision by inspiration, for the thinking of the social scientist is oriented toward pattern and organization, while the situation we face here is one of randomness and disorganization.

If these situations occur it probably is seldom by design. Nevertheless, an attempt to deliberately construct such a situation might be instructive for the student of organization.

What we are trying to build now has been labelled by Durkheim as a state of *anomie*, normlessness, or deregulation. As a rough approximation, anomie occurs when former goals or values have lost their meaning or significance or when such goals appear unobtainable with the means available. Thus, our problem is to create a situation of chaos, but to do so with an aggregation of persons who in some sense can be considered to constitute a group or collectivity. We will therefore call for the following constraints: (1) the individuals or groups must be interdependent and thus have some incentive for collective problem-solving, (2) there must be a multiplicity of preference scales and therefore of factions, with each faction of approximately equal strength, (3) more information must be introduced that can be processed, and it must be routed through multiple communication channels, and (4) each member must have access to the major communication networks, in case inspiration strikes.

While it is doubtful if empirical cases of organizational anomie are deliberately created, there seems to be evidence that the more carefully structured organizations do sometimes find themselves in a state of anomie. The routed military organization, for example, is characterized by de-emphasis of military values and an abundance of rumors, contradictory information, and loss of contact or faith in nominal leaders.

Anomie and inspiration probably appear in less stark form in formal organizations, for the most part. Befuddled administrators of organizations caught up in forces which are not understood may and sometimes do rely on decision by inspiration in one of two forms: (a) imitation of more prestigeful and successful organizations, or (b) importation of prestigeful and authoritative management consultants to tell them what they should want and how to go after it.

MIXED SITUATIONS

There are a variety of reasons why the purity of our illustrations may be relatively infrequent. A major proposition of this essay is that usually an organization adopts one of the four strategies—

computation, collective judgment, compromise, or inspiration—as its dominant strategy, and bases its structure on that strategy.

To the extent that this is true, we can expect or predict several kinds of organizational difficulties which will be presented to administrators when the organization faces issues or problems which do not fit the formal neatness of our pure types. We can also expect difficulties if the appropriate constraints are not present within the particular decision unit. Finally, it can be predicted that problems will arise if an issue calling for one strategy is presented to a decision unit built to exercise a different kind of strategy.

Confusion of Issues

The difficulties of means-ends distinctions are as real for operating organizations as for scientific observers. Psychological time perspectives have much to do with whether a particular issue is seen as one of means or ends. Despite the fact that social system of various kinds generally are expected by members to persist through time, their members may attach different valences to varying periods of the future. The holder of the short-run viewpoint may see an issue as one of preferences, while the long-run adherent sees the issue as one of causation.

In a dynamic and complex organization, moreover, the range of possible outcomes widens rapidly as the time-span is extended. If this is true, then members of an organization probably are less inclined to grant the competence of experts for long-run decisions, even when they would grant the ability of the same experts for short-run matters.

Thus, different members of an organization or of its decision unit may respond to the same stimulus in varying ways, some seeing it as a matter for computation, others as a judgement matter, and still others as requiring bargaining.

Absence of Structural Constraints

One constraint common to all of the pure structures described earlier, except for the case where the decision unit is an individual, was that each judge, each bargainer, each faction, had equal power to influence the choice. While this usually is a formal specification for such units as trial juries, legislatures, or boards, we know that such units in fact exhibit inequality of membership. Strodtbeck, for example, reports that sex and social status affect the amount of participation of jury members in the decision process, the perceptions that fellow jurors have of their competence as jurors, and the degree to which they influence the outcome. Such factors as partly loyalty and party discipline, seniority, political skills, and the endorsement of pressure groups may affect the legislator's ability to make his voice heard as loudly as the next one. Within bureaucracies there are well-known inequalities between offices and divisions which formally are equal, and such scholars as Dalton have documented some of the reasons why computational experts may temper their computations with other considerations.

Another constraint common to all but the anomic structure was that each participant in the decision unit have access to all available, pertinent information about causation. In fact, despite all of the attention given to communication in modern organizations, the condition called for by this constraint is at best approximated but seldom achieved. Colleagues of the expert in a bureaucracy, then, may grant the competence and good intentions of an official, but refuse to honor his decision on grounds that he did not know the local or "real" situation. Well informed minorities may control the collegial body whose other members are ill-informed, and "private information" obtained by one faction may make a mockery of the compromise situation.

This listing is intended to be illustrative rather than exhaustive. Relaxation of other constraints, peculiar to particular structures, will be discussed below.

If organizations were completely pliable, it would be a relatively simple thing to assign each problem to a decision unit designed especially for it. But, of course, organizations would cease to be organizations if they were completely pliable. Regularity, pattern and structure are inescapable.

Presumably the basic structures which prescribe the standing or regular decision units of organizations are established because they are expected to be appropriate for the *typical* problems those organizations will face. In some organizations, at least, precedent and tradition lead members to expect that *all* decisions will be made by the decision units and processes established for typical decisions. This undoubtedly will vary with the history of the organization and with the social and cultural attitudes surrounding it. In our own society and decade, it is not unusual to hear officials of bureaucracies complain that committee participation (on judgment problems) interferes with their work—by which they seem to mean expert computation in their own offices. On the other hand, we frequently hear university faculty members, conditioned to expect collegial decisions, complain when department heads or deans make purely computational decisions. There are also situations, particularly in certain types of military units, when members are dismayed if leaders so much as ask their opinions. For some in the military organization, the commander must be an expert and every issue must be a computational one.

Thus the attitudes and expectations of members may make it difficult for organizations to create *ad hoc* or alternative decision units to deal with problems for which basic, traditional structures are ill-suited.

Another important source of structural rigidity is the shifting nature of human knowledge. Types of problems which at one time are identified by members of a group as appropriate for judgment may at another time be defined as computational problems, as the group changes its beliefs about cause-and-effect relations.

Decision issues appear to be broader, more complex, and more time-consuming as we move from computation issues to voting to bargaining issues. There is reason to believe that, left to their own devices, members of social systems tend to expand decision issues. In a revealing summary of community issues and the course of their disposition. Coleman notes a tendency for transformation of issues from specific to general, and from disagreement to antagonism. Bales also notes in small problem-solving groups, that interpersonal tensions mount as the decision process moves from orientation to evaluation to control.

As knowledge becomes increasingly pluralistic, in the sense that new specialized logics are developed, the bureaucracy encompasses not one but several sets of beliefs about appropriate means to organizational ends. Thus the competence of the single expert becomes doubted and members define issues as calling for judgment rather than computation. If, for example, the expert can be forced to admit that his is but a professional opinion—a tactic in jury trails—the way is cleared to insist that others be consulted and a balance of judgments obtained. This has also been a common practice in communities where public health experts have decided to introduce fluoride into the public water supply.

With problems which appear to call for judgment, the heat of debate can lead proponents of the several alternatives to overstate their cases and discount missing information; often it also leads them to refer to more general but extraneous organization preferences as a means of finding moral justification for the selection of the alternative they endorse. When this occurs, the issue is no longer one of judgment regarding causation, but becomes one of dispute over (relevant) ends and thus subject to compromise.

The issue which seems a natural for bargaining may verge on the anomic, since it frequently generates difficulties in the identification and exploration of causation. Inherently emphasizing preference conflict, the bargaining structure leads its members to discount causation theories endorsed by opponents and to overemphasize their own. This hampers the effort to get the "facts" and where preferences already are at issue, disputes over facts create anomic situations. Moreover, if one faction is adamant or unwilling to "bargain fairly", there is a tendency for the other faction or factions to seek to expand the issue into a larger, more general category, and to threaten the adamant faction with trouble on unrelated matters. This too, tends toward anomie.

INFLUENCE OF ADMINISTRATION ON DECISION-MAKING

We can now offer the general proposition that an important role for administration is to *manage* the decision *process,* as distinct from *making the decision*. We are not suggesting that administrators do one to the exclusion of the other, but if issues are not automatically crystallized, the ideal structural constraints are not automatically present, or appropriate decision units are not automatically selected, it may fall to administrators to take action which will facilitate decisions.

The following discussion is not offered as exhaustive, but as illustrative of the potential utility of considering administrative roles with respect to the decision process.

Where a time dimension is not clearly implied by the nature of the issue, one role of administration is to delineate by fiction or otherwise, such a time dimension. This facilitates the sorting out of means from ends, by the decision unit, and thus tends to contain the issue from expanding into a more complex one.

When there are many alternatives available, a role of administration is to provide machinery for elimination of all but a few. This can be particularly important when an issue is assigned to a voting unit, which seems to be able to operate effectively only on binary problems. At one level of generality this is an important role for Congressional committees. At a more general level of analysis this is the function of political parties in the two party system; the necessary compromises of platform and candidates are achieved before the issue is put to the electorate. By way of contrast, in multi-party France the function of compromising a plurality of interests developed on the legislature more than on intraparty processes, and was an important factor in the lack of effectiveness of the Fourth Republic.

In the bargaining situation the important role of administration may be to obtain initial mutual commitment to reaching agreement, and to maintain this commitment as taking priority over factional preferences. This approach may guard the issue from expanding into one of anomie., for as Dubin points out, mutual commitment to the necessity for reaching agreement in effect moves the issue in the direction of judgment and voting. One method of handling the bargaining issue, and seemingly an indispensable one when the preference scales do not contain common items, is to place the particular issue in a larger context. This can be done by "horse-trading", thus assuring the losing faction on the present issue of priority treatment on a future issue.

A suggestion regarding possible roles of administrators in facilitating organizational decision-making concerns the extremely complicated kinds of issues that frequently face administrators of "loose" organizations. We have in mind such social systems as the community (as viewed by a mayor, council, or manager); the school district (as viewed by the superintendent or board), or the bloc of nations (as viewed by their diplomats and officials). We refer to these as "loose" organizations because only a portion of the relevant "members" are directly subject to the hierarchy of authority. In the legal sense, that is, some of the groups are not "members", although in the behavioral sense they are.

When such organizations face important and complicated issues, we believe, it may become necessary for administrators to redefine the issue into a series of issues, each assigned to an appropriate decision unit. It may also be that there are patterns in the sequence in which the series is handled. For example, in order to achieve a "community decision" on a fluoridation or school bond issue, it may be necessary to *first* get agreement and commitment of the powerful elements on preferences. This might be done "informally" in the smokefilled room, by compromise, and it might include the important choice as to whether to tackle the issue at all. After that decision is made, the *second* step might be to frame a judgmental issue for presentation to an electorate. Finally, within the limits of the majority decision, specialists can be presented with such issues as the proper equipment for fluoridation or the most appropriate timing for bond issues.

We feel rather safe in predicting that there is a cumulative effect in this sequence. Weakness in the first step probably forecasts trouble in succeeding steps, and so on.

9

QUANTITATIVE MEASURES IN DECISION MAKING

THE decision situations examined earlier were well structured and clearly defined. They involved a single individual with the power to make the decision. This individual had a single, we defined objective, such as maximizing profit, minimizing cost, maximizing flow, or minimizing the duration of a project. Success in achieving this objective was assessed in terms of a single, well defined measure expressed in easily understood units such as dollars, barrels of oil, or days. Situations of this nature are well understood. They can be treated in most instances by a well structured analytical procedure.

Simple, well defined measures of the benefits and disbenefits of courses of action may not be available in many practical decision situations. This chapter discusses the problems of establishing quantitative measures and the manner in which decision makers can proceed if such measures cannot be used. In the text that follows, the term "disbenefits" is taken to mean not only money value costs, but also any disadvantages that may arise from a course of action that do not immediately appear to be measurable in terms of dollars. Examples of such disbenefits include loss of public image of a corporation, reduction in the standard of living of a person or a community, and reduction in the aesthetic value of an object or of a geographic location.

ESTABLISHMENT OF QUANTITATIVE MEASURES

The purpose of establishing quantiTative measures of benefits and costs is to facilitate comparison of the effectiveness of alternative courses of action in a decision situation. We need quantitative measures so that comparisons between numbers are easy to comprehend and unequivocal. We are all used to the idea that 5 units of a benefit are better than 3 units. Comparisons of the profit or costs arising from each of several alternatives are easily made in this fashion. It is extremely important, however, in establishing such quantitative measures to ensure that the basic objectives of the decision maker are known and understood. In situations involving maximization of profit or minimization of costs, there may be no major problem in this respect. However, in other situations in which objectives are less well defined, it may be more difficult to establish quantitative measures that relate to the true purpose expressed in the objective. The chance that a measure is suggested that does not represent exactly the nature of the objective of the decision maker is correspondingly increased. For example, the objective of a corporation which is commonly expressed as "being a good corporate citizen" is open to a number of interpretations. One such interpretation may be in terms of the corporation's dealings with the community in which it operates and its relations with the people in that community. Another interpretation might be with respect to the percentage of gross earnings devoted to the public good. Very different measures of achievement might apply to these two interpretations.

In other cases, alternatives may need to be considered against a range of objectives, and quantitative measures may need to be established for each of these objectives. For example, in consideration of alternative proposals to meet a transportation need, the desires for shorter travel time, safe travel, and low cost are frequently expressed. The effects of the proposals on the environment, on service to industry, on recreational areas, and on the disruption of neighborhoods may also have to be taken into account. The measures of benefits and disbenefits relating to these factors are different and each must be established before the evaluation of alternatives can start.

Efficiency and Effectiveness

Two particular types of measurement in common use in practical situations are concerned with *efficiency* and *effectiveness.* In general, efficiency relates to the best use of resources used in a process or in carrying out a course of action. An alternative that results in the greatest amount of output for a given amount of resources used (or the least amount of resources for a given amount of output) is regarded as the most efficient. A measure of efficiency might be concerned, for example, with the greatest amount of flow through a pipeline or the maximum use of space in a building. Measures of effectiveness, on the other hand, relate to the degree of achievement of objectives. Such a measure might be concerned, for example, with the degree to which a particular course of action contributes to an objective of diversification of the activities of a company.

Efficiency and effectiveness sometimes coincide. For example, if the sole objective of a company were to make a profit, maximum efficiency would result in maximum effectiveness. However, the two concepts do not always run in parallel. In the administration of a health care unit, for instance, maximum efficiency might be thought of in terms of the number of patients treated in a given period. Pursuit of maximum efficiency in these terms might lead to a situation in which the amount of time devoted to each patient was insufficient to provide satisfactory health care. The effectiveness of the unit might therefore be jeopardized by adherence to the concept of maximum efficiency. On the other hand, if standards of health care could be established, it might be possible to define situations of maximum efficiency while ensuring that the prescribed standards are met.

Measurements of workload that are possibly good indicators of efficiency are not necessarily equally good indications of effectiveness. A report of the number of purchasing departments visited by a sales representative is not always an indication of the potential effectiveness of that individual in increasing sales. A record of the number of inspections made of manufacturing plants is not necessarily an indication of the effectiveness of the visits in increasing safety at these locations. In similar fashion, the establishment of standards such as are frequently used in government planning agencies does not necessarily indicate a certain level of effectiveness unless these standards are related to products that are directly concerned with objectives. For example, that a community has a certain number of dentists per 1000 of the population does not necessarily imply a particular level of effectiveness of dental health for the community.

The aim in most decision situations is to choose an alternative that provides the greatest effectiveness relative to the objective or objectives of the decision maker. If the alternative chosen also provides the greatest efficiency in the use of resources, this is well and good. However, it is possible to be effective while not operating at maximum efficiency. It is also possible to be not at all effective while being very efficient. Furthermore, it is possible for the relationship between effectiveness and efficiency to change as conditions change. Consider, for example, a manufacturing plant that makes a product from certain ingredients. The objective is to make maximum profit consistent with meeting certain standards in production. If the market for the product is very good, high efficiency contributes to high effectiveness in meeting the objective. Suppose, however, that the market for the product disappears, as happened, for example, when certain types of pesticide were banned for general use. The plant may continue to work at high efficiency, but the effectiveness of the operation drops to zero because no profit can be made from the sale of the product.

More on Decision Situations

Many practical decision situations exist in which there are no immediately apparent quantitative measures of benefits and disbenefits. The objectives in these situations are such that well understood quantitative measures relating to money, time, and effort do not describe completely the results of progress towards their achievement. Many of these situations are in the public sector and have to do with health, welfare, and the provision of services to the public. It is frequently very difficult, for example, to describe in simple quantitative terms, the benefit of a course of action that leads to an improvement in the health or quality of life of a segment of the population. However these problems are not confined to the public sector. Similar difficulties arise in measuring the degree of success of a corporation in achieving a desired level of social responsibility or public image.

The natural tendency in such situations is to try to represent the benefits of a course of action in terms of easily measurable items such as money. This practice is often justified by the premise that the usefulness of an article or a situation to an individual is directly measurable by the amount of money he is prepared to pay to obtain or achieve it. This argument is tenable only as long as a market exists for the article or situation being considered. In many cases, however, such a market does not exist. It is very difficult, for example, to put a price on good health or public esteem.

Attempts to represent benefits in easily measurable terms have been reported in a number of studies. The most frequently referenced of these studies is that of the Roskill Commission on the Third London Airport. In this study, the research team appears to have established quantitative measures of benefits and disbenefits with little thought for the consequences or the implications with respect to the results of analysis. For example, the team placed a value of about Rs. 25,000 on each human life likely to be lost in an aircraft accident. Furthermore, it is explained in this report, that approximately Rs. 13,000 of the total represents the effects of the loss in terms of such factors as the grief of the next-of-kin, and the remainder accounts for the economic loss to society of the individual's premature death. The team made similar assumptions with respects to measurement of the convenience of an airport site to the traveling public. In this respect, it assumed that convenience could be measured in terms of the value of the time taken to travel to the airport by the users.

Defenders of this type of quantification make the point that a choice between alternatives implicitly puts a value on such factors as human life. It is argued that an openly discussed process of quantification is now worse than an implicit valuation. It may, in fact, be preferable, insomuch as some of the major factors involved are at least brought out in explicit discussion. There is some validity to this argument. A municipal authority allocating funds to ambulance and rescue services or to the removal of grade crossings implicitly puts a value on human life. If human life were priceless, there would be no alternative but to allocate an infinite amount of money to services that would save just one individual.

However, practical considerations always dictate that a finite sum be assigned in such circumstances.

There are many situations in which readily available measures of benefits and disbenefits cannot be used. In such cases, it may be possible to conceive of a *proxy measure* that can be used instead. A proxy measure is one which does not measure a benefit or disbenefit directly but does measure something closely enough related to it to provide an indication of the value of a course of action. Hatry has suggested, for example, that the response time of an ambulance service might be a suitable proxy measure for assessing alternative proposals for such services. Similarly, the street price of a narcotic might be a proxy by which to measure the effectiveness of efforts to reduce the flow of drugs to the consumer.

Good analytical practice requires that proxy measures of benefits and disbenefits represent as faithfully as possible the effects of courses of action in relation to the objectives in the decision situation. Furthermore, it is essential that no significant aspect of the benefits and disbenefits be left unrepresented by the proxy measures that are adopted. Particular care must be taken in assigning proxy measures in situations in which the health, safety, welfare, or quality of life of persons or segments of the population are concerned. There has been a tendency, for example, in some of literature on cost-benefit analysis to measure the benefits of programs affecting individuals in terms of their production on behalf of society (in dollar terms) less the dollar cost of their consumption. An assumption of this nature neglects altogether considerations of human happiness and nonmonetary aspects of the welfare of the individuals involved. It can lead to conclusions from analysis that certain segments of the population should receive less attention because of their relatively smaller contributions and relatively greater needs. Further extension of the arguments based on these premises could lead to the conclusion that society would be better off if certain elements of the population were eliminated. This position not only is morally indefensible; it also demonstrates a strong discrepancy between the results of some analytical studies and decisions that are reached by responsible administrators.

It is most important therefore in dealing with proxy measures to avoid choices that automatically build undesirable bias into the analysis on which decisions are based. However, selection of this proxy measure may introduce a bias into the analysis against programs that are beneficial to women, because women are generally paid less than men in today's society. It is important also to consider the effect that selection of different proxy measures can have upon the conclusions drawn from analysis.

Leaving aside for the moment the appropriateness of the second measure, the two criteria are seen to provide very different orderings between the programs. Arthritis and syphilis, diseases that result in crippling rather than in early death, appear high in the ordering against a measure of cost to the community, but not at all in the list in terms of deaths averted. On the other hand, uterine cervical and breast cancer are high on the deaths averted listing but lower on the cost to the community ordering, primarily because those affected by these conditions are women. This differentiation brings into question once again the validity of measures in which gross earnings by members of the population are a factor.

UTILITY CONCEPT

The desire for a quantitative basis of comparison of alternatives has led to the development of the concept of utility. The foundation of this concept is that if an individual demonstrates a preference for one alternative over another, that person can be said to have a greater utility for the chosen alternative than for the other. There is little basis for argument against this idea. Problems arise, however, when an attempt is made to measure utility in quantitative terms. Such measurement is necessary to much of the recently developed techniques of decision theory. It is appropriate, therefore, to investigate the nature of utility as it has been described over the past two hundred years and the more recent attempts that have been made to measure it as the basis of comparisons between alternatives. These matters will be the subject of the following sections of the text.

The word utility has been used in the technical literature to describe a number of different but related concepts. The question of the utility of money was considered in the early eighteenth century by the Swiss mathmematicians Cramer and Bernoulli. Their basic premise was that the usefulness of an additional amount of money decreases with the amount of money possessed.

Under this premise the value of an additional dollar to an individual having one thousand dollars is less than that to a person having only ten dollars. This concept has come to be known as *Bernoullian Utility.*

In line with the philosophy of his day, Bernoulli assumed that all men, being rational, would behave in the same way. He therefore proposed a fundamental law which he maintained governed such behavior. This law stated that the utility of money to an individual could be measured in terms of the logarithm (to any base) of the amount of money. Both Cramer and a French scientist named Buffon argued in favor of different laws (Cramer for the square root and Buffon for the reciprocal of the amount of money) as a measure of utility. However, each of the proposals resulted in a curve of utility for money plotted against money that had the general concave-downward shape shown in Fig. 1. With such a curve, incremental amounts of money contribute less utility as the level of money involved increases.

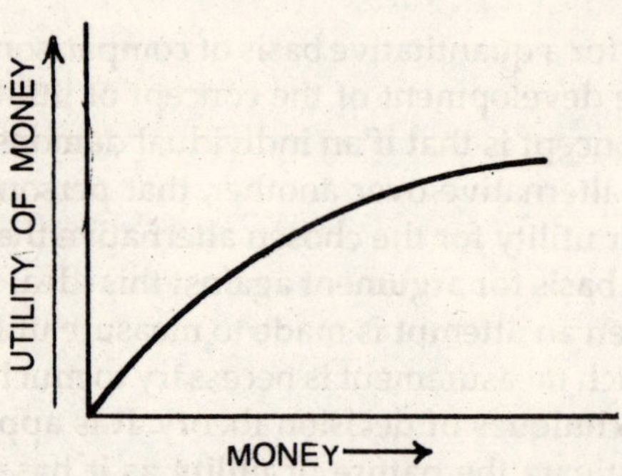

Fig. 1. Bernoullian utility of money

Much more recently, Friedman and Savage put forward the idea that every individual has a utility function that reflects his utility for money or some other commodity. Starting from a basis of Bernoulli's work, they tried to construct a utility function that would reflect observed human behavior under a variety of circumstances. They noted, for example, that any such function would need to take into account two aspects of human behavior that are apparently inconsistent: namely, gambling and buying insurance. In gambling, the individual gives up a sure thing (the stake) in return for participation in a risk, whereas an individual buying insurance gives up a risk (for example, that his or her house burns down) in favor of a sure thing (the relatively minor loss represented by the premium).

It had previously been pointed out that the shape of the utility curve suggested by Bernoulli and his contemporaries did not explain gambling behavior. The Bernoulli curve supposed that people had less and less utility for money as the amount increased. Some types of gamblers clearly have more and more utility for money as the amounts get larger, at least up to a point. This latter type of behavior can be described by a utility function of the (concave upward) type shown in Fig. 2.

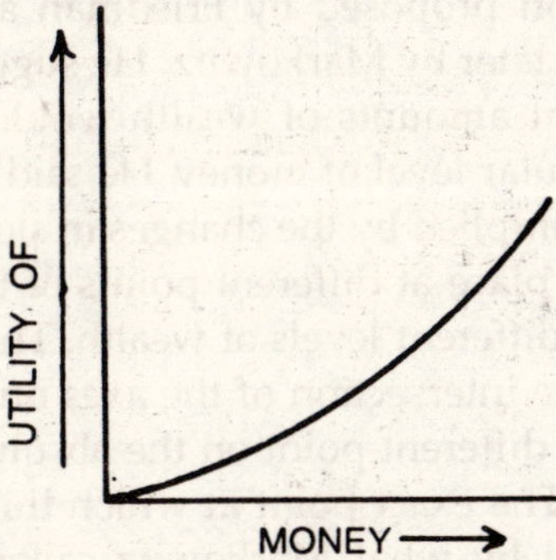

Fig. 2. Concave upward utility function

Friedman and Savage suggested further that behavior in buying insurance could be explained by a curve in the negative quadrant similar to that shown in Fig. 3. With this curve, additional amounts of loss contribute greater amounts of disutility as the loss increases. They then combined these curves to produce a proposed general utility function of the type shown in Fig. 4. The portion of this curve in the negative quadrant was said to explain behavior in buying insurance and the part in the upper, positive quadrant to explain gambling behavior. Note that the portions of the curve near the intersection of the two axes are close to straight lines, although the curve is not necessarily continuous in the region of the origin.

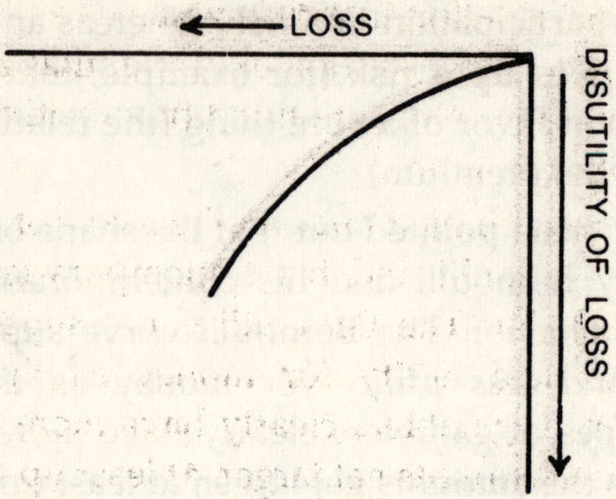

Fig. 3. Function representing disutility of loss

The utility function proposed by Friedman and Savage was modified some years later by Markowitz. He suggested that individuals with different amounts of wealth would not act in the same way at a particular level of money. He said, rather, that the changes of behavior implied by the changes in slope of the utility function would take place at different points of the money scale for individuals with different levels of wealth. This is the equivalent of saying that the intersection of the axes on the diagram in Fig. 4 would be at a different point on the absolute money scale for each individual. The exact point at which this intersection is placed is determined by what Markowitz called the *customary wealth* of the individual.

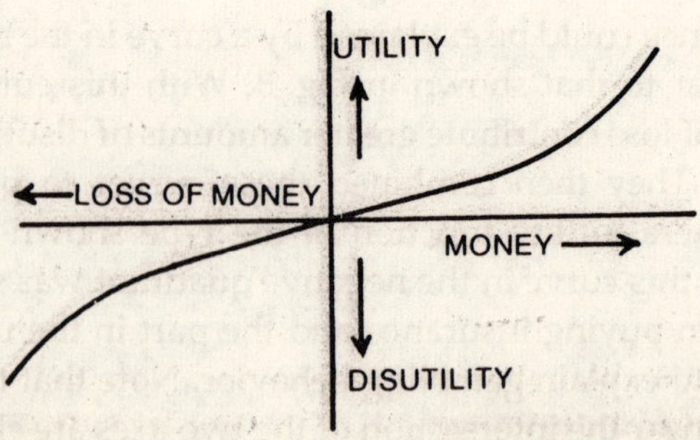

Fig. 4. Friedman-Savage utility function.

Markowitz proposed further that there should be a modification of the shape of the Friedman-Savage function at each end of the curve. He said that there must surely be a point at which an individual becomes satiated with gain and that the right hand end of the curve should therefore turn downward in a manner to reflect this condition. Similarly, there is presumably a leveling off of disutility at some very large amount of loss. The left hand end of the curve should therefore reflect this disregard of further loss. These arguments lead to a curve for the utility of money of a form shown in Fig. 5. The intersection of the axes is at the customary wealth of the individual to which the curve refers.

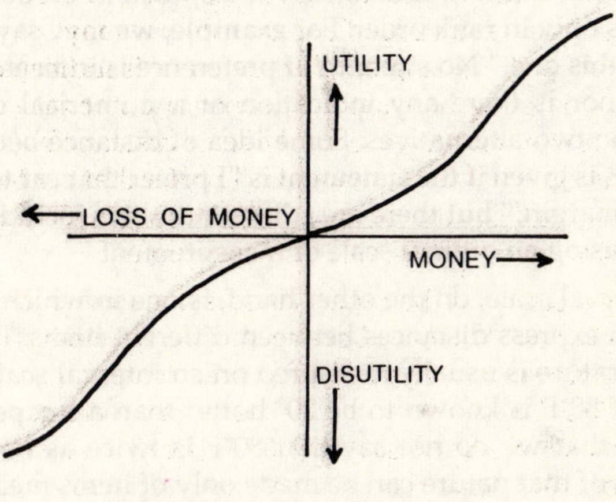

Fig. 5. Markowitz utility function

MEASUREMENT OF UTILITY

Given that the utility function of an individual for money or for some other commodity is of the general form shown in Fig. 5, the question now arises of whether that individual's utility for various amounts of the commodity involved can be measured in a manner suitable to the construction of such a curve. In particular, it is necessary to know the units in which utility is to be measured and also the type of scale on which these units are to be placed.

Scales of Measurement

There is a hierarchy of scales that can be used in measurement. Individual scales are distinguished from one another by the extent of the restrictions that they place on the process of measurement. There are three types of scale that are in common use today. Listed in increasing order in the restrictive conditions they impose, these types of scale are:

1. *The ordinal scale* in which entities are shown ranked in order of preference in relation to some expressed objective or condition.

2. *The interval scale* in which entities are placed according to their distance from some arbitrary origin.

3. *The ratio scale* in which entities are placed according to their distance from some nonarbitrary origin.

The ordinal scale is used when it is possible or desirable to show items only in rank order. For example, we may say "I prefer that car to this one." No strength of preference is indicated by this statement nor is there any indication of a numerical difference between the two alternatives. Some idea of distance between the alternatives is given if the statement is "I prefer that car to this one by a wide margin," but there are still no numbers included in this statement using an ordinal scale of measurement.

The interval scale, on the other hand, is one in which numbers are used to express distances between different items. For example, temperature is usually measured on an interval scale. A temperature of 80°F is known to be 20° hotter than a temperature of 60°F. Note that we do not say that 80°F is twice as hot as 40°F. Statements of that nature can be made only of items measured on a ratio scale. There is no unique zero on an interval scale. The zero on the Fahrenheit scale is chosen at 32 degrees below the freezing point of water, whereas that on the Celsius scale is at that freezing point. If two interval scales are used to measure the same thing (for example, the Fahrenheit and Celsius scales) there is a relationship of the form $y = ax + b$ (called a linear transformation) that allows conversion between the two scales. To convert from Celsius to Fahrenheit, y in Fahrenheit equals 9/5 times the Celsius reading plus 32°.

By comparison, a ratio scale is one in which there is very little arbitrariness in the measurements. There is an absolute zero on a ratio scale. Items like the length or weight of an item are measured on a ratio scale because they can take an absolute value of zero. If two different ratio scales are used to measure the weight or length of an item (pounds or kilograms; inches or centimeters) there is a direct multiplication factor between the units on the two scales. Conversion between the two scales is governed by a relation of the type $y = kx$. Furthermore, a weight of 2 tons is said to be twice as heavy as one measuring one ton in weight.

Experimental Measurement of Utility

The results of an experimental study of the utility functions of a group of corporate executives engaged in decision making on behalf of their firm has been reported by Swalm. The first step in this study was to establish a planning horizon for each executive in terms of the amounts of money that he or she was customarily involved with in decision making. The planning horizon was set for each individual as twice the amount of money that he might recommend be spent in any one year. Each individual was then questioned using the standard gamble procedure, and the utility for gain or loss was determined on an arbitrary scale. The same scale was used for all individuals taking part in the study. The results of the study showed widely different attitudes to gain and loss on the part of the individuals involved. Typical utility functions found in the study are illustrated in Fig. 6.

The utility functions of the executives found in the study illustrate managerial behavior that ranges from extremely conservative to that of a gambler. A majority of the functions contained the sharp drop in the negative quadrant (as in Fig. 6 (a)) which denotes conservatism in situations involving loss to the corporation. The proportion of individuals showing inclination towards risk (as in Fig. 6 (c) and (d)) was small. This attitude no doubt inhibits the selection of alternatives in which the possibility of gain justifies the assumption of some risk of loss. They indicate perhaps that in organizational decision making the penalty for obtaining a bad outcome is considered by some managers to be much greater than the reward for choosing an alternative that works out well.

A similar set of experiments to determine utility functions in a practical situation has been reported by Spetzler. In these experiments, thirty-six executives from the same company were interviewed and utility functions were obtained using a variation of the standard gamble method. The subject matter in each of the interviews was investment decisions in which the company was or could be involved. Each executive was asked to express his

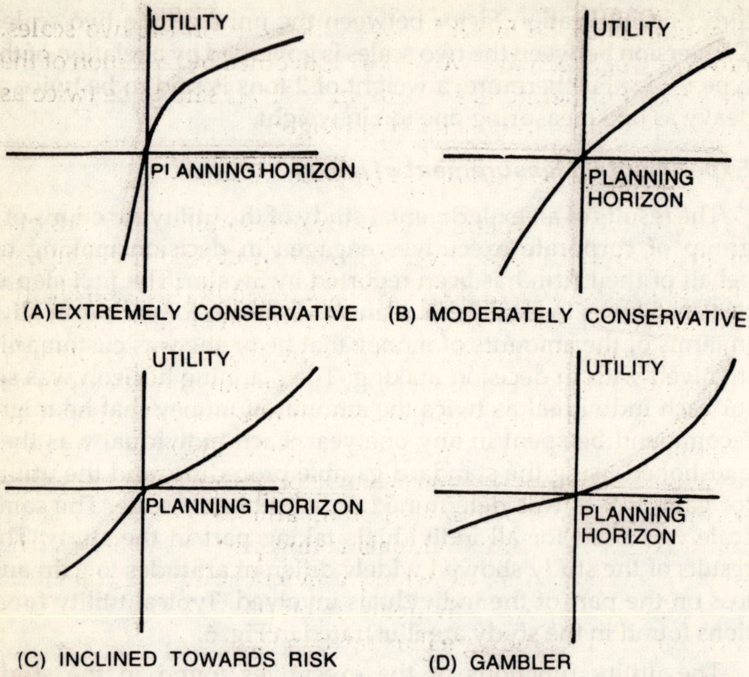

Fig. 6. Utility function of executives determined in an experimental

preferences between alternative investment situations that involved some degree of risk. This set of experiments is interesting in that the participants were asked to express opinions on the alternative investments from the point of view of the company they represented. The utility functions obtained represented therefore the impressions of the individuals involved of what might be called a corporate utility function. As set of experiments with similar objectives has been reported by Cramer and Smith.

EVALUATION OF THE CONCEPT OF UTILITY

The concept of utility is one that seems acceptable at first sight to those who have been involved in the study of decision making. It appears reasonable that if alternatives can be placed in an order of preference, then the relationship between these preferences should be capable of being expressed in numeric form. The major reservations with regard to the concept center on the manner in which utility can be measured and the way in which the measured utility can be used in practical decision situations.

The two assumptions involved in the standard gamble procedure that have attracted the most comment are those of transitivity and attitude to gambling in the individuals involved. Transitivity is essentially a mathematical concept. Most individuals follow it when dealing with preferences with respect to a single objective. It appears to represent logical behavior. It seems to be normal and consistent that if an individual prefers *A* to *B* and *B* to C with a particular objective in mind that he or she will prefer *A* to C with respect to that objective. However, most of those involved in managerial decision making seldom have only one objective to consider. A manager is likely to say, "On the one hand, I prefer *A* to *B* and *B* to C but under some circumstances I prefer C to *A*." Such a statement does not obey the strict mathematical condition of transitivity. It may however represent practical conditions better than a purely transitive statement with respect to one objective. Nevertheless, if preferences do not obey the transitivity condition, the standard gamble procedure is placed in jeopardy.

The standard gamble procedure also requires the individual involved to choose between a sure thing and a gamble in establishing the interval-scale utility. This procedure could be disrupted if the individual has an aversion to or a liking for gambling that would influence the choice. The establishment of interval scale utility requires that the choice be made entirely on the basis of preferences between the alternatives available to the decision maker. Any influence on this choice introduced by the behavioral characteristics of the individual involved would cause errors in the interval scale measurement.

The concept of the "customary wealth" of an individual or of an organization which is incorporated into the Markowitz utility function is far from clear. Whereas this concept is similarly intuitively acceptable, there may be difficulty in defining the customary wealth applicable to an individual or organization with sufficient accuracy to permit the determination of a utility function. There are similar reservations with regard to the establishment of utility for alternatives that involve considerations other than gain or loss of a commodity such as money. Situations involving objectives that are concerned with matters for which money is not an appropriate proxy measure (such as health, welfare, public esteem, and social responsibility) may not be amenable to representation by a numeric quantity such as is derived by the interval scale measurement.

Some of these concerns have been investigated experimentally in the laboratory, notably by Mosteller and Nogee. In these experiments, subjects were offered a series of gambles involving real money. Utility curves were constructed on the basis of responses and an attempt was made to determine whether future behavior in similar situations could be predicted from the experimentally determined utility functions. The predictions did not match the behavior of the subjects exactly. Nevertheless, the experimentors found that the higher the expected utility of a gamble, the greater was the probability that a subject would choose it. However, laboratory experiments involving persons with less immediate responsibility than executives have and sums of money far smaller than are involved in real life are probably not a satisfactory representation of the conditions under which managers must make practical decisions.

Even given that a utility curve can be constructed that represents the behavior of an individual at a given time, there is reason to question whether such a curve can be used to predict the future behavior of that individual. Interval scale measurements of utility are at best *descriptive*, in that they describe the preferences and behavior of an individual at some time in the past. There is no immediately-acceptable reason why such descriptive measurements of past behavior should be used in a *prescriptive* fashion to predict future behavior. Conditions may have changed since the measurements were made and the individual's preferences may have changed along with them. The individual's view of his or her personal life and prospects may have altered considerably since the utility measurements were taken. His impression of the position of the company for which it is proposed that a utility function is being used in decision making may have changed since the function was determined. Nevertheless, repeated adherence to the same utility function over a long period of time might be regarded as evidence that future behavior will follow the same pattern. There is, however, always the chance that some event or change in conditions will bring about a change in decision making behavior.

A further serious reservation to interval scale utility results from the nature of the scale on which it is measured. The basic characteristic of the interval scale is that the zero point is chosen arbitraily and the units on the scale can also be changed at will. In practice, therefore, the utility of one person can be measured on a scale of, say, 20 to 200 and that of another person can be measured on a scale of say 0 to 100. Furthermore, the scales of each person can be multiplied by an arbitrary factor without loss of applicability. The difference of scales matters little until an interpersonal comparison of utilities is made. However, if attempts are made to compare the utilities of different individuals for alternatives, serious difficulties arise unless a relationship between their two utility scales can be established.

Additions of individual utilities is sometimes proposed as a means of constructing a "social welfare function" for use in group decision making. Functions of this nature have been used in the assessment of the desirability of alternative social programs with respect to populations that contain segments with different views, needs, and preferences. The validity of a social welfare function obtained by adding individual utilities is in serious question amongst authorities in decision making at the present time. Apart from the difficulties inherent in the measurement of utility, questions have been raised about the nature of the function that is used. The manner in which the function is constructed clearly implies a weighting of the preferences of the individuals whose utilities contribute to it, even if all utilities are originally measured on the same scale.

CONCLUSIONS

Doubts exist on the feasibility in may situations of establishing quantitative measures of benefits and disbenefits that are truly representative of progress toward achievement of objectives. Situations in which all the benefits and disbenefits of all the participants can be represented by well understood quantitative measures are limited in number. There are considerable concerns and constraints with respect to these of proxy measures. The concept of utility, while intuitively attractive, is surrounded by reservations, primarily with how it can be measured and the applicability of utility to situations involving more than the gain or loss of a simple commodity. Notwithstanding these concerns about the availability of appropriate quantitative measures of benefits and disbenefits, the bulk of the recently developed theory of decisions is based on the assumption that such quantitative measures can be determined. A large proportion of recent articles in the technical literature start with a sentence like, "Let us assume that the utilities of the decision maker for the alternatives take the following form...." The question arises as to how the practical decision maker should approach the comparison of alternatives in these circumstances.

First and foremost, most authorities agree that the decision maker should earnestly seem appropriate quantitative measures of benefits and disbenefits and adopt them whenever this course of action is acceptable and feasible and necessary to the choice between alternatives. Having adopted these measures with a clear conscience, the decision maker has available a number of powerful methods and techniques involving quantitative measures to assist in the decision making process. Second, the decision maker should avoid the temptation of adopting quantitative measures merely for the sake of simplifying the decision process or of using a particular methodology. The penalties for yielding to this temptation may be severe in terms of wrong conclusions and partial rather than complete appreciation of a decision situation. Third, the decision maker should take heart in the fact that most individuals are able at least to express preferences between alternatives. Furthermore, there are methods and techniques available to assist the decision making process that can be used when only the preferences of the participants are available.

10

CORPORATE STRATEGIES

In shaping and defining the success of an organization corporate strategies play a major role. Corporate strategy describes a firm's primary performance objectives, product-market scope, and major operating policies. Formulating strategy involves analyzing and synthesizing the environment and resources of a firm with the values of its managers and external constituents. Implementing strategy involves designing and administering the formal organization to elicit individual and collective behavior required by the strategy. Managing strategy involves orchestrating and influencing organizational renewal and growth through strategic change over time.

Strategic decisions are major resource commitments which affect a firm over long time periods. These commitments determine how the parts of a firm relate to one another and how a firm postures itself toward the environment. The pattern of resource commitments reflects a firm's priorities and establishes its level of risk. The sequence and timing of strategic decisions determine the efficiency and effectiveness with which a firm obtains, transforms, and deploys its resources.

Background

Business policy as an academic subject began at the Harvard Business School in 1912. The course attended by top executives and senior faculty had three characteristics which remain with the field today: (i) integration of other areas of business; (ii) adoption of top management's views; and (iii) solving problems of importance. The field was descriptive.

Having gone through some changes during World War II, the concept of strategy began to provide the field a conceptual structure and normative orientation in the 1960s. From his business history research about "Strategy and Structure", Alfred Chandler concluded that environmental shifts induced strategy reformulation which required organizational change to implement it. Building on Chandler's work and on a decade of collaborative research, Kenneth Andrews first articulated "The Concept of Corporate Strategy," and prescribed an analytical approach to its formulation and implementation. Simultaneously, Igor Ansoff developed a normative methodology for formulating "Corporate Strategy" based on his corporate experience and on available management theory.

By 1980, corporate strategy was well accepted as a concept useful to the managers of a firm. The concept is most valuable in helping sophisticated and complex organizations anticipate and respond to their turbulent environment satisfactorily. Business policy is part of the curriculum in most schools of business, suggesting that future managers will rely on it increasingly.

Definition of Strategy

Corporate strategy describes a firm's primary performance objectives, product-market scope, and major operating policies. Primary performance objectives state the criteria by which management judges the success of the firm and expects others to judge it. Product-market scope limits the firm's range of activities and therefore sets some of its environmental boundaries. Major operating policies stipulate how the firm conducts its activities, uses its resources, and faces its environment. Business policy indicates how managers should define, formulate, implement, and manager corporate strategy.

Primary performance objectives describe what the firm wants to accomplish. As economic entities, firms often focus on financial performance objectives. However, as societal entities, firms increasingly espouse objectives for their impact on the broader environment. These objectives can include many dimensions from employee welfare or community improvement to political impact or philanthropic contribution. All objectives constrain the selection of other strategic choices and thereby guide the search for strategic alternatives as well as provide criteria for evaluating a strategy retrospectively.

Good strategic objectives have four common characteristics: they should be measurable, temporal, comprehensive, and realistic. *Measurable* objectives need not be quantitative; however,, they should permit observers to agree on their meaning both when set and when reviewed. *Temporal* objectives specify a deadline for achievement, although appropriate horizons may vary by industry. *Comprehensive* objectives enable the firm to specify a small number of objectives that reflect the overall performance of the firm while permitting considerable latitude in how they are to be accomplished. *Realistic* objectives are achievable, even if challenging, and fully utilize the resources available to the firm.

The product-market scope of a firm describes the range of products it provides and customeıs it serves. This scope highlights two different types of firms and strategies. An integrated firm is one business, usually comprised of major organization units responsible for stages or functions in the development and delivery of a single product line to a market. Its scope is the breadth or focus of its product line and customer base. The objectives for integrated firms often relate to their industry positions and conditions.

By comparison, a diversified firm (generally a multinational firm) operates several distinct businesses, each as a separate orgnizational unit. For a diversified firm, product-market scope specifies the kinds of businesses it enters or exist, nourishes or starves. This specification may include criteria such as size, minimum profitability, potential growth, desired market share position, and other statistical criteria. In addition, it may specify commonalties among its businesses, such as common technology, raw materials, customer characteristics, or geographic coverages. In some cases it specifies the resources shared among businesses.

The major operating policies of an integrated firm define its approach to competition. Some of these policies guide the major functional areas of the business, such as marketing, production, research and development, personnel, and finance. Functional policies are guidelines or decision rules for the managers of these functions. They shape decisions that develop and deploy the resources of the firm by changing its capabilities and limitations over time. Other operating policies guide the timing and sequencing of changes in functional policies or define priorities in interfunctional decisions such as resource allocations. These policies also indicate the kind of coordination required among functional areas to compete effectively. Finally, operating policies indicate how some of the nonfinancial objectives of the firm will be achieved.

Operating policies in a many-faceted firm usually indicate how corporate management relates to its businesses or divisions, and how the businesses relate to one another, rather than how the businesses themselves compete. They address how the firm is financed and organized, how businesses are entered or exited, and how resources are allocated and shared among the divisions. Businesses are acquired, internally developed, or created by dividing existing businesses; they can be divested, liquidated, of consolidated. The policies can define the roles of businesses in the firm, such as providing growth, profitability, stability, or resources. They also stipulate what functions or decisions belong to corporate management and which belong to the businesses, such as accounting and planning systems, research and development, or personnel.

Formulation of Strategy

Formulating strategy involves distinct steps of analysis and decision. Since the steps are interactive and repetitive, people disagree about the content and sequence of the steps. The content of the steps is somewhat different for integrated firms than for diversified firms. The sequence does influence the effectiveness and efficiency of formulation. Two early steps generally are to identify the current strategy and to select preliminary performance objectives for the future.

The next steps for most firms are to assess the major conditions and trends in the environment, to evaluate the capabilities and limitations of the firm, and to articulate the values of key managers and external constituencies. A firm scans the environment to identify social values, customer needs, technological changes, governmental regulations, economic movements, and competitor shifts, and to estimate their potential impacts on its future strategy and performance. These suggest opportunities or risks for the firm. A firm also evaluates its capabilities and limitations in absolute terms, both current condition and future potential. These suggest areas of strength or weakness relative to the environment. Values are inherently difficult to articulate and categorize, however, they often have significant impact on the assessment of environment, the evaluation of resources, and the choice of strategy.

The next three steps are to generate major alternative strategies, to forecast the likely performance results of each (including the current strategy), and to evaluate the resource utilization and risk associated with each alternative. Major strategic alternatives include changes in performance objectives, product-market scope, or operating policies. They are usually ways to seize opportunities, reduce risks, utilize capabilities, or overcome limitations either by changing the resource configuration or the arena in which it is deployed. A major impetus for generating alternatives is a realization that the future performance of a firm will not meet its objectives without strategic change. Alternatives seek to fill the gap. A second impetus is the realization that an existing strategy does not fully utilize the firm's resources. Alternatives seek to improve performance through their better or different utilization.

Finally, the firm compares the forecast performance results against the objectives and either selects one of the alternative strategies, searches for additional strategies, or revises the objectives. These steps are all iterative as analysis proceeds and repetitive as more information becomes available. Many techniques are useful for each of the steps; specific techniques depending on the situation. Before fully committing to a new strategic alternative, the firm should reassess the consistency among its strategic elements and the major factors which should be considered in its formulation. One of these factor is the firm's ability to implement a new strategy.

Implementation of Strategy

Implementing strategy is making strategy an accurate description of a firm by transforming a statement of its strategy into decisions, activity, and performance. This transformation involves directing and motivating individual and group behavior toward the successful accomplishment of the tasks implied by the strategy. Organizational design and political leadership help managers implement strategy. Organization is important in implementing strategy because through it, senior executives can influence many people continuously and pervasively. Organization design influences behavior in at least two important ways: (a) it directly influences people's jobs and their perceptions of what the firm expects them to do and (b) it partially shapes the informal organization or corporate culture. Political leadership provides further opportunities to shape the informal organization of managers near the top of the formal organization.

Implementing strategy involves designing the structure and systems of the organization. Structure is the formal framework of job definitions, authority relationships, and communication channels which specifies how the work of the organization is divided and coordinated. Dividing work and defining jobs can focus attention and activity on the key tasks required by strategy. Authority relationships and communication channels influence the independence or coordination among those tasks as required by strategy.

Organizational systems further influence strategic behavior. These systems include those of planning and control, measurement and evaluation, reward and restraint, recruitment and selection, and training and development. Collectively, the pattern of these systems provides the knowledge, skills, and attitudes of job encumbents and determines how they use these attributes to contribute to the accomplishment of objectives through their behavior. Some of these systems may be pervasive throughout an organization, and others may be tailored to the specific requirements of parts of the organization. Through experience, people perceive what the organization expects of them and develop patterns of behavior reflecting those perceived expectations. Implementing strategy involves shaping those responses to conform to strategic needs.

Political leadership recognizes that many business decisions are the outcome of an influence process. Managers with varying degrees of authority and power bring their influence to bear on decisions that are important to them. The political leadership of senior management utilizes, develops, and influences this process so that decisions support the selected strategy. Organization design and political leadership partially shape the social and political structure of the firm. This helps to stabilize and routinize continuing activity, to establish and reinforce norms of acceptable behavior, and to highlight and resolve important conflicts.

Strategy Management

Strategic management refers to the roles of various executives in formulating and implementing strategy. The role of senior executives is process-oriented in firms that confront broad and turbulent environments and that adopt complex and decentralized organizations. In these firms, formulating and implementing strategy requires the continual involvement of many managers throughout the organization. Through new information, they perceive changes in environment, resources, and values. They each gather this fragmented information incrementally. Each manager brings a different organizational, political, and personal perspective to the information processing. Therefore, managers with different perceptions and perspectives prepare and support different proposals for strategic and organizational change.

Top executives increasingly recognize that correctly managing the process of organizational renewal through strategic change is more important than critically evaluating the substance of proposals for strategic change. The argue that if the process is appropriate, the substance will be likewise. Managing the process involves analytical, organizational, and political skills to understand, structure, and administer it.

Senior executives manage the process of formulating and implementing strategy through organizational design and political leadership, the same factor used to implementary strategy. These factors provide a context within which proposals are generated, advocated, and adopted. This creates a tension between the use of organization as a way to stabilize operating behavior and implement strategy on one hand and to promote desirable strategic change on the other. In this sense, formulating and implementing strategy are inseparable processes which senior executives must manage through organizational design and political leadership.

One other way senior executives manage the process is by providing broad statements of corporate strategy which provide a framework for other executives to challenge or detail. Senior executives can articulate areas of particular interest or concern which strategy should address, and they can establish criteria for selecting strategy proposals submitted by others these criteria stimulate and guide lower level managers who formulate and advocate strategic proposals.

LONG-RANGE CORPORATE PLANNING

The term Long-Range Corporate Planning came into popular management use during the middle 1950s. By 1960, a minority of large industrial companies had some sort of formal long-range planning process under way. Some of these companies introduced planning on too grandiose a scale, and abandoned it after a year or two because it was more trouble than it was worth, only to reinstall it a few years later on a more moderate, step-by-step basis.

The concept of formal planning gained continued acceptance during the 1960s. By 1980, probably 80% to 85% of the *Fortune 500* engaged in some form of long-range planning (not always of outstanding quality), as did perhaps half of the industrial companies down to the $ 25 to $50 million sales range. Companies significantly smaller than this are usually subject to close, personalized management, under which the need for the formalized planning and formal communications discussed here is less evident.

During the past 15 years, large banks, insurance companies, and other non-industrial organizations also began to undertake formal long-range planning to a significant degree. Today, formal programs of this sort are being activated by universities, professional and trade associations, units of city governments, and other nonprofit groups. On the other hand, only a few of the largest firms in the securities and brokerage industry have, as of 1980, undertaken any significant formal forward planning.

Typically, "long-range" in this context may be five years, sometimes ten, with possibly even longer periods in natural-resources industries such s forestry and minerals. Typically, a time span is chosen that embraces at least one decision-making cycle, such as from the conception of a new plant or new line of products to getting them on stream. The "long- range planning" span is almost always longer than one year, but it is not unusual to find the designation "one-year profit plan" applied to the first year of the long-range plan. In such cases the first year is spelled out in considerably greater detail than the second, third, or succeeding years. The first-year financial data may be the same as the one-year budget.

In further clarification of terminology, a distinction is frequently made between two basic types of planning effort. The first is usually called *strategic* planning, and is concerned primarily with questions of major strategy and new growth directions for an enterprise. Major decisions may be involved, as for example those having to do with a merger or entry into a new business.

The second type is frequently termed *operating* or *divisional* planning. Such planning is usually centered under the heads of the individual operating units or divisions of an organization. In contrast, strategic planning calls for the heavy involvement of the corporate chief executive.

How Long-Range Planning Differs from Budgeting

Documents coming out of the planning process differ significantly from budget documents, both in content and use. Budgets are prepared for financial and operating control. They typically aim for maximum accuracy in the dollar quantification of authorized activities rather than the formulation of imaginative new objectives. They usually concentrate on financial results, with little elaboration of the "whys" and with little background, descriptive analysis, or text material on programs. In contrast, planning documents covering more than one year tend to have somewhat ambitious goals, and good deal of analytical and text material, and discussion of impending programs. They are used for communication, setting policy, decision-making, and long-range thinking on resource allocations, rather than month- to-month controls.

In many cases the financial statements in planning documents are much more simplified than those found in budget statements or monthly operating statements. In one form or another the plans address themselves to the questions, "Where are we now?" "Where do we want to go?" and "How do we want to get there?"—the last including the items of "Who" and "How much will it cost?"

Why Growth of Planning?

A program for *strategic planning* is often undertaken by highly successful companies simply to assure continuation of existing momentum. The motivation for initiating strategic planning may be either offensive (e.g., to exploit an attractive opportunity) or defensive (e.g., to minimize future risk).

Planning is often inaugurated because management sees an upcoming threat to its business and recognizes the need to develop new sources of earnings to overcome the threat. Many defense contractors have attempted this type of planning, albeit with only spotty success, when threatened by cutbacks in defense spending. As a specific example, a paper company foresaw that its main profit-producing product line would undergo greatly intensified competition in the years ahead. Through formal, organized strategic planning it succeeded in adding new product lines both through internal development and acquisition, so that earnings are now many times the size they were when the threat to the one line was first recognized.

The growth of *operating* or *divisional* planning has received much of its impetus from the growing complexity of business (and also non-business) organizations. The head of a moderate-size company with two or three divisions may in many cases have an adequate "feel" of the future of each, so that he can, for example, decide which unit should get the lion's share of new investment expenditures, without formal planning. In contrast, the head of a company with twenty or thirty divisions or major product groups cannot do this, and must use formal planning as a tool to help make such resource allocations rationally.

The growth of formal planning is often attributed to the acceleration of technological and social change, and to similar external and uncontrollable factors. While these may be underlying causes, it is usually something much more concrete that provides the actual impetus to more formal planning. For example, many companies have initiated formal planning because their banks or other financing institutions asked to see their long-range plans in connection with loan applications.

For completeness here, it should probably also be added that a small percentage of companies have undertaken long-range planning simply because it is the fashionable thing to do. However, unless such organizations can direct their planning in a way to provide tangible returns, it can be expected that they will soon abandon those efforts for resumption at a time when they can make them practical. In any event, long-range corporate planning can never be an "ivory-tower" undertaking. Guidelines for operational and divisional planning can be set in terms of the broad parameters of strategic planning—but constructive divisional involvement in a long-range planning program sponsored by corporate headquarters will only be secured if the divisions see "user benefits" in terms of their own operations.

How to Implement Operating Planning?

Operating long-range planning (also referred to as divisional planning or profit improvement planning for present operations), typically begins with the generation of a series of forward plans by the individual operating units. They frequently have a three- to five-year time span. In concept, the head of the individual operating unit is responsible for executing it; however, he may receive assistance from his own staff or the staff of corporate headquarters.

It is quite common for the corporate headquarters staff to issue a five-year set of economic and other basic assumptions at the beginning of each year's planning cycle. This facilitates coordination so that each unit bases its planning on similar assumptions, in contrast to one unit's predicating its planning on more prosperous overall conditions than another. This planning cycle is undergone annually, adding a year on the future end and dropping a year gone by. It is not uncommon for the planning cycle to begin with the issuance of the aforementioned assumptions in the summer, followed by a month or two or compiling the plan by the operating units, a period of review by headquarters staff, and final approval or modification by headquarters line management toward the end of the year.

The budget for the upcoming year may be approved at the same time. Some organizations have found it useful to phase the long- range planning at a different time of year from the one-year budget preparations. The justification usually cited is that the attention to the details of the budget process overshadows the more conceptual thinking generally considered to be the hallmark of effective planning. Still other organizations engage in more or less continuous planning which plays down the prominence of the annual planning cycle. Such organizations may update long-range plans or introduce new long-range programs whenever circumstances warrant.

There appears to be a growing feeling that the financial summary should indeed be merely a financial representation of the conditions discussed above. Many organizations have found that so-called long-range plans that deal only in financial material, or that lay too much emphasis on financial detail.

Robert W. Haigh, group vice president of Xerox Corporation, has put forward the ideal that division plans can sometimes become so complex and detailed that fundamentals are lost sight of. He prefers, as an indication that his people are doing effective planning, that the head of a unit be able to cite without reference to notes the key factors in his business. These include such elements as:

- ☐ The new major trends in the business environment.
- ☐ The few major objectives of this business unit in fairly specific terms.
- ☐ The few major programs to be featured in achieving the objectives.
- ☐ How the foregoing relate to the short-term plan of the unit.

It is quite common for the divisional plans to be summarized or consolidated by headquarters planning staff into a total plan for the present units of a company. There may be negotiation between headquarters management and division management as to goals to be achieved and programs to be undertaken. In some cases, negotiation and at least preliminary approval take place at the objectives-setting stage, so that the lengthy job of working out detailed programs does not have to be reworked because of changed objectives.

It is not uncommon for some headquarters managements to include a positive or negative "fudge factor" in their own private thinking to offset what they consider under optimism or pessimism on the part of individual units. They may also add a factor for objectives or expectations from new sources of earnings, that is, new earnings coming from sources other than the present divisions, such as new acquisitions or ventures. (This is discussed further immediately below). Thus the "corporate long-range plan" is born, although it may never exist as a single document in one place.

How to Implement Strategic Planning?

The underlying concept of *Strategic* long-range planning is that it provides the vehicle for the enterprise to reposition its business mix or basic pattern of doing business, in order to achieve superior objectives, i.e., results which would be superior to continuing on substantially an "as is" basis. Thus some textile organizations have successfully made a conversion from being primarily weavers of commodity greige goods to organizations which supply, say, fashion-oriented finished goods, knit as well as woven constructions, consumer end products, and other specialized items less vulnerable to low- price commodity import competition.

In actual practice, formal strategic planning is often done on a more spasmodic basis than operational long-range planning. Thus a formal strategic plan is usually not redrawn in total annually, adding and dropping a year, as in formal operating long-range planning. Rather, parts of a strategic plan may be revised several times a year, for example as new studies disclose new areas of opportunity or possibly indicate the desirability of de- emphasizing some traditional areas. Other aspects of a strategic plan, for example to expand in certain European businesses through ventures and internal expansion, may continue without change in basic concept for some period of years.

Some literature on strategic planning has advocated a doctrinaire attitude, putting forth "cookbood recipes" as to how it should be done. In contrast, it is the writers' observation, based on consulting with companies which have had successful results in strategic planning, that effective planning of this sort may be carried out in many different ways, with various degrees of formality and with varying frequency of updating. However, the main factors to be considered as part of the overall strategic planning process include elements such as the following:

(1) **Establishing Financial Objectives.** For publicly-held companies, consistency of growth in earnings per common share is generally the overriding financial objective. Companies usually wish to do at lest as well as their own past record, or at least as

well as their own past record, or at least as well as other companies in their field.

(2) **Measuring the Earnings "Gap."** In comparing the financial objectives with the outlook as portrayed by the sum of a company's operating long-range plans, it is frequently apparent that there is a gap between what is *desired* and what is *anticipated.* It is the job of the strategic planner to fill this gap by laying plans for developing new sources of earnings or redirecting present resources into more productive lines. As in operating planning, it is the line management (i.e. the chief executive) which has the ultimate responsibility for strategic planning decisions.

(3) **Appraising Internal Strengths Weaknesses, and Issues.** In many organizations, strategic planners make an inventory from time to time to determine where there are strengths which can be capitalized or weaknesses to be circumvented or offset.

(4) **"Pullers-Draggers" analysis.** The writers have coined this term to describe the process by which the strategic planner analyzes the component businesses within a company. This pinpoints the need to force-feed the "pullers" (businesses with attractive earnings and prospects) and lay specific plans for doing this, and to correct or withdraw from the "draggers" (components of the business with unattractive earnings or prospects). In an analysis of this type, other segments of the business may be identified as cash "milk-cows," each requiring appropriate treatment.

(5) **Analysis of Business Environment.** Strategic planners will also from time to time attempt to portray future trends in their business environment. This includes their markets, their competition, their technologies, the social climate, trends in governmental regulation, and the like. It is the job of the strategic planner to see that a company capitalizes on such trends where possible, and avoids being trapped by surprise in disadvantageous trends.

(6) **Directional Planning.** Selecting new growth directions for a company, when done on the most rational basis, involves setting criteria for evaluating new growth directions, screening the full range of possibilities against these criteria, and establishing priorities for implementation, Criteria can be based on three principal factors, each of which has sub-factors in turn. The first is *profit*

opportunity: "Does this field give us an opportunity for the size, growth, consistency, and level of profits which we are seeking?" The second criterion relates to *compatibility*: "Is this a field which we can understand and to which we can make some unique contribution based on our marketing strength or technical strength, or the like?" The third criterion has to do with *feasibility* or *prospects for successful entry*.

Screening the full range of possibilities against the criteria is less difficult than it may at first sound. It is important that a variety of factors be considered, such as growth markets, growth business areas, horizontal and vertical integration and all possibilities which closely relate to a company's strengths, such as its own type of technology, as well as the screening of all acquisition candidates within certain established limits. By this process, it is possible for a strategic planning group to say truly it has considered all possibilities for new growth directions and has established priorities accordingly. Reorienting priorities as conditions change is more-or-less an ongoing job in many organizations.

(7) **Implementation.** Many strategic planning groups also have responsibility for acquisitions, divestitures, and setting up or ventures. If these activities are not housed organizationally within the planning group, there must obviously be a close liaison. Close liaison is also required with the technical people responsible for developing altogether new products for a company. This implementation stage, calling as it does for somewhat different activities than strictly planning, is sometimes referred to as the "development" or "planning and development" activity.

A Practical Approach

In the foregoing material, the authors have endeavored to spell out the practices typically employed in organizations which are well managed and experienced in the techniques of long-range planning. However, one common departure is frequently found in unquestionably successful companies (although it is now less common). This is an acquisition program to acquire new companies, based more on opportunism than on reasoned planning of suitable growth directions for the parent company. In other words, if an attractive "deal" can be made, the business the acquired company is in is not considered to be especially important. This may still be justifiable where the parent company is threatened with immediate disastrous prospects in its base business.

Planning theory says that objectives must be spelled out so that all concerned can be working toward a common goal. However, professional planners sometimes encounter chief executives who are reluctant to spell out the real objectives of the company. These company heads apparently feel that they had best keep their options open by articulating only vague or highly generalized goals—for example, "to maximize profits." Obviously, unless this attitude at the top is changed, the planner will have to develop proposed programs based on his own assessment of needs and opportunities, and secure separate approvals on a ad-hoc basis.

Another problem encountered by planners is a tendency for managements to be biased by existing conditions—i.e., to make overly optimistic plans in good times and overly pessimistic plans in poor times. Use of professional economists' inputs to the planning process will provide more objectivity in this regard.

How to Organize the Planning Function?

A competent planner should be a specialist in the techniques of planning, but he should also be a generalist who knows the requirements for success in his particular industry. The head of planning typically reports to the chief executive (or division head if the planner is on a division level). In large organizations having an "office of the president" the planning function may report there. In other large organizations the planner may report to the executive vice president for administration.

Planning staffs for operating planning are typically small, perhaps consisting of only a few people even in a large company. This is because their focus is to see that the operating planning gets done, rather than actually doing the actual planning. However, to the extent that there is major emphasis on *strategic* planning, study of new growth directions, acquisitions, and venture work, the planning staff can consist of a dozen or even several dozen persons.

New Developments in Planning

There has been considerable interest in the application of computer techniques to planning matters. Certainly computers have been used for many years in dealing with such "planning" problems as warehouse location and transportation networks; however, for most companies, matters of that nature are peripheral to the main issues of business planning.

Computer models have been constructed which provide helpful answers to "what if" questions which sometimes have to be faced in planning—for example, "What if we were to change our price...?" or "What if we were to increase the size of our sales force...?" Citibank of New York among others has developed a computer model for use with its customers which forecasts under certain assumptions the effect of a merger for five or more years ahead. Such techniques can be useful aids to planning decision making where many "what if" question must be (or should be) answered. However, they are still only aids to decision-making. No one is yet "planning by computer" in the literal sense of the phrase.

Some interesting work has gone into developing massive econometric and corporate models as an aid to planning. While again these show signs of promise especially on peripheral matters, the fundamental planning decisions are still being made by seasoned executives on the basis of their conviction and judgment. It seems that this will continue to be the case.

Management by Objectives, which can be described as medium-range personal planning by individual managers, has come into widespread use. However, where companies have both long-range corporate planning and management by objectives programs, the link between the two is generally indirect. In setting his own objective, say for the forthcoming year, an individual manager must be guided by the immediate objectives of his unit of the company. Obviously, none of his objectives can run counter to long-range operational planning. However, they must be very specific for short-term results in his segment.

In the coming years, formal long-range planning can be expected to continue to spread to industrial organizations which do not now practice it, and to an increasing degree to non-business organizations.

Formal planning has already achieved a foothood in numerous educational institutions, charitable organizations, hospitals, and the like. Nevertheless many business executives who insist upon sophisticated long-range planning in their own business organizations, sit on the governing boards of nonbusiness organizations where formal long-range planning does not exist. However the changing pressures of the times are beginning to work for the installation of formal long-range planning in such organizations.

NEW-PRODUCT AND PROMOTION DEVELOPMENT

New-Product Development is certainly not new. Its appearance on industrial organizational charts as a recognized area of responsibility is however, a post World War II phenomenon. Also, sometimes called *New Product Planning*, this activity is generally considered to be part of the overall responsibility of Marketing Management. It does involve, however, an active relationship with the technical operations of the company located in the Research and Development and the Engineering organizations. New-product development is concerned with getting ideals for new products, screening them by a selective process, and, through technical research and development, translating them to tangible products ("hardware") which can be mass-produced and sold at a profit.

Companies depend on new-product development for many reasons, among which are: (1) to counteract a slowdown in company growth rate; (2) to replace short lived products; (3) to capitalize on surplus capacity, including both physical facilities and managerial time, ability, and desire; (4) to employ surplus funds or available borrowing power.

It is important to have a working definition of the term "new product." A noted writer on this subject. Peter Hilton, has defined a new product as "any product, which, regardless of the length of time it has been marketed, is still unknown by name or application to 75% of its potential users." He points to that "a new product need not, of necessity, employ a brand new concept. It can be an improved product or an established product with a new feature or a new application."

In this article, major emphasis is placed on the development and commercialization of those products that embody ideas or knowledge which are new to the company seeking product diversification.

The Process of Development

New-product development compasses all activity from idea conception to full-scale introduction of the product to the market. The process is highly complex, requiring successful coordination of many individual activities. It may be looked upon as a sequence of six separate and distinct stages: Exploration, Screening, Business Analysis, Development, Testing, and Commercialization. The following is the description of six stages:

(1) **The exploration** stage comprises the seeking of new ideas which may come from many sources, among which may be listed the sales force, which is in constant contact with customer needs and applications, and the personnel handling sales inquiries. Also useful is a study of the products of competitors and of products that are allied and substitutable. Ideas may originate with management, stockholders, or consultants, or may come from a study of foreign products and markets, reports from trade associations, Government or university laboratories, the Patent Office, trade journals, or from papers delivered at technical or trade meetings. Research and development organizations are expected to be alert to new product possibilities, and their effectiveness in this direction is directly related to the knowledge they possess of the marketing conditions. Engineering and manufacturing departments often get ideas from proving-ground tests, performance records, observing products in use, and from other work. Suggestions systems, market analyses, cost studies, and feedback from service organizations may also prove to be fruitful sources of new product ideas. Emphasis in the exploration stage should be placed on quantity, not quality, of ideas.

(2) **Screening** is the selection of the most promising ideas for further consideration. If a company as good sales and research and development organizations, there will be no dearth of ideas to exploit. The greatest problem facing management is that of proper selection and rejection. Whereas in the past this was done by shrewd guesswork or by hunch, today every bit of quantitative and factual information is assembled and arranged to eliminate chance as much as possible from the decisions made by management.

Prerequisite to any successful screening procedure is a clear understanding of company objectives. These should be written down in an appropriate top-management policy statement. This should eliminate many suggestions, which although intriguing, are entirely unsuited to the production facilities or the sales organization.

Concerning the ideas that survive, many questions must be answered such as: Is there a market opportunity? Is the concept technically feasible? What is the patent position? What is the status of needed raw materials or supplies? How stable are the sources of supply? Are production facilities suitable? If not, how much will it cost to obtain them? Many companies have evolved specific written new product criteria which spell out such items as short-term and long-term profitability requirements, estimated profit margin, dollar volume of production each year for a period of time, estimated amount of new capital required, etc.

It is important that management prepare such questions and make certain that they are answered quantitatively, if possible. If not possible, then they should be answered qualitatively by the best informed and least biased persons available. A number of books and articles given at the end of this article offer lists of representative questions.

Once these data are available (and they should be in writing), then the difficult job of decision making occurs. Screening at this point should not be exclusively logical; neither should it be whimsical. Too much logic leads to too safe a position which results in trivial new product advances. If there is too much whimsey, survival of the enterprise is possible only with continued good luck.

(3) **The business analysis** stage consists of establishing a project with man-hours and funds budgeted to permit the analysis of the technical and economic factors in sufficient detail to evaluate the commercial feasibility of the idea. This may include some preliminary testing and analytical studies. The end result is usually a capital budget.

(4) **The development stage** determines the practicality of the idea by producing a working model embodied in a new producing a working model embodied in a new product design. At this

stage a preliminary study of acceptability to customers may be conducted.

(5) **The testing stage** comprises redesigning the working model into a production prototype, producing a limited quantity, and usually testing the market before proceeding to full-scale production.

(6) **The final stage, commercialization**, involved deciding whether to make or purchase component parts, developing mass production methods, and activating a distribution organization. New Product Development is completed when the new product is fully integrated into the company's normal operation and is achieving satisfactory sales volume and profit.

In proceeding successfully through the stages, the following are essential:

(1) An R & D organization with competence, interest, and enthusiasm to solve the problems involved.

(2) An engineering organization equal to its part of the job.

(3) A production organization oriented to new products.

(4) A marketing organization that is interested and motivated by the challenge of selling new things.

(5) A service organization that is capable and interested, should post-sales service be required.

Mortality Rate of New Products

Published data show that it takes anywhere from 50 to 500 new product ideas at the exploration stage to result in one successfully introduced new product. Since each succeeding stage of the process is more expensive, it is imperative that only the most promising ideas be allowed to progress. Even the idea which survives and eventually leads to a new product on the market is subject to further mortality. Depending on the sample and the definition used, anywhere from 50% to 98% of new products introduced into the market fail for various reasons, and a large majority fail in the first year on the market. Some companies have estimated that 75% of the annual corporate expenditures of new products are unproductive. One company reported that, of the products that are considered successful, only one in four significantly contributes to company profits. To help reduce the high mortality in new products on the market, it is imperative to review periodically all planning for new products in the light of changing customer demands, introduction of competing products, increases in production costs, and general changes in the economic outlook.

Organizational Factor in New Product Development

It is generally conceded that it is the function of the president of the company to assume responsibility for the product line. Since the successful development of new products involves so many entirely separate operations of the company, there is a need for high-level coordination. Neither the president nor any of his immediate staff are apt to be competent on such a broad front as to be able to provide the best detailed supervision. Two methods to effect coordination have been used: either a committee has been appointed or a new department established to take responsibility for new product development. Before establishing either of these organizational devices there must be a clear definition of authority, responsibility, and functions assigned. The activity must be located within the company so that it can function effectively, and the selection of personnel must be careful planned.

If a committee is appointed it should be clearly spelled out whether the committee is *advisory* or *action-taking* and to whom it reports. If it is an action-taking committee with authority over some of the line officials, this should be clearly spelled out in a written charge or charter. It should be made very clear whether the president is prepared to accept the recommendations of the committee unless there is good reason to do otherwise, or whether he is seeking advice which he may or may not accept. If a committee is appointed, it must be provided with statements from the top management regarding company policies which serve as the first filter in the screening operation.

The persons selected for the committee must be chosen carefully and it must be made clear whether they are appointed for their personal abilities and experience, or because of their particular position in the company. This is important to know when it becomes necessary to replace anyone. Also it must be decided whether committee service is a full-time or part-time obligation. If it is full-time, some provision must be made to introduce new blood into the committee. This may be done by releasing persons for other duties and replacing them on some kind of schedule.

Persons who possess the knowledge and abilities to be extremely valuable on such committees may not have the temperament to serve for long periods in an advisory and coordinating capacity. This is particularly true if the committee is set up as an advisory committee only.

If a department is established, the duties must be clearly defined so that it does not overlap the responsibilities of other departments. There appears to be a trend to establish the new-product development function in a separate department.

A department would usually consist of a small number of specialists who do not become involved with routine responsibilities. To this small nucleus there are generally added persons from other operating divisions to provide information and advice. Thus *ad hoc* task forces are formed with different membership, depending on the product being developed.

If a committee structure is used, the chairmanship may change as the product passes through different phases from research to final production. Selecting persons on a part-time basis from these different operations and keeping them as a team from start to finish has the advantage of acquainting all responsible people with the whole project. Their own operations may thus be more effectively integrated to save time and money. In a departmental structure, this technique might also be used, but generally the department supplies the chairman, and others are brought in as needed.

New-product development activities are controlled through appropriate reports, and through accounting-type data such as man-hours expended through budgets, but most importantly through the constant personal contact of responsible parties. The chairman of such efforts is, in effect, a little president with the responsibility of getting the product planned, developed, and marketed, making use of the organization existing in the company. He must constantly strive to minimize cost and time, and maximize the utilization of resources available.

Conclusion

New-product development is a very active and growing part of the management function. Experimentation is constantly being carried out to determine the most effective method of operation.

There is no unique formula, since this depends on many company variables such as size, location, personnel, etc. The increased numbers of publications on new product development appearing in the business and trade journals provide ample evidence of the nation-wide concern of industry with these problems.

MANAGERIAL DECISIONS ON NEW PRODUCT DEVELOPMENT

The following points are representative of the type of questions to which answers must be secured—factual or estimated—before extensive developmental commitments are made. On many of these the Research Department will be expected to have answers or opinions. In some companies, a director of planning, or of commercial development, will coordinate the gathering of facts and opinions needed for a decision. The check list can form a guide for a report to management.

(1) A brief description of the proposed product.

(2) At what broad market target areas would this product be aimed?

(3) With respect to our company, is this a new product, an extension of size or application of an existing line of products (i.e., additional model), or an optional accessory to an existing product?

(4) If a new product or model, start development of a "factor comparison" chart, comparing the proposed product features with competing products.

(5) A succinct statement as to possible "pluses":

(a) Is this an entirely new invention, marking a new departure in terms of labor-saving or in the sense that it produces something not heretofore in existence?

(b) Possible technological advantages over similar products of entrenched companies in the field.

(c) Possible style appeal beyond that of potential competitors.

(d) Possible company advantages in deliveries or service.

(e) Are our background and standing *vis-a-vis* a product of this type such that our name would add special prestige?

(6) Into what price range dos this product fall? Is there a chance that under our manufacture there will be a "plus" in price?

(Include prices of comparable existing products in factor-comparison chart, item 4 above).

(7) Bibliography of pertinent literature having to do with necessary descriptive information, market possibilities, etc., with possible excerpts or photostats of key items.

(8) Names and makers of all principal commercially available items of this type, including principal imported units, if any. Who dominates this field?

(9) As to existing competition:

(a) Names of leading companies in the field, with estimate, if possible, of the share of the market each is apparently enjoying in the product in question.

(b) What is the parent corporate control of key companies in the field?

(c) Analysis of published financial figures of key companies, showing profit record in recent years, with possible analysis as to profits from the products in question.

(d) Start a special library of catalog information, advertising brochures, annual reports, etc.

(10) Is this product seasonal in usage, and if so, how?

(11) What published data can be quoted (U.S. Dept. of Commerce, trade associations, directories, trade papers, etc.) as to *current business* being done? (If possible, assemble for five past years, with estimate for current year. If an authoritative source can be cited for future years, do so; if any estimate for future years, is that of the Market Research or Planning Division, cite rational behind it. In the foregoing, give units as well as dollars, if possible also, break down by domestic manufacture, exports, and imports).

(12) List leading trade journals and trade associations in the field. Should any of these be contacted for possible surveys they may have conducted or know about, showing share of market by leading producers, etc.?

(13) At what kind of expositions or trade shows are products of this type shown? What was the most recent? When and where will the next one be held?

(14) What data from the Sales Department and other contacts exist, that will throw light on opportunities in this product?

(15) What *potential business* (for all companies) is foreseeable?

(16) A "bird's-eye-view" of *potential market breakdown* (give sources for statistical information):

(a) Classification of users—as by kinds of industries or companies, areas, income group, or other identifiable categories.

(b) Analyze above for logical size breakdowns to use: numbers of employees, dollar sales, income group, or the like.

(c) Give estimated numbers of establishments (or other logical unit) in above breakdowns.

(d) Give rating as to prospective buyers ("Limited," "Fair," "Good," or "Excellent").

(e) Are any of the above prospects for multiple sales?

(f) Can an estimate be made of the frequency of purchase?

(17) Which of the foregoing are worth considering for any special surveys? Does the company have any special contacts in any of them? Should any of them be surveyed by an outside market research organization?

(18) What steps, if any, should be taken with respect to our own dealer or sales organization?

(19) Would the *sale* of this product be:

(a) Largely through existing company sales organization and channels?

(c) To users to whom we are quite well known, but who would require well different selling organization and approach?

(c) To users to whom we are not well known?

(20) What sales channels are the leading factors in the field now using?

(21) What is the private-brand situation?

(22) What is the mail-order house situation?

(23) What are the customary discounts to dealers, markups, etc.?

(24) Would the manufacture of this product be classed as:

(a) Mass-produced?

(b) Semi-massed-produced (perhaps mass-produced parts, with relatively limited assembly)?

(c) Custom-built?

(25) If a model of drawings or samples have been submitted, what is R&D's report with respect to the product's technical feasibility and function?

(26) Does this type of product require special research and production-development know-how? If so, do we have it in out organization? If not, is it readily available on a consulting basis? If not on consulting basis, how difficult and expensive would it be to expand our own company staff?

(27) Are our research, engineering, and manufacturing know-how particularly applicable to this type of product?

(28) Are our present manufacturing facilities particularly suitable?

(29) Is a big plant investment involved, and/or is intricate equipment required to compete? (What leads can be obtained from suppliers of the type of equipment involved?)

(30) Can important components be subcontracted for?

(31) Does this product require extensive tooling investment?

(32) Are there existing "bugs" in the product? Is it possible to estimate the extent of additional development work which would have to be done?

(33) What is the patent situation?

(a) Secure patent numbers on patents issued, if this is a new product brought to the company by the inventor.

(b) Secure photostatic copies, when needed, of patent applications.

(c) Arrange for a preliminary report on above by our patent department.

(d) Does the company now dominant in the field have comprehensive basic patents? If so, are they approachable regarding licensing?

(34) Even if the product is to be manufactured by us, are important component parts to be purchased? If so, are these dominated by a single producer who might create problems later on?

(35) Is the principal material to be used a by-product of some large, unrelated operation (unrelated insofar as markets for the proposed product are concerned)? If so, would a company that is not in the first kind of business stand a chance against such a first

company which, through a subsidiary, may have brought out a product of the type under consideration?

(36) Is the principal raw material subject to violent price fluctuation?

(37) What synthetic materials worth investigating have come to the fore?

(38) Is there a company in the field which may be acquired?

(a) Check to see whether our company was in contact with it previously.

(b) Is there a special line of contact through a present board member, official, or affiliated company?

(c) Roughly what order to magnitude of investment would be involved?

(d) Is this company in sound financial condition now? (Secure credit information—analyze last five year's financial statements).

(e) What is this company's reputation?

(f) What can be said at this time about its physical facilities? Is a detailed engineering survey in order?

(g) Does it have special research or engineering know-how worth acquiring?

(h) Does it have special sales facilities worth acquiring?

PROFITABILITY PROJECTIONS

Numerous formulas and projection techniques have been developed to measure the value of a proposed new product or project in relation to others proposed. In discussing these, Asbury points out that a note of caution must be raised in the application of formulas or equations. A prudent research director or management will not allow judgment and experience to be displaced by a premature economic analysis.

Indexes

An example of an equation quoted by Asbury for determining a project index for product development projects is reported by a chemical research organization:

$$PVI = \frac{CTS \times CCS \times AV \times P \times \text{squatL}}{TPC}$$

where:

PVI = project value index

CTS = chances for technical success,, on an arbitrary rating scale, say 0 to 10

CCS = chances for commercial success, on an arbitrary rating scale, say 0 to 10

AV = annual volume (total sales of product in units)

P = profit, in dollars per unit—simply price minus cost

L = life of product in years

TPC = total project cost,, in dollars.

A simple index formula has been advanced by the Industrial Research Institute. This is an index of net probable monetary return per research dollar. When it is properly developed, the elements of good judgment, experience, and intuition are reflected in the number itself:

$$I = (PN/C)$$

where:

I = Index of relative worth

P = overall probability of commercial attainment of the goal

N = estimated net return for an arbitrary five–year period

C = estimated future research cost.

Point System

A variation of the formula approach is a point system of weighted factors, cited by Blake. In this system, chances of success are rated from 10 (good) to 2 (poor); pay-off in years (total costs divided by annual earnings) is rated from 20 to 2; and cash position in two years is rated from 10 to 2. Cash position is defined as one half the difference between ten years' gross earnings and the total investment in research and plant. In addition, the formula gives one point each to ten miscellaneous factors, such as good raw material position, etc. With this system, two proposed projects can be compared, or one project can be measured in relation to an acceptable minimum score or rating standard.

Graphs

Another system which uses no formulas but does use graphs and charts is described by Brozen. In this method, up-to-date graphs are kept which chart for each of the company's products the percentage of the total market sold by the company. Further graphs are kept which chart the gross margin, in percentage, received on each product. If either of these graphs begins to drop for any single product, work is started to improve the product, reduce its cost, or find a new product which will do the job better or more cheaply.

Product Profiles

A technique involving a series of screening of proposed new products has been developed by the New Products Study Committee of Dewey and Almy Chemical Company.

First appraisal is a preliminary screening as to probable suitability of the product for the company's type of business, and with relation to general policy. If the new product idea passes this preliminary test, the next step is a set of profiles, divided into three categories: *stability, growth,* and *marketability*. These are shown in the first three of the accompanying profiles. For each of the profiles, the new-product idea is rated on the scale as very good, good, fair, poor, or very poor.

The next step is a series of specific profiles but developed in similar vein, concerning the proposed product's suitability for the company's *manufacturing program*, and how it fits into or desirably augments the *research program*.

Finally, the new-product idea is profiled on a series of *position factors*.

If the new-product idea has succeeded in clearing all of these analytical hurdles, more detailed analyses are made. If the new product is to be recommended to top management, the committee accompanies its report with a project evaluation. This is usually based on careful market research and on preliminary technical research, and includes a reasonably thorough estimate of the manufacturing cost and the projected profit-and-loss statement.

Dewey and Almy considers the ultimate measure of attractiveness of a new product to be the return on investment which can be expected from it. To give uniform evaluation to new product ideas, we well as to provide sound, recurrent re-evaluation of existing product lines, the company has established certain principles and definitions.

The definition of "investment" includes working capital and fixed investment.

Working capital consists of accounts receivable and inventories. The company does not deduct accounts payable, because in its business the amount per plant would have to be estimated on an arbitrary basis and because the cash on hand is practically an exact offset. Inventories are evaluated at standard direct cost.

Fixed investment includes land, buildings and equipment (normally before depreciation). Occasionally a project arises contemplating converting existing unused equipment to new products. This calls for including only the current realizable value rather than the new value of the equipment involved. The company considers that it would be a mistake to use the original book value of such equipment blindly, or even its depreciated book value. The true value of the equipment is determined by its alternate usefulness *other than* for the project under consideration. For example, if the equipment is otherwise useful only for junking, under this concept it should be evaluated into the new project at its junk value.

In calculating percentage return on total investment, the operating margin is normally used as the "return." This is the net earnings before deduction for income-tax and interest expenses. However, the return *after* taxes is also estimated. This gives a better measure of the comparative attractiveness of two propositions, one of which can take heavy advantage of accelerated depreciation rates for tax purposes, while the other cannot.

As a third way of appraising an investment project, an estimated *cash flow* is projected—that is, operating margin after taxes, but with the depreciation write-offs added back in—and related to the time required for the original outlay in the project to be returned. This is an aid to long-range financial planning, because it indicates the future availability of cash for dividends, modernization, debt retirement, exploratory research, and reinvestment in other projects both as fixed capital and as new working capital.

In this case, the company includes in the original outlay what it terms the "grubstake." This is one half the cost of product development, start-up expenses, and market development, based on present corporate income tax conditions. (Obviously, this reasoning can be used safely only by a going concern operating at a profit).

Cash Flow

James W. Russell, formerly Manager of Planning, American Machine & Foundry Company, has contributed the following discussion and on the assessment of tangible risks that can be defined and measured in terms of dollars, i.e., engineering cost estimates, production cost estimates, market forecasts of sales volume at various price levels, and organizational costs of getting into business. He points out, however, that the evaluation of a proposed new product necessarily includes the consideration of *intangible risks*, i.e., advantages and disadvantages that cannot be reduced to numerical terms. These include product fit with the present business, possibilities of future growth in lines allied to the proposed product, and probable reactions of competition. Such factors involve guesses, "feel", and judgment, as does an assessment of the general chances of success for the proposed program, although the latter may be expressed as a percentage, as in the first two formulas quoted.

The fact that working capital will be tied up is recognized, however, by levying an artificial working capital charge against the enterprise. This change is deducted from the profit after taxes to give a "criteria" investment, which is used to calculate the discounted rate on the speculative investment.

Engineering development cost estimates, and costs of manufacturing, tooling, start-up, and production are also entered, together with normal product engineering and appropriate general and administration expenses. In this case, the product development and tooling expenses are burdened with a 30% miscellaneous and contingency allowance, arbitrarily spread over the first five years.

The working capital requirements are forecast at 50% of annual gross sales, and the charges on use of working capital are assessed at 5% after taxes.

Thus, the business estimated for the proposed machine amounts to 20 million gross sales over a six-year sales period. Preceding this is a four-year engineering development, testing, and tooling-up period which, together with initial marketing expense, will cost 1 million. Most of this money must be committed before any return can be anticipated.

In order to compare this investment with other investment possibilities, the "criteria" investment is obtained, and the discounted rate of return;n on investment is found to be 31.5%.

The discounted rate of return represents the rate at which compound interest would have to be earned by the outstanding investment in order for the interest plus the principal to provide sufficient funds to pay the cash flow-backs anticipated at the times predicted. This one figure can serve as a realistic measure of the desirability of the venture, and it is an important criterion in evaluating the proposal as a favorable or unfavorable company move.

11

VENTURE MANAGEMENT

THE business of money invested in business ventures that do not have access to conventional sources of capital such as the stock market, banks, or near banks (such as leasing companies or commercial factors) usually fall into three categories:

(1) Start Ups.

(2) Growing young businesses which need additional capital to continue their growth.

(3) Leveraged buy-outs. This is a phenomenon that has been particularly prevalent in recent years, in which a management group is assisted by venture capitalists to acquire a business—usually from a large public company or a private individual.

The chief ingredient in all of these situations is an intrepreneurial team. The entrepreneurs generally prepare a detailed business plan that describes the nature of the business and forecasts the future activity and future incomes. This business plan is used to attract venture capital. Venture capital investors are interested in and will only invest in situations that will ultimately produce sizeable capital gains. Because the investments are made in unproven situations, or with large amounts of debt, venture capital investing is risky and very dependent on the ability of the entrepreneurs to turn their ideas into a successful company.

The investment in the enterprise is made by buying stock (generally from the treasury) or by lending it money, or combinations of both. Debt instruments such as direct notes or convertible debentures are often the mode of investment, but "sweeteners" in the form of warrants or stock are invariably part of such arrangements, so that capital gains can be realized when the investor ultimately "unlocks" his investment. Venture capital investments are often described as "lock-ups" because of the long time between investment and realization.

The extent of the possible capital gains is indicated by the outcome of the investment of AR&D—American Research & Development Corporation—in Digital Equipment Corporation, the company that created the minicomputer. AR&D, which is one of the most successful professional venture capital organizations operating in the United States and (until it was merged with Textron) one of the four listed on the New York Stock Exchange, saw its original $70,000 investment in DEC in 1957 reach a peak value of over $500 million by 1968. In a similar way, F.S. Smithers & Co., Inc. invested in IBM back in 1911. The appreciation of its initial investment in IBM substantially exceeds that of AR&D's in DEC, although over a longer time.

Until a few decades ago, the primary sources of venture capital were wealthy families or partnerships of affluent individuals looking for capital gains. For example, the Rockefeller family has funded several venture capital pools. There is one venture- capital group based on the private fortune of a wealthy European family that has been operating for centuries. Currently, the fifth generation has funds in venture-capital pools operating in several countries outside of the parent country where the fortune was founded. This particular venture capital investment group has the interesting philosophy that it is investing for the benefit of the next generation. To its members, the common problem of venture capital—the long lock-up—obviously presents no problem.

In the past, only a few investment banks and brokerage houses were involved in venture capital. However, the activity of brokerage houses in venture capital has in recent years been simulated by the enormous interest in new issues. At the beginning of the 1960s, and again during the extraordinary bullish period of 1968–69, new issues of untried companies enjoyed unparalleled market acceptance. Realizing that the capital appreciations prior to going public were often the greatest, many brokerage houses became interested in grooming companies and investing in them before they went public. The venture capital route of investing in new or young companies was a logical consequence of this desire to become involved at a much earlier stage of growth. However, this source of venture capital tends to be extremely volatile and follows the same cycles as the new issue over-the-counter market. When this market is "hot." plenty of risk money seems to be available. When the over-the-counter market is in the doldrums, the brokerage world becomes a very poor source of venture capital.

Growing Sophistication

Beginning after World War II, a variety of professional institutions were established specifically to invest in venture capital. These new groups changed the original frontier character of the industry to a sophisticated, institutionalized, professionally-managed network of organizations whose full-time activity is the investigation, analysis, and investment in venture capital situations. This movement began in 1946 when American Research & Development Corporation was founded, with a capital of about $4 million. AR&D was the brain-child of Senator Ralph Flanders when he was still president of the Federal Reserve Bank of Boston. New England was in an economic decline at that time, primarily as a result of the shrinking of the textile industry and the loss of some traditional machine industries directly involved with textiles. Flanders, believing that the region's trouble was not the loss of old industries but the lack of new ones, came to the conclusion that the area's birthrate for new enterprises was too low. He concluded that this low birthrate was due to the lack of capital for new enterprises, in spite of the fact that the region had enormous technical resources in the world-famous educational institutions located in and around Boston. He felt that the large reserves of capital available in Boston, which traditionally were invested in Government bonds and in the securities of blue-chip corporations, had to be tapped, and sums set aside for the support of new enterprises.

One of the landmark policies was the creative and unorthodox decision to establish a policy that AR&D would willingly consider minority positions in the establishments. The policy made it possible for AR&D to make investments in a company at a much later stage of the company's growth without the need for capital reorganizations to the disadvantage of the founders and original investors. The policy also opened to the possibility of joint ventures (while not a regular practice of AR&D). This became a common practice of other organizations, particularly the private venture-capital partnerships. Unless they were prepared to take minority positions, two or more venture capital organizations obviously could not jointly invest in one company. AR&D's first investment was in a company called Tracerlab (now part of LFE). It did not make its famous investment in DEC until 1957, nearly twelve after it was founded.

The U.S. Government entered the picture in 1958 with financial support for organizations giving loans to small businesses through SBIC (Small Business Investment Corporation) operating under the auspices of the Small Business Administration.

Recent Development

During the late 1960s and early 1970s, there was a rapid growth of venture capital companies, paralled by a growth in internal venture departments of large corporations. This growth became particularly rapid after the lowering of capital gains tax rates in 1978.

The largest of the venture-capital organizations at this writing is the Chicago-headquartered Heizer Corporation Launched in December, 1969, with a capitalization of $81 million supplied by 35 institutional backers, it now has approximately $300 million in assets. Running close second is Citicorp's venture capital group with assets of over $200 million.

Formal venture-capital organizations with professional management and significant capital pools are also springing up in Europe. An example is Technical Development Capital Ltd. which has branch offices in many of the major cities of England and regularly advertises its desire to invest in companies with a technological base. In France, there is European Enterprises Development, which is partnerned after AR&D. Scienta, which is headquartered in Brussels, in a consortium of several European industrial companies. As with the two previous groups. Scienta is primarily interested in investments in technical companies.

A noteworthy development is the establishment of internal and external venture capital operations by many of the largest corporations in the United States, with a sprinkling of the same activity by some Canadian and U.K. companies. These corporate venture activities take two very distinct and separate forms. One is the independent operation which is strategically (and sometimes geographically) independent of the parent. The second is the venture operation within the framework of the parent corporation, in effect operating as a captive activity. In both instance the objective is to promote the diversified growth of the parent.

The corporate venture capital activities usually operate relatively independently of their corporate sponsors. Generally, they have their own charter, their own company-supplied pool of investment capital, and their own personnel—a small group of "bright young people" presenting an independent cluster of marketing, technical, and financial skills. The use of a supracorporate team for corporate venturing has the prime virtue of liberating the venture team from the limits of the sponsoring corporation's capabilities. This frees the venture group from having to operate within the constraints of the corporate resources of technology, market research, personnel, plant facilities, and probably most important of all, the self image of the company. A maker of synthetic fibres, for example, generally does not present a good environment to develop an activity in disposable paper garments.

Two other interesting variations of venturing can occur within the corporate framework. First is the intra-corporate team or department. This venture group functions largely as an internal operating unit. This approach is often termed Venture Management. The second is the intercorporate team or joint-venture where a company double-teams with another corporation to explore and perhaps enter a new era. The Bunker-Ramo Corporation is an out- growth of this type of approach.

Limited Partnerships

A quite recent significant development has been a large growth in limited partnerships for venture capital.

Through the centuries, investment groups have been formed to invest in specific ventures. This indeed was how West Indies Tea Company, which had so important an effect on the development of the American Colonies, was started—as was the Hudson's Bay

Company, which led to the development of Canada. However, these investment groups were *ad hoc* in nature; that is they were brought together for the one investment, and there was no continuity in their investment actions.

A later development was the creation of pools of capital for investment in a *series* of risk situations. These venture-capital groups were generally formed as limited partnership. The limited partners would be wealthy individuals interested in providing corporate venture situations. Management of the pool would rest in the hands of one or two general partners who were responsible for making investment decisions and monitoring the investments. The limited partners would be passive investors.

This method of investment has been refined and there are several very well known partnerships operating in the United States now. Customarily the general partners form a separate management organization which receives a management fee commonly reckoned as a percentage of the assets. Additionally, as an incentive they receive a portion of the capital gains. In some partnerships the annual management fee is equal to 3 ½% of the invested assets at the commencement of the partnership. All of the limited partnerships generally have a specific life period, often seven or ten years. At the end of this time, the limited partnership is dissolved and the assets—cash and stock—are distributed to all partners.

Probably the most famous such partnership was the Davis & Rock partnership which was founded in 1962 and was terminated in 1969. The original investment was $3.4 million and at the conclusion of the partnership's life, $76 million was distributed. The most successful investment of the partnership was in Scientific Data Systems, which was its first investment. Davis & Rock saw SDS grow until it was acquired by Xerox for $940 million of Xerox stock.

Small Business Investment Companies (SBICs)

These are companies qualified to borrow money with the guarantee of the small Business Administration (SBA) of the U.S. Government with the mandate to invest their funds in operations defined as small businesses. The fundamental purpose of the Government supported SBIC program was to create a system that would provide risk capital to smaller companies. Although the investments in their companies was generally in the form of a loan, the risk attached to the loan exposed it to virtually the same jeopardy as equity in the common stock of the company.

The basic concept of the SBIC legislation was that private capital could be induced to invest in small companies with Government backing leading to high leverage. In effect, the Government realized that sman companies needed venture capital, which would not be forthcoming without special incentives, Spurred by studies that showed that the equity financing gap for small companies might be as high as $500 million per year, Congress passed the Small Business Investment Act in August 1958, twenty-five years after the initial effort for such legislation. Probably the unique aspect of this remarkable legislation was that it did not propose direct Government subsidization or a Government administered capital bank. Instead, it proposed the creation of a series of completely new sources of capital to be called SBICs.

The newly organized industry suffered through the usual early growing pains encountered by any new type of financial industry. From their inception, the number of active SBICs rose to a peak of 649 in 1964, then sank to 248 in 1973 before rising to 350 at the end of 1980. More significantly, the private capital and total assets of the industry rose to record levels of $625 million and $1.375 billion, respectively. Total financing disbursements also attained a new high of $295 million. Now coming into maturity, SBICs have proven to be of great assistance to smaller businesses in the United States, investing over $3 billion in 43,000 small business in the 21 years of their existence. There are also numerous MESBICs (Minority Enterprise SBICs) which specialize in financing minority businesses owned and run by minority groups.

Preparation of a Business Plan

The most important preliminary step in organizing a new venture is the preparation of a business plan. This should describe the market for the proposed product or service, the capabilities of the team constituting the original entrepreneurs, the production, marketing, and financial program of a new company, and finally what type of deal the entrepreneurs are seeking. One of the best guides for the preparation of a business plan for a new business was prepared by Kley is given below:

Guide for the Preparatiion of a Business Plan

1. Provide a one-page summary of the venture idea.
2. Describe the key goals and objectives. Specify what you are setting out to achieve, particularly your sales and profitability goals.
3. Provide an in-depth market analysis. If you can support your own probe with some solid numbers from a recognized research institution such as Stanford Research Institute or Arthur D. Little, Inc., so much the better.
4. List the names of close competitor firms, and briefly analyze their strengths and weaknesses.
5. List the anticipated selling, lease, and maintenance price to your ultimate consumer for each product in the projected line. Include also a brief summary of comparison prices.
6. Provide a list of potential customers, particularly indicating those who have expressed an interest in your projected products.
7. Provide a one-page summary of the functional specifications of each product in your overall spectrum. Cover the total line, but don't get down to individual models.
8. Show the physical forms of the products, with photographs of prototypes if possible, or art renderings.
9. Provide a profile of key patents (where and when and what device is being covered).
10. List and categorize the key technologies and skills required to develop and manufacture the products. Indicate which fronts of the art are being pushed hardest.
11. Describe the alternative channels of sales distribution; indicate whether you intend to sell direct, through manufacturers' representatives, or to original-equipment manufacturers.
12. Describe the basis for determining if your products will be typically "lease" or "buy" items. This will depend upon the propensities of your potential customers, who must be sorted out.
13. Describe the type and geographical distribution of your anticipated field service organization.

14. Tell how you can modularize your product line with changeable subassemblies. This is critical from an inventory point of view, and can mean tremendous cost savings.
15. Show cost-volume curves for each module, with breakdown for material, labour and factory burden.
16. Describe the manufacturing process involved, and illustrate it with block diagram.
17. Describe the types and quantities of capital equipment needed and when.
18. Present a flow-event-logic feedback chart, illustrating achievement milestones and showing stepped levels of when and how additional funds should go into the venture.
19. Project staff and plant space requirements over a five-year period.
20. Describe the rational for choosing any single manufacturing plant location.
21. Present cash flow projections, monthly for the first twelve months, and then quarterly for the next three years.
22. Provide pro-forma balance sheets for five years.
23. Provide pro-forma P&Ls for five years.
24. Present your position on the degree of ownership control you and the other founders seek, and the limits to which these can be varied with time and profitability.

To raise expansion capital for an existing business, or purchase capital for a leveraged buyout, the information can be simpler, but should definitely include:

(1) A one- or two-page summary.

(2) Background of the key people involved in the venture.

(3) History of the company.

(4) Description of the product or products.

(5) Description of the market and the competitors.

(6) Historical financial information.

(7) Pro forma P&L and Balance Sheet information for three to five years.

(8) Amount of financing needed and how it will be used.

VENTURE MANAGEMENT AS CORPORATE STRATEGY

Venture Management is a corporate strategy for building new businesses. It places primary emphasis on the use of internal resources as the means to grow, rather than on mergers and acquisitions. While it is currently being used only by a small number of large U.S. industrial companies its applications may increase in the future as the natural advantage of venture management become more important to the success of large organizations.

Venture management is different from venture capital investments in that the initiating company usually has 100% ownership of the venture and supplies significant management and technical assistance. It is also different from new-product development because it is concerned with the building new businesses rather than the extension or modification of existing product lines.

Being venturesome is not new to American business. What is relatively new is that this venturesomeness is being channeled and directed by these organizations in formal organization structures. (A 1970 survey of venture management functions in 36 corporations revealed that twenty-six of these had organized their functions within the prior two years.) Venture departments are established, usually at the corporate level, as separate organizational units. The central concept of venture management is that responsibility for initiating new business is separated from responsibility for operating existing businesses.

Why Venture Management?

Common reasons cited for venture management are:

1. *To help reach long-term growth objectives.* If growth projections from existing operations do not meet company growth objectives, a planning gap exists. Companies turn to venture management to help fill this gap.

2. *As a major alternative to acquisitions.* The diversification movement continues strong in American industry. In past years the major vehicle for diversification has been mergers or acquisitions. However, a number of changes in the accounting, tax, financial, and anti-trust aspects of acquisitions have made this route more expensive and less certain.

3. *To aid diversification in new areas.* Some companies use venture management to enter attractive new business areas where there

may not be any good acquisition candidates, or, if there are, they may be too expensive. A related objective is helping the large company respond to segmented, small, or temporary markets that may be highly profitable but not worth the disruption of its existing operations.

4. *To improve the effectiveness of a company's research and development expenditures.* It is well known that a number of companies are disenchanted with the output of their laboratories in relation to the fund being expended. Several companies are using venture management to increase this output by commercializing new research discoveries that do not quite fit into existing markets and hence might not be fully exploited.

5. *To overcome organizational constraints to entering new business areas.* Most large organizations are set up on a divisionalized, decentralized basis. This model is effective for managing existing operations, but it does not facilitate the development of new business areas. That is why responsibility for new ventures is most often lodged at the corporate level under the chief executive officer, even though successful new ventures may be transferred to divisional responsibility at a later point. Overall, venture management represents a split in the organization. One part runs today's businesses; the other builds new businesses for the divisions of the future. This can cause resentment and conflict between divisional executives (who are responsible for producing current income) and the venture function, which is viewed as a risky and expensive proposition, at least in the early years.

6. *To provide entrepreneurial opportunity to employees within the large-firm setting.* Many talented younger managers are somewhat disenchanted with large organizations and would prefer to work in smaller organizations where their efforts are more visible and have more impact and where they have more independence. One of the reasons cited for venture management is to overcome this advantage of small companies in the attraction and retention of talented employees.

There are situations where venture management may not be appropriate. These include companies whose long term growth objectives can be fully met by expansion of existing divisions, who do not have adequate capital or management resources to invest in new business, and whose management climate is not conducive to the innovativeness required to succeed in venture management.

How Venture Functions Can Be Organized

There are three different ways of organizing for venture management: (1) Task force or project management approach, (2) venture management division or department, and (3) venture management company.

The *task force approach* is the most informal of all the methods employed. There is no staff assigned full-time to investigate and develop new ventures. One person in the organization, perhaps the head of corporate planning, is responsible for establishing and managing task-force investigations into new venture areas. Employees assigned to task force usually have other responsibilities in the organization and are only on loan to the venture function. The task force leader should be an individual highly interested and knowledgeable in the product concept of the potential venture. The members of his team should be carefully chosen for the skills they bring to the project. Some may work on the project full time; others on an as- needed basis. Members of the task force could change as the skill needs of the project change. Under the task-force approach, projects are handled as they come along rather than on a planned basis. A fixed budget for task-force investigations may not exist.

The *venture management division or department* is a more formal structure. There are usually more individuals involved on a full-time basis than in the task-force concept. There also tends to be an established budget and criteria for evaluating new ventures. The department itself might be composed of a number of venture analysts. Their job is to investigate new venture ideas generated internally or brought to the corporation's attention. As ideas are translated into new ventures, the venture managers would also be assigned to the department, usually until the venture reaches or passes its commercialization stage. As such, a venture management department tends to have both line and staff attributes: staff in that it investigates new business opportunities for corporate decisions, and line in that it manages new ventures until they are ready to take their place in the existing organization structure.

The *venture management company* is the most formally structured of the three approaches. It is a separate legal entity, wholly owned by the parent organization. Its major responsibility is to investigate, build, and manage new business ventures for the parent.

Each of the three types of venture organizations can be effective for a particular company. The chosen structure needs to reflect a particular company's objectives, current situation, and commitments to new ventures. Those organizations using the task-force approach to venture management tend to be process- manufacturing oriented, functionally organized and fairly centralized in their decision-making processes, in terested in new business ventures that are closely allied to their existing businesses and which tend to be offshoots of their R&D efforts, and only interested in exploring a small number of potentially large ventures, after which the function could be disbanded.

Organizations using the venture management department or company approach tend to be highly decentralized, already engaged in a wide variety of new business areas, interested in exploring a still broader spectrum of new businesses, many of which could be fairly limited in potential size, concerned with the need to maintain a separate environment conducive to new ventures, and fairly certain that the need for venture management will be long.

How the Venture Process Works?

Building a new venture can be visualized as a six-step process: (1) idea search, (2) idea screening, (3) idea investigation, (4) venture development, (5) venture commercialization, and (6) venture disposition.

The venture process begins with the *idea search.* One individual in the organization may be designated as the person to whom all new business ideas are sent. He gathers new ideas from a variety of sources, both internal and external.

The second stem is *idea screening.* Broad criteria are used to avoid rejecting a venture which does not look promising at first but which may, in the long run, have great potential. A sample of the criteria used at this stage is: (1) compatibility with existing technology and resource strength; (2) market needs; (3) uniqueness of product and patentability; and (4) economic considerations (investment required, sales and earnings potential). New venture ideas that pass screening may be ranked in terms of priority and placed in a "pool" from which they are drawn for further analysis and investigation as time and funds permit.

The *idea investigation* stage involves the gathering and analyzing of information necessary to determine whether the organization should enter a particular business area. Many companies have developed specific criteria (strategic, financial, marketing, and technological) against which all new ventures are measured. The existence of such criteria helps guide the venture staff in their collection and evaluation of potential ventures. Some examples of criteria employed at this stage are: "compatibility with long-range plan:" "capital intensive:" "20% return on investment;" "fifth year sales volume: $50 million;" "fifth-year profit contribution: $5 million;" "market growth rate: 20% annually;" "minimum share of market: 30%;" "proprietary product."

In most companies, the return-on-investment (ROI) criterion for new ventures is higher than returns from existing operations. This compensates for the risk involved in a new venture. Some companies have developed quite elaborate computer models to help in evaluating potential ventures. In some cases, the ROI requirement may vary in proportion to the risk involved.

The end result of the investigation stage is a report to senior management recommending that the idea should proceed into development as a venture, or be dropped, shelved, sold, or licensed. A venture development plan, evaluating the potential venture in terms of all the pre-established criteria, may be presented. The decision for entering a new business area is usually made by the chief executive officer, by a committee of senior executives, or by the board of directors if major funding or a reorientation of business activity is required. The decision at this stage is not a final one—it merely authorizes development of the venture.

In *venture development* a venture team is formed with a venture manager in charge. The team may be the group that originally investigated the idea. Likewise, the venture manager may be the person who headed the investigation. It is important that the venture manager be carefully selected for his skills, experience, and interest in the venture.

All necessary steps are now taken to build the venture: product refinement and testing, prototypes, consumer and market research, pilot plant, test marketing, pricing, advertising campaign, production, distribution, and sales facilities. The development process is guided by the venture plan, which is modified as additional factors become known. The process of venture development is reported to the chief executive periodically. Funding may be on a short-term basis, with additional funding dependent on progress. The development stage may take a long time and be quite expensive, especially if a new area of technology is involved.

In the fifth step, *venture commercialization*, the success of the venture should be apparent rather quickly. The business is usually run by the same venture team that brought the venture through the development phase, and it continues to report to the head of the venture function.

The final step in the venture process is *disposition of the venture*. Successful ventures may either join an existing division become a new, independent division, join a special division composed of other successful ventures, or be sold to another company or to the public. New ventures that fail may either be dropped or sold, the technology could be licensed, or the company could seek a partner for a joint venture in a further effort to gain success.

The venture process is far easier to explain than to carry out. In most cases the time and funds required are great, and the outcome is risky because by definition the company is entering an area with which it is somewhat unfamiliar. If a company does not recognize and accept this in advance, it should steer clear of the concept.

The Venture Manager

The venture manager performs the classic entrepreneurial function of combining idea, resources, and people to form new enterprises, but he does so within the large-company setting. However, the typical individual described in the literature as a classical entrepreneur probably will not be an effective venture manger: he would be stifled by the somewhat restrictive atmosphere of the large firm. What is needed is a person who has both the skill and drive necessary to build a business on his own, and the ability to put up with the requirements placed on him by the parent company.

The process by which companies select their venture managers is not scientific, nor is it ever likely to be. There are no systematic testing and selection mechanisms for venture managers. Such mechanisms would undoubtedly be helpful even though the criteria for selecting venture managers are likely to vary from company to company in response to different organizational structures, operating environments, and objectives.

Deciding how to pay venture managers is a problem for any company. The key question is, Should the compensation arrangements for the venture manager differ from the arrangements for other managers in the company? Some companies say "no,"citing the disruption it would cause in the management ranks. They also feel the recognition and speed of advancement that can come from building a successful new venture are sufficient motivation. Other companies say "yes," special compensation is appropriate and supportable by the economics of the situation, but have not instituted such programs, again for fear of disrupting the other managers. Others say special compensation arrangements are vital to the success of the venture process and have instituted them.

Requirements for Success in Venture Management

Companies that are successful in venture management seem to exhibit to following attributes:

1. *Top management support*. Such support on a continuing basis is essential because of the long time and high risk involved in building new business.

2. *Clear relation to planning*. Tie-in between corporate planning and venture selection helps insure that the venture function fulfills corporate ends.

3. *Clear organization lines*. Clear definition of responsibilities and authority helps overcome the conflicts likely to be generated by an active venture function.

4. *Strong management control*. Such control helps insure objectivity and minimize losses.

5. *Proper climate*. A free environment (within mandated controls) conducive to new ventures is essential. The separate department and company venture approaches help create and maintain this environment.

6. *Capable people.* The head of the venture function and the venture mangers are keys to the success of the venture function.

7. *Good estimates.* While ventures always seem to take longer and cost more than originally estimated, every attempt should be made to secure estimates that are as close to the work as possible.

8. *Adequate funding.* Sufficient capital over the venture development period helps insure continuity of the venture. Several companies have run into problems here and have had to curtail otherwise successful ventures. A few companies have established separate capitalization for their ventures. These funds can be committed at the discretion of the head of the venture function within specified limits.

The success requirements for new ventures are not unique to venture management—they are required in operating any business. However, costs of mistakes in venture management are large. But then so is the payoff from successful new ventures.

Unless a company has a highly innovative environment and a flexible structure, a separate organization for new ventures would seem to be called for. This permits the major portion of the organization to concentrate on managing and improving today's businesses, while in another part of the company, a separate unit is evaluating and building new businesses that may be the operations of tomorrow. The two functions are joined together and coordinated at the top through corporate planning, other staff functions and top executive control.

Venture management activity to date has been concentrated in large industrial companies. Other types of organizations as well could benefit from applying the concept. These include banks, railroads, insurance companies, utilities, foundations, schools, medical institutions, and government units. In fact, any type of organization that wants or needs to undertake new activities—activities that are not direct extensions of current operations—might find venture management applicable as a means of accomplishing this objective.

MERGERS AND ACQUISITIONS

The terms Merger, Acquisition, Consolidation and Amalgamation are commonly used interchangeably. They all describe the event of two or more companies combining into one economic entity. In the technical jargon of finance, however, a *merger* is the absorption of one or more corporations by another with the acquiring firm retaining its corporate identify and the other firms disappearing from the corporate community. A *consolidation* occurs when all the combining firms disappear as distinct and separate corporate entities and a new consolidated corporate entity is created. Mergers also include the acquisition of the working control of an acquired firm that may leave the legal corporate entities undisturbed. The financial press tends to use the term merger for all types of combinations and we adopt that convention for the purpose of this article.

Types of Mergers

Business mergers are generally classified by the market relationship that exists between the merging parties. Mergers can be classified as *congeneric* or *conglomerate*. A congeneric merger occur when firms combine in the same or related industries, while conglomerate mergers occur when firms in different or unrelated industries combine. *Horizontal* mergers and *vertical* mergers are both of the congeneric variety. A horizontal merger unites two or more firms engaged in the production or sale of the same or similar products. Horizontal mergers, in particular, are generally considered as eliminating competition and increasing the concentration of economic powers in surviving firms.

A *vertical merger* unites one or more firms engaged in the production of a given product at different levels or stages of the productive process. Frequently the merging parties have a buyer/seller relationship with one being a customer of the other. Vertical mergers are also classified as:

(1) Backward—merging toward earlier stages of production (i.e., toward raw material source).

(2) Forward—merging toward later stages of production (i.e., toward consumers of the final product).

Mergers that are not congeneric are conglomerate. Conglomerate mergers may involve the addition of new products, entry into a new industry, or the combination of different production technology, or marketing channels.

A *concentric merger* occurs when merging firms are in different product areas but are related in raw materials, production technology, or marketing channels. Concentric mergers are classified as a subset of conglomerate mergers.

Historically, mergers have played a central role in determining the level of concentration and the amount of competition in many U.S. industries. Merger activity has also been instrumental in determining the relative size and diversification of many large U.S. corporations and has left an indelible mark on the structure of the U.S. economy.

Historical data on merger activity are incomplete, but sufficient information is available to provide valuable insights concerning merger movements. Corporate mergers and acquisitions in the United States have occurred in three major "merger movements." The first merger movement occurred at the turn of the century, beginning with a trough in 1897, reaching a peak in 1899, and bottoming out with the stock market slump in 1904. The second merger movement occurred in the late 1920s, and extended from a trough in 1922 to a peak in 1929 and receded quickly after the stock market crash in 1929 to a trough in 1933. (A "mini- merger" was occurred in the 1940s, peaking out in 1945.)

The third major merger movement began in the 1950s, continued through the 1960s, peaked in 1968–69, and receded to a trough in 1972. This movement is commonly called in merger wave of the 1960s. After the peak in 1968–69, merger activity fell to levels that existed in the first half of the 1960s. Substantial merger activity continued into the 1970s with the years 1976 and 1977 characterized as a "merger binge" of companies of large size. A decision concerning the place of the merger activities of the late 1970s and early 1980s will have to wait an historical perspective.

The first merger movement was preceded by the so-called "trust movement" of the 1890s. The major trust activity began with the organization of the Standard Oil Trust in 1879. The following decade ushered in substantial trust activity in many industries, including cotton-seed oil, lead, and sugar. But merger and trust activity, although important prior to 1890, was almost insignificant when compared to the enormous activity in the 1890s. The turn-of-the-century merger movement was of relatively short duration, but the magnitude and the quickness of the movement had a profound and lasting effect on the structure of industry in our economy.

The magnitude of merger activity is exemplified by the 1895–1904 period, when 170 firms disappeared into the U.S. Steel Corporation, and 162 firms were absorbed by the American Tobacco Company, while 65 and 64 firms disappeared respectively into E.I. duPont de Nemours and the American Can Company. In the year 1899, at the peak of the merger movement, 1.028 firms disappeared from the corporate community. By 1903 it was estimated that there were 318 important industrial consolidations in the U.S., and that of this total, 236 or over 70% had occurred in the preceding five years. The economic impact is revealed by the fact that these large consolidations controlled about 40% of the total manufacturing capital in the U.S. economy at that time.

Horizonal mergers dominated the activity at the turn of the century. As a result, the first merger movement greatly increased the proportionate size and control of a few firms over production and marketing in many of the major industries in the U.S. This activity resulted in high levels of economic concentration in such industries as steel, tin cans, farm machinery, tobacco, copper, chemicals, and typewriters.

Primary factors contributing to the increase in merger activity at the beginning of this century were changes in state incorporation laws and the formation of larger and more efficient capital markets. Until the early 19th century, corporation laws usually did not permit mergers and did not allow corporations to hold stock in other corporations. New Jersey, starting in 1889, removed many of the typical restrictions on corporate acquisitions and consequently became the leading state of incorporations for merger activity. New Jersey corporations alone accounted for over 50% of mergers by dollar value in the period 1889–1920.

It is argued that good capital market encouraged merger activity and were a necessary ingredient for the merger activity of this period. It is also argued that merger activity and subsequent security flotations provided the basis for the development of a healthy securities market. As with many economic phenomena, the growth of both variables occurred jointly and their respective growth was in part dependent upon the others existence and condition.

Of significance at the turn of the century was the role of the professional promoter in merger activity. In many cases the compensation of the professional promoter was very large (i.e., up to 20% of the capitalized value of the merging firms), and evidence seems to indicate that it was the existence of promotional profits rather than operational efficiencies that motivated many mergers in this period.

In general the merger movement of the 1890s co-existed with and was an integral part of the times. Expansion of industrial activity and technological advances permitted large-scale production and resultant economies. The growth of the railroad system and the settling of the west expanded the markets for many products. The development of the New York Stock Exchange coupled with a bullish stock market and a rising economy provided the financial incentive and opportunity for new stock issues to finance mergers. These factors also provided the opportunity and the environment for large promotional profit and the feverish promotional activity of the period. While mergers increased at a feverish pace in the 1890s, the demise of the merger movement was equally rapid. In 1901 prices on the stock market started to fall. A great many mergers were not financial successes, and the disillusioned investor was not as easily enticed by the professional promoter. These factors ultimately ended the first merger movement, aiding and aided by the economic downturn of 1903.

The second major merger movement began in 1923, reached a peak in 1929, and declined rapidly after the stock-market crash, to be finally choked off by the Great Depression. The merger wave in the "roaring 20s" resembled that of the turn of the century in many respects. It was coincident with a bouyant stock market and an increase in economic activity and general prosperity. As with the earlier merger movement, the merger wave of the 1920s was largely horizontal in nature; but the movement also included an increase in vertical integrations and in concentric types of mergers.

As with the earlier period, merger activity in the 1920s played an important role in creating and preserving the oligopolistic structure that prevailed in many industries, and in increasing the degree of concentration in our economy. Between 1925 and 1930, the largest 100 manufacturing corporations increased their share of corporate manufacturing assets from 26.1% to 43.3%. Merger activity accounted for nearly all of this increase. The second merger movement resulted in larger concentrations in major industries, including food manufacturing, public utilities, oil, commercial banking, motion pictures, hotels, and retail stores. The importance of the chain store movement should be singled out. The development of the chain store resulted in a change in retailing from small individually owned stores to the retail chain store that sold approximately one-fourth of all food, drugs, tobacco, apparel, and general merchandise by the end of the 1920s.

One important aspect of both the turn of the century and the 1920s movements was the important role of the professional promoters. Since merger activity generated a profitable activity for both investment bankers and brokers, some investment bankers employed commission men who did little else but search for potential merger candidates. Of course, the merger activity and promotional profits were again coincident with a strong and rising stock-market and a feeling of economic prosperity.

Mergers did provide economies for firms in many industries. Merchandising economies could be achieved through the chain store development, and economies of scale could be achieved through large scale production. Both real economies of scale and the opportunity for financial profits provided a stimulus for mergers in the 1920s.

Innovations in organizational techniques went hand in hand with merger activity in this period. Decentralized management and multidivisional organizational techniques provided managerial effciencies that were used extensively by such firms as General Motors, Du-Pont, and Standard Oil. Other factors commonly cited as fostering and enabling the merger movement in the 1920s were the improvements in transportation and in communications (especially the growth of radio). The growth of a good transportation system and the advent of radio greatly enlarged marketing areas and provided the basis for large-scale distribution and production, and consequently the potential for economics of scale.

The merger wave of the 1960s was unprecedented in magnitude, in United States history, regardless of the measure used. It contributed to even further increase the concentration of control over economic activity in a relatively small number of corporations. This merger movement started in the early 1950s and grew steadily throughout in 1950s and 1960s to reach dizzy heights in

1967, 1968, and 1969. In 1968 alone approximately $15 billion of assets were acquired by firms in manufacturing and mining. In that single year nearly 10% of all independent manufacturing corporations of over $10 million in assets were acquired by other firms. After 1969, if activity is measured by the value of assets acquired, merger activity declined by one half in 1970 and continued to decline through 1972, to turn around, and return to the 1970 level by 1976. Available data indicate that the turnaround has continued through 1979. The most recent wave of mergers followed the trough of 1972 and has grown in size yearly through 1979.

The major distinguishing factor of the wave of the 1970s is the size of the acquired company. In the 1970s well over 100 companies of over 100 million in asset size were acquired. Also, this period evidenced an unprecedented number of billion-dollar acquisitions. Toward the end of the decade of the 1970s, the 100 largest firms controlled about the same proportion of the nation's assets as the top 200 did in the 1940s. Additionally, the largest 200 manufacturing firms at this writing control over two thirds of corporate manufacturing assets, a greater amount of assets than did the largest 1,000 manufacturing corporations in 1941.

Although there has been some congeneric merger activity in the recent merger movement the great bulk of merger activity through the 1960s and 1970s has been of the conglomerate variety. Congress has been investigating the possible adverse effects and suggested remedies of the recent conglomerate merger movement and various government agencies responded by increasing their supervisory activities. In 1978, for example, the Federal Trade Commission established new rules under the Hart-Scott-Rodino Anti Trust Improvement Act of 1976 requiring increased disclosure for acquisitions of large size. It is clear that the effects and the possible impact and reaction to the merger activity in the last two decades will be felt for years to come and will probably result in further anti-merger legislation.

Reasons for Mergers and Acquisitions

The primary justification for a merger or acquisition is the "synergistic effect" of combining two or more firms. The combination is assumed to provide some real economies, a reduction in risk or both. Since any increase in earnings or reduction in risk has the effect of increasing the value of a going concern the value of the firms combined is presumably greater than the sum of their values separately. The synergistic effect will occur when a merger produces economies in production costs or the elimination of duplicate facilities. It may also occur as a result of reductions in marketing costs. A reduction in marketing costs may result from either an expansion of product lines, or the easing of competitive pressures. Reduction of risk in the combined firm by virtue of diversification may also occur through merger. However, this reduction in risk may not result in a benefit to the stockholders. Stockholders can achieve comparable diversification through portfolio selection and therefore should not realize a gain from mergers specifically done for risk reduction. Finally, there may be economies in either the management or the financing of the firm.

The logic of economies of scale is persuasive: however many recent studies designed to measure or identify the existence of such economics have failed to find statistically significant evidence of these benefits or have concluded with conflicting results.

Since expectations are not always realized empirical data are an imperfect measures of motivations. Interviews in depth with officers of firms which have been involved in mergers or acquisitions also provide an indication of merger objectives. Specific motives indicated by acquiring corporations include the following:

(1) To obtain diversification.

(2) To offset product obsolescence.

(3) To acquire new customers or expand the market area.

(4) To offset an actual or threatened loss of market.

(5) To obtain a greater rate of growth.

(6) To add glamour to the company.

(7) To improve cyclical and seasonal stability.

(8) To exploit a product, a productive process, or a basic raw material.

(9) To improve the effectiveness of the marketing effort.

(10) To obtain cost reductions through elimination of duplicate facilities.

(11) To support increased product development work.

(12) To improve credit position.

(13) To secure or use a tax loss.

(14) To acquire management with specific technical competence.

(15) To enhance power and prestige of owner or management.

(16) To substitute efficient management for inefficient management.

Motives for Selling. Quite often, the small corporation with one or a few products comes to realize that its size is a handicap in a national market. The owners are then apt to decide that joining forces with a larger corporation would yield a better return on their accumulated capital than the yields they would receive through expansion with funds generated internally. Also, many small firms cannot generate sufficient internal funds or raise funds as rapidly as needed to finance their desired growth. Small firms lacking sufficient stature to raise funds advantageously in the capital markets often find that their principal alternative is to merge.

Reasons for selling are frequently personal as well as economic. Personal reasons are generally most important in small, closely-held firms and include the following:

(1) Retirement. Owner-manager wants to retire and does not have capable managerial talent available internally.

(2) Stock not listed on an exchange. Merger with firm listed on organized exchange would give seller a marketable security with greater liquidity and capital gains treatment on the subsequent sale of the country.

(3) Estate taxes. The reason most cited for sale or mergers of closely held firms is the anticipation of estate taxes. The problem of liquidity to pay estate taxes and the problem of valuation of the ownership interest are eased when the estate is in marketable securities.

Economic reasons cited for the sale or merger include the following:

(1) Financial problems.

(2) Inadequate distribution and incomplete product lines.

(3) Rapid change in technological product design and manufacturing processes.

(4) Lack of qualified managerial talent. The firm may be too small to afford a well staffed management group, but too large to be run efficiently by one or two men.

(5) Attractive offers. The price the acquiring firm is willing to pay may be too attractive to turn down.

Methods of Acquisition

Many of the fifty states have statues spelling out procedures for merging two or more firms. These normally call for an exchange of common stock. Whenever a merger is executed in conformity with the statutes of the states in which the acquirer is incorporated, it is called a *statutory merger*.

The method of compensating the firms being acquired may involve cash, securities, or a combination of cash and securities. The securities offered may be common stock, preferred stock, or bonds. Convertible preferred stock and convertible debentures were particularly popular means of payment during the last half of the 1960s. While cash seems to have been the popular alternative in the 1970s.

Acquisition by Purchase of Capital Stock. The acquiring company may purchase all, or a majority, of the outstanding common stock from the owners of the company to be acquired. This may occur with the support of the management of the companies being acquired, or despite their opposition. Once the purchase of stocks has been accomplished, the company of the selling stockholders becomes a wholly or partially owned subsidiary of the acquiring firm.

Acquisition by Purchase of Assets. The acquiring company may purchase the tangible and intangible assets of a firm and make payment in either cash or securities. Frequently, all the liabilities of the selling company are assumed by the purchaser as a condition of sale. However, this is not mandatory. It is possible to purchase only a portion of the assets and to assume responsibility for only selected liabilities.

After the sale, the selling company may distribute proceeds of the sale to its shareholders and terminate its corporate charter. On the other hand, if the company continues as a legal entity it may invest the proceeds from the sale of its assets in a portfolio of marketable securities and become, in effect, an investment trust company. It may also use the proceeds to acquire new assets as an operating company in some new area of economic activity.

When the property and assets of a corporation are sold, formal approval of the sale by the stockholders of the selling corporation is required. Typically, holders of two-thirds of the shares entitled to vote must vote in favor of the sale. The percentage required for approval is set in the company's charter and/or in its bylaws. Dissenting shareholders generally have the right to receive a cash payment equal to an appraised value of their shares, but it is unlikely that the appraisal value of dissenting shares will exceed the pro rata distribution of the proceeds of sale if the transaction is arranged in good faith. Therefore, the right of appraisal becomes the right to receive cash in lieu of securities if the terms of acquisition provide for payment in securities.

Purchase of Control The purchase of less than 100% of the outstanding common stock may occur as a matter of policy or strategy if the acquiring company is simply seeking corporate control. Such a transaction can have serious legal implications and should be approached cautiously by both buyers and sellers.

If a buyer limits his purchase of shares to the amount necessary to achieve control, and pays a premium for the control shares, the sellers can be held liable by the minority stockholders for the premiums they received. It is rather clearly indicated that control shares should not be acquired unless the buyer is willing and able to offer the same price and terms to the minority shareholders. Holders of control shares carry the responsibility of ascertaining the good faith of the buyer in order to avoid sale to a buyer who would proceed to loot the corporation, an act for which the sellers of control shares can be held liable.

Unfriendly and Friendly Mergers

When a merger is opposed by the management of the firm to be acquired, it is called an unfriendly merger while friendly mergers have the support of the management. In an unfriendly merger the potential acquirer may attempt to accomplish the merger by initiating a "proxy fight" or making a "take-over bid." In a *proxy fight*, the stockholders of the firm to be acquired retain their shares, but are asked to vote in favour of a slate of candidates that will favor the merger of the firms. If the insurgents win the proxy fight, the new Board of Directors can be expected to replace the management team that was opposed to the merger and the new management will work out the terms of the combination.

In the 1960s and the 1970s *take-over bids* replaced proxy fights as the dominant method of achieving mergers when there was management opposition to a combination. A take-over bid represents a direct offer by the acquiring firm to purchase all, or a majority, of the outstanding stock from the stockholders of the target company. If the offer to buy the stock is made for cash, the take-over bid is called a *tender offer*. If the offer to buy is made in terms of securities that will be exchanged for the shares of the target company, the take-over bid is called a *registered exchange offer*.

Requests to "tender for cash" are regulated by the Williams Bill which added Section 14(d) in 1968 to the Securities and Exchange Act of 1934. The Williams Bill makes it unlawful for a corporation to make a tender offer for any class of equity involving more than 5% of that security unless the offering firm has field a statement with the Securities and Exchange Commission. This statement must include an identification of any position that the potential acquirer already has established in holding stocks of the target firm, disclosure of the source and amount of funds that will be used to acquire the shares tendered, and a statement of the purpose, or purposes, behind the tender offer. If the tender offer will result in transferring control, the statement must disclose any plans to liquidate the target firm or to sell any significant portion of its assets. The Williams Bill also places restraints upon the management of the target company. Before the management can make any recommendations to their shareholders either to accept or reject the tender offer they must file a supporting statement with the Securities and Exchange Commission justifying their recommendation.

Accounting Treatment

The Accounting Principles Board recognizes two methods of recording business combinations—"purchase" and "pooling-of-interests." The earlier practice of using a mixture of techniques, part-purchase and part-pooling, is no longer acceptable. In the 1950s and '60s the accounting treatment adopted was frequently determined by management's preferences based on the effect of the accounting procedure upon future income tax payments and/or the short-run impact on reported earnings per share. However, *Accounting Principle Bulletin* No. 16 issued in 1970 establishes a series of criteria that must be met if a combination is recorded as a "pooling-of- interests." As a result, the accounting method for recording a merger is supposed to be based on the facts in the case rather than the preference of the parties.

The essence of "pooling-of-interests" consists of those combinations where two or more independent stockholder groups lose their individual identity and are combined by an exchange of common stock and thereafter share the same risks and rights. The essence of a purchase is found where all or a portion of the assets of the company being acquired are paid for with cash and/or securities other than the common stock of the acquiring firm.

The "pooling-of-interests" method records the value of assets and liabilities of the separate companies as they are reported on the books of the firms being combined. This treatment also results in the combining of stockholder equities. The new total equity is the sum of the equities of the combining firms and the new retained earnings account is the sum of the retained earnings of the companies involved.

No positive or negative goodwill is recognized under "pooling-of-interests." The financial statements for periods prior to the combination are restated as though the firms had been combined throughout the period being reviewed even though it may cover years when they were separate entities. The income statement in the year of the combination is reported as if the combination had occurred at the beginning of the year, even though it may have occurred on the last day of the year.

In accounting for a purchase, the acquired assets are recorded on the books of the acquiring corporation at the cost to the purchaser. Cost is measured by the amount of cash payment or of securities issued as consideration. If the acquisition is effected through issuance of securities, the fair market value of the securities delivered determines the cost of the assets acquired.

Frequently, the acquiring corporation will pay a price in excess of the net book value of the assets of the acquired firms. This excess must be recorded in some manner on the balance sheet of the acquiring firm. If, as is frequently the case, some of the assets being acquired have a market value well in excess of their book value, then those assets should be assigned a new cost basis equal to their current market value.

Restating the value of the assets acquired affects the tax position of the acquirer and the future earnings per share that will be reported after the merger. Writing up assets to market value can increase tax-deductible expenses for the purchaser. If fixed assets are restated, depreciation expense will change and if inventory is written-up, the next year's cost of sales will increase. This reduces future income tax liabilities but it also depresses the level of reported future net income and earnings per share. For the closely held acquiring company, the emphasis is clearly on minimizing income taxes and maximizing after-tax cash flows. However, the publicly owned firm may worry about how this treatment may affect the price of its common stock. If the market value of its common stock is a function of reported earnings, this treatment would depress stock prices.

To the extent that the seller's tangible assets cannot be written up to reflect a purchase price in excess of book values, the balance is recorded as "goodwill" on the acquirer's balance sheet. Companies subject to the regulations of the Securities and Exchange Commission must observe the requirement that goodwill be amortized over a period not to exceed 40 years. On the other hand, the Internal Revenue Code has ruled that the amortization of goodwill cannot be deducted as an expense for income tax purposes. This has the effect of reducing reported earnings without any compensating income tax benefits.

If patents of material value to be business are part of the acquired assets, they may be assigned an appraised value and amortized as a tax-deductible operating expense over their remaining lives. Similarly, if the seller agrees not to complete for a specified period of years with the acquirer of the business, such an agreement has a value which the acquirer should fix and amortize as an expense over the stated period.

The "pooling-of interest" accounting treatment became widespread after 1954 and was the primary method of reporting in the 1960s. This was a period when the purchase price was typically well in excess of the book value of the company being acquired and the method of payment was primarily via exchange of voting securities. In the 1970s the purchase method of accounting dominated. Purchase prices, particularly in the last half of the 1970s, were frequently less than book value, and the acquisition was frequently accomplished by cash payments via a tender offer. It is not clear whether the accounting treatment permitted by APB No. 16 affected the method of acquisition employed in mergers during the 1970s or whether the more rigorous standards of APB No. 16 were introduced in a period when the "pooling-of- interest" technique was no longer particularly attractive to corporate acquirers.

Tax and Legal Considerations

While tax considerations may not be a significant factor in deciding to execute a merger, tax problems will undoubtedly be important to both parties and may dictate the method of effecting the transaction. For the most part, the tax problems derive from Sub-chapter C of the Internal Revenue Code. This is one of the Code's most complex areas, and at an early stage both parties should retain competent tax counsel. The following discussion does not purport to interpret the tax laws, but merely outlines principal aspects of importance.

Taxable vs. Nontaxable Transactions Essentially, a taxable merger or acquisition is one under which the seller has a recognized gain or loss for tax purposes in the year the transaction is completed. A nontaxable transaction, usually referred to as a "tax-free" merger or exchange, is one in which there is no immediate recognition of gain or loss. In a tax-fee transaction, the sellers realize a taxable gain or loss when they sell the securities received in payment. Buyers realize gains or losses as they dispose of or amortize, the assets acquired. In a taxable transaction, the seller has a realized taxable gain or loss in the year of the transaction. Taxable gains and losses are equal to the difference between the tax basis of the property disposed of and the fair market value of the consideration received.

Types of Nontaxable Mergers and Acquisitions Essentially, the Internal Revenue Code provides that a merger or acquisition may be "tax-free" if it is consummated.

(a) As a statutory merger or consolidation.

(b) Through exchange of voting capital stock of one corporation for that of another if, immediately after the acquisition, the acquiring corporation has control of the acquired corporation.

(c) Through exchange of voting capital stock of one corporation for all, or substantially all, of the assets of another firm.

In "Type A" mergers the stock issued by the acquiring corporation does not have to be voting stock. Furthermore, a part of the consideration to the stockholders of the acquired corporation may be an obligation, such as notes or debentures, without disqualifying the transaction as tax-free. However, the use of debt securities, being an obligation and not an equity, will be treated as "boot" and regarded as a dividend taxable at ordinary income rates. In the exchange of stock for stocks designated as "Type B." the emphasis is on issuance of a voting stock, common or preferred, to effect the acquisition. The transaction may qualify as nontaxable to the shareholders of the acquired corporation even if less than all of the shares are exchanged. In the exchange of voting stock for properties of the other corporation, designated as "Type C," the acquiring corporation may assume the liabilities of the other or provide cash for their discharge.

Other Qualifications for Nontaxable Transactions In addition to statutory requirements, several doctrines derived from judicial decisions are important. Failure to observe these issues may negate the tax-free status of the merger.

(a) *Business Purpose.* It has been held that there must be a rational bona fide business purpose for the organization, not one "masquerading as a corporate reorganization." The usual type of merger or acquisition would have little difficulty satisfying this requirement, but it is an aspect which must not be overlooked in planning the transaction.

(b) *Continuity of Interest*. The courts have interpreted the law to mean that to secure the benefit of non-taxability, the stockholders of the acquired corporation must retain an equity interest in the new or surviving corporation consistent with the value of the stock or property transferred to it. This condition is generally satisfied by the issuance and exchange of voting stock. A serious question is raised, however, when a statutory merger involves a disproportionate amount of debt securities being delivered to the sellers.

(c) *Step Transactions.* In cases where the plan has been devised in the form of a series of transactions, each of which is designed to be tax-free under the Code, the courts have held that the net effect of all the steps becomes the determining factor.

Section 306 Stock Section 306 of the 1954 Code established severe restrictions on issuance of preferred stock in a corporate reorganization, as well as in transactions commonly referred to as the "preferred-stock bailout." "Section 306 stock." as it is termed in the Code, is defined to include preferred stock if the effect is substantially the same as receiving a stock dividend. Thus, as often occurs, if a portion of the earned surplus of the acquired corporation is capitalized as a result of issuing preferred stock, and if such stock is disposed of by the recipient shortly thereafter, the proceeds would constitute, in net effect, a cash distribution out of surplus. Consequently, although received in a non-taxable transaction, the proceeds of subsequent sale of "Section 306 Stock" may be subject to tax as ordinary income rather than as a capital gain.

Antitrust Factors

Corporate mergers and acquisitions involve compliance with, often interpretation of, Federal and state laws. Early discussions with legal advisors on the antitrust implications of proposed acquisitions is frequently essential.

Corporations entering into a merger transaction, particularly those of substantial size, or those holding a large share of a relatively small market, are confronted with the uncertainties of possibly violating one of more sections of the Sherman Act or the Clayton Act. Notwithstanding the many cases decided under these laws, attorneys still regard their provisions to be relatively undefined and subject to flexible interpretations, with the possible result of civil or criminal liability.

Management should be fully aware of the implications of Section 7 of the Clyton Act as amended in 1950 by the Celler-Kefauver Act: it provides that mergers and acquisitions are unlawful "where in any line of commerce in any section of the country the effect of such acquisition may be substantially to lessen competition, or tend to create a monopoly." It should be noted that "substantially to lessen competition" has in recent actions been interpreted to include *potential* competition as well as competition already existing. Thus, management may expect counsel to examine aspects such as size, rate, and manner of growth (i.e., record of previous acquisitions), share of the market before and after the transaction, and how that market is defined, the pattern of distribution, the effect upon customer and supplier relationships, the relative ease of entry of new competitors into the pertinent market, and the question whether the acquirer possesses a "...dominant ability to produce and sell which threatens...extremely adverse competitive effects."

Congressional comment in the course of amending Section 7 in 1950 and in the 1978 hearings on mergers and industrial concentration was to the effect that the Section "applies to all types of mergers and acquisitions, vertical and conglomerate as well as horizontal." Further, even though the corporation to be acquired does not make products competitive with those of the acquiring corporation, the fact that it has facilities adaptable to such manufacture may be grounds for a change that "potential competition" is lessened or precluded.

Planning Mergers and Acquisitions

The planning phase starts with the task of defining the specific objectives of the firm. If objectives such as growth, stability diversification, product line improvement, etc., cannot be attained efficiently by internal development within the desired period of time, the merger route is a natural alternative. The reasons for seeking acquisitions establishes the criteria that should be used in selecting the firms to be acquired.

As a general rule, the best acquisitions are made among companies which are not openly available for sale or are being "shopped about." The soundest procedure is to search and predetermine the targets by deciding which companies will bring to the combination the desired assets, tangible and intangible, quickly ruling out those that fail to meet the acquiring firm's established criteria.

Approach to Negotiation Formulating the strategy of approach is a critical step. Success or failure may hinge upon the initial and preliminary discussions. Data compiled in the early search procedures should be augmented by other published information about the company which could be useful in developing the reasons why the acquirer's proposition should be seriously considered. If the company is listed on a stock exchange, the Form 10-K reports to the S.E.C. are a valuable source of information on ownership of the stock, salaries of the highest paid executives, incentive compensation plan, and other pertinent information. The prospectus of any recent public offering of securities, the registration statement, and the attached exhibits on file with the Securities and Exchange Commission also provide information on takeover targets.

The age of the major stockholders, the probability of estate problems in a closely held company, the connections of the officers and directors, and the company's principal banking connections are valuable information in planning the strategy of approach. It is just as important to initiate merger discussions with the right individual as it is to present the merger idea effectively. (For example, if analysis of the company's financial statements indicates heavy current loans as well as long-term debt, a talk with the loan officers of the company's bank may lead to a better entree than a direct approach to the president.) In some situations, an unequivocal rejection may result from a direct approach to the president, who may be concerned primarily with protecting his position, whereas a more effective approach may be made through an "outside" director who is fully aware of his responsibility to the shareholders.

Essentially, the strategy is to identify a company's needs and problems, (e.g., capital shortage, inadequate distribution, lack of management succession, lack of marketability for its stock) and present the advantages of this merger in solving those problems. It is also appropriate to demonstrate that, through merger, the stockholders of the acquired company can improve their prospects for growth and market value appreciation for their shares.

An important factor is the determination of who should initiate the merger discussions. Sometimes it is inadvisable for the president of the acquirer to make the initial approach because his presence in the company's offices could set afoot rumors when secrecy is of utmost importance. Delegating the initial approach to an investment banker or to a consultant is a common tactic which has the added advantage that, should the proposal be rejected, the president of the acquiring corporation remains free to make another attempt by changing the strategy to meet the reasons given for rejection.

Use of a Business Broker. Commercial and investment bankers may act as intermediaries. This may include finding firms for acquisition, or simply handling the negotiations. After the reputation and reliability of the intermediary have been established, and as a prelude to his disclosure of a candidate, it is essential to confirm in writing: (1) the amount of the commission; (2) the conditions under which the commission becomes payable (usually only in the event the acquisition is consummated); (3) if negotiations are initiated by an intermediary representing a company seeking to sell, the authority of the intermediary to represent the seller (usually a letter from the president or controlling stockholder of the seller).

The fees of a business broker are negotiable and should be governed by the services performed and the amount involved. The seller may expect to pay 5% of the first million dollars, 3% of the second million, and 1.5% on the balance, with a further step down for large deals. If finding a buyer is difficult or if the negotiations are protracted and require the broker to maintain the continuity and equilibrium of the trading, the broker may justifiably bargain for a higher fee.

The fee is payable irrespective of whether the transaction involves cash or stock. Although the obligation to pay the fee commonly is that of the seller, the net effect often is that the total purchase price is increased by the amount of the fee, or that the net assets received are reduced by the fee payment.

Negotiation. The first few discussions are usually confined to generalities on why the two corporations should be combined. These discussions would include the firms' respective strengths, organizational structure, staffing financial position, and economic prospects. Preliminary information exchange will concern areas where economies from the merger are anticipated. The information would include marketing, manufacturing, and other expense and revenue data. It would also include the certificate of incorporation, the bylaws, copies of loan agreements and, frequently, an auditor's report.

The terms proposed by the acquirer are submitted subject to a full investigation of the corporation to be acquired, and consequently must be regarded as a preliminary indication of terms. On the other hand, the sellers may demand that the terms be final if the investigation does not disclose any material misrepresentations or any adverse factors not previously disclosed. Failure to resolve divergent views on price frequently is overcome by authorizing a consulting firm to make a comprehensive examination of both corporations and recommend an equitable ratio of exchange.

Not all negotiations are preceded by the planning selection, and approach strategy just described. Frequently, a prospective acquirer is approached by an investment banker, a business broker, or other intermediary acting on behalf of the seller. Obviously, under these circumstances, the prospective acquirer is entering the negotiations without the benefit of previous investigation. There is then a tendency for top management of the acquirer to request opinions of middle management and sales personnel regarding the products and reputation of the seller. Such an approach inevitably results in rumors which can be adverse if not disastrous to the negotiations. Consequently, it is usually advisable to gain such information through a confidential survey by a professional firm or through the acquirer's commercial bank and its correspondents.

Preliminary Agreement. Upon reaching agreement, the negotiating officers of the two corporations generally will draw up a simple memorandum stating: (1) the basis of the agreement—i.e., the terms of the merger or acquisition: (2) that it is subject to approval by the respective boards of directors; (3) that it is subject to authorization by the shareholders of each corporation (in a cash purchase, the acquirer usually does not need approval of its own shareholders unless securities are to be issued); (4) that the acquirer shall have access to the business, properties, books, records, agreements, and operations of the corporation to be acquired and the right to examine them completely, and that the agreed upon terms are contingent upon a favorable finding in such examination; (5) that the effective data of the merger or acquisition shall be on a specified day or as soon as practicable thereafter; and (6) that in the interim, until stockholder action is taken, neither corporation will make any substantial change in its operations or enter into unusual commitments unless the other is informed and gives prior approval.

Approved by the Board of Directors. The boards of both corporations should be kept informed of the progress of the negotiations. Each board must take formal action to approve the terms and conditions of the merger or acquisition as expressed in the preliminary agreement. Such approval, unless the terms were based upon a comprehensive examination made in the course of negotiation, would be a preliminary action providing authority to the respective managements to pursue the various procedural steps. If the terms and conditions are not subject to adjustment, the approval by the respective boards would be a definitive action followed by submission of the matter for shareholders' approval.

Announcement. Unless there are substantial reasons for withholding disclosure until the notice of the meeting of stockholders is sent out (assuming such action is required), it is advisable to make prompt announcement of the pending transaction, indicating advantages to both corporations, their employees, and customers. This is usually done by simultaneous letters from the president of each corporation to the stockholders, executives, key employees, distributors, customers, etc., by notices to clerical and plant employees, and by releases to the newspapers and trade publications.

Organizing the Procedural Activities. There are a great many tasks to be accomplished by the closing date. Here we can merely indicate the major procedural matters, since the detailed program will be different in individual situations.

(1) Final agreement of merger or contract of purchase—usually drafted by counsel for the acquirer but with participation by counsel for the seller.

(2) Investigation of the corporation to be acquired (unless this was performed previously)—sometimes by a task force of executives and key personnel of the acquirer, but generally by a consulting firm.

(3) Review of audited financial statements of the corporation to be acquired and a reconciliation of differences in accounting policies and practices to make its statements comparable with those of

the acquirer—almost always performed by the certified public accountants of the acquirer.

(4) Examination of commitments and liabilities of the corporation to be acquired, whether or not reflected or reserved against in the balance sheet. Consideration must be given to undisclosed contingent liabilities for assessment of additional income taxes (for prior years not yet audited by the IRS), for patent infringement, for customer claims under product warranties, etc. It is also important to ascertain whether adequate reserves have been provided for future pension and retirement benefits to which the acquired corporation may be committed.

Post Merger Audit. When the corporate marriage has finally been consummated, a new set of problems arises that need attention if the long-run benefits of the combination are to be achieved. A suggested check list of some of the more important post-merger activities includes:

(1) Effecting the merger by:

- ☐ completing legal arrangements (e.g., new corporate charters, transferring title on assets).
- ☐ designating agents of the new corporation for suppliers and vendors.
- ☐ changing corporate signs and logos.
- ☐ preparing necessary public-relations releases.

(2) Maintaining momentum immediately after the merger by:

- ☐ clarifying reporting relationships.
- ☐ ensuring the continuity of credit lines and insurance.
- ☐ making financial authorizations.

(3) Bringing the new organization into the corporate structure by:

- ☐ installing a reporting system for the new company.
- ☐ consolidating financial reporting press relations, and stockholder communications.
- ☐ reviewing compensation and personnel policies of the acquired company.
- ☐ consolidating tax return preparation.
- ☐ reviewing accounting practices and policies, developing a new audit program.

- ☐ eliminating activities not appropriate to a division.

(4) Realizing short-term profit-improvement potential by:

- ☐ consolidating the headquarters staffs.
- ☐ closing down unnecessary facilities.
- ☐ eliminating redundant executive positions and unproductive personnel.
- ☐ centralizing functions (e.g., purchasing insurance, data processing).
- ☐ cutting unnecessary frills (i.e., cars, planes, club memberships).
- ☐ consolidating banking relationships.

(5) Realizing long-term profit-improvement potential by:

- ☐ integrating operations (e.g., raw materials, manufacturing, distribution, marketing),
- ☐ and transferring technologies and methods.

Valuation of Company Being Acquired

The terms upon which an acquisition or merger is consummated may require a determination of the value of the acquired corporation or simply the relative value of the securities to be exchanged. There is no standard formula or set of rules for this evaluation: however, there are basic concepts which may be applied.

The management of the firms involve frequently have difficulty agreeing upon a fair price or a fair rate of exchange if the combination is accomplished by an exchange of securities. If the exchange ratio differs substantially from current market prices of the securities involved, it is not uncommon to seek the help of an impartial outsider. This role is frequently filled by either an investment banking firm or a consultant.

A variety of procedures may be used by outside experts to establish reasonable values of the firms involved in a merger. The basic principle is that the value of business assets is determined by their expected or potential earnings power and the degree of risk or uncertainty associated with these expectations. Confirmation and application of this principle are found in numerous court decisions, one of the most succinct statements being by Mr. Justice Brewer of the Supreme Court of the United States who in 1894, said, "The value of property results from the use to which it is put and varies with the profitableness of that use, present and prospective, actual and anticipated."

The theoretical value of the acquired firm would be the present value of the incremental cash flows that would be attributed to the acquired firm discounted or adjusted for the risk of the acquired firm. The risk measure should consider the portfolio effects of the combination. The use of the capital asset pricing model and the evaluation of systematic risk has gained support as a possible approach to the valuation problem when risk is present.

The theoretical value of the combined firm would be the present value of the estimated future earnings of the combined firm discounted or adjusted for its risk. If synergism exists, the post-merger value of the combined firms should exceed the sum of the pre-merger values of the merging firms. A number of studies have attempted to investigate this concept (value additivity) as well as other real gains of merger activity. Results of these studies are mixed, and although some studies indicate that there are real benefits accruing to stockholders of merged firms, most studies indicate little support for synergism. Yet, executives and managers cite many potential gains from these combinations, and actively seek acquisitions.

An appropriate evaluation method would estimate the expected future earnings stream of the combined firm, discounted at a discount rate that recognizes the risk associated with the combined firm. The maximum value of the acquisition would be the difference between the value of the acquiring firm with the acquisition, less the estimated value of the firm without the acquisition. The minimum value of the firm would be its value in liquidation. The final price or terms should be within this range and would depend upon the bargaining positions of the firms. If the synergistic effects exist, it is probable that stockholders of both firms would benefit from the combination.

It is not unlikely that the acquiring firm will offer an exchange ratio that represents a premium over the market price for the stock. This reflects the normal results of bargaining when the incentives to reach an agreement are not equally divided among the parties. Assuming there are "synergistic" possibilities in a business combination, the distribution of the increased economic values is not necessarily based on relative contributions, but rather on the relative bargaining powers.

The evaluation techniques that may be applied by impartial experts observing a business combination are many and varied. While the basic concepts of valuation can usually be agreed upon, the methods of measurement are subject to dispute. As a result, a fair ratio of exchange should be visualized as a range rather than a specific value.

Pros and Cons of Mergers

The bulk of the voluminous literature developed on the subject tends to be critical of corporate expansion through mergers and acquisitions. The basic criticism of merger activity rests upon the resultant reduction in competition or potential competition. The impact on competition may occur not only as a result of the reduction in the number of firms, but also through an increase in the frequency of "price leadership" or "conscious parallelism." Even though socially undesirable mergers may exist, there may also be economic benefits which results from mergers and acquisitions that should not be overlooked. Economic and technological innovations frequently demand larger and larger economic units in order to take advantage of economies of scale. In the absence of mergers and acquisitions, the economics of the market place would still create the needed economic size in surviving firms, but it would simultaneously increase the rate of business failures as smaller units were driven out of the market rather than being absorbed by other firms.

Mergers involving large publicly owned companies probably do not involve any significant economies of scale, but the threat of future take-over bids may well have a beneficial effect upon the activity and efficiency of entrenched management groups. The concept of corporate democracy is appealing, but it is not very compatible with the frequently expressed attitude that if a shareholder is unhappy with the performance of the management of his company he should simply sell his stock. The possibility of proxy fights and/or take-over bids represents potential corrective devices when the machinery of corporate democracy breaks down.

While the merger process may contribute to economic efficiency and growth, there is no doubt that some mergers and acquisitions may also be socially undesirable. However, such disadvantages and social costs should be controlled with appropriate legal restraints and supervision rather than by eliminating a process that can be both socially and economically valuable.

12

MANAGEMENT SERVICES AND PRACTICES

MANAGEMENT AUDIT

Management Audit concepts were originally developed as a tool for investment appraisal. Within the past twenty years, however, their use has been expanded to cover virtually all kinds and sizes of business organizations, as well as non-profit enterprises ranging from individual hospitals and colleges to the worldwide operations of the Roman Catholic Church. (While the term *management audit* is sometimes used to denote any evaluation of management, it is properly applied only to the systematic method of appraising administrative performance developed and validated by the American Institute of Management, and used by it in its evaluations of American businesses and other organizations.)

The management audit may be defined as a procedure for systematically examining, analyzing, and appraising a management's overall performance. To determine this overall performance, the management audit combines the evaluations of ten categories of appraisal, each a determination of the worth of the subject management in one category of the analysis, viewed historically and in comparison with other organizations.

As applied to a business organization, the management audit presents the qualities of the subject management relative to those of other management in its particular industry, as well as in relation to the finest managements in other industries.

The ten categories of the management audit of business organizations are as follows:

(1) Economic function.

(2) Corporate structure.

(3) Health of earnings.

(4) Service to stockholders.

(5) Research and development.

(6) Directorate analysis.

(7) Fiscal policies.

(8) Production efficiency.

(9) Sales vigor.

(10) Executive evaluation.

These categories do not represent single functions of management, or pure variables.

In actual practice, preparation of a management audit of an organization consists of two distinct parts. The first is the compilation of data for analysis and evaluation. To insure completeness as well as comparability with data collected on other organizations, the American Institute of Management uses detailed prepared questionnaires covering management's performance in each appraisal category over a number of years. The information obtained through the Management Audit Questionnaire (Questionnaires have been developed for a wide range of industries and types of business) is supplemented by interviews with members of management, directors, and a wide range of others associated with the company as employees, suppliers, competitors, customers, or investing owners. At the same time, material is assembled on the subject company's industry to provide the comparative basis.

The second and significant portion of the management audit is the analysis of all information obtained. This results in the appraisal of individual categories and from these of the overall performance of management. It must be stressed that management appraisal, even with the systematic approach of the management audit, cannot be considered a science in the full sense of that word, since subjective judgment ultimately enters the appraisal. One of the values of the management audit, however, is the extent to which it permits judgment to rest on the widest possible base of substantive information, and on a uniform and general conceptual foundation. The most basic concept underlying the system is that management, wherever it is found, is *the art of purposeful action.*

Economic Function

The category Economic Function in the management audit assigns to management the continuing responsibility for the company's importance to our economy. In effect, economic function determines the *public value* of the company. This value is based on what the company has chosen to do—what products or services it produces—and how it does these things in the moral and ethical sense. It comprises such intangibles as the company's reputation and management's view and enlargement of the purpose of the enterprise. The *public* as referred to in economic function includes not merely the consumers of the company's products or its share owners, but a number of distinct groups, all with varying interests, which the business organization must seek to satisfy (among them its employees, suppliers, distributors, and the communities in which it operates).

The fulfillment of economic function is cumulative, in the sense that time alone can test a company's public value. A new corporation may quickly become an important element in our national life, but until it has endured trade cycles, met competition over the years, developed and replaced its management teams, and earned its reputation among its various publics, it cannot have achieved maximum economic function. It is by such outstanding companies as Eastman-Kodak and Minnesota Mining and Manufacturing that the public value of new companies must be measured.

Corporate Structure

The category Corporate Structure appraises the effectiveness of the structure through which management seeks to fulfill its aims. The organization structure of any company must expedite making and executing corporate decisions, must permit control of the enterprise, and must establish the areas of responsibility and authority of its executives. These are requirements that must be met regardless of the specific form of organization a company adopts.

In actual practice, the real form of organization of a company under study is seldom that of the nominal organization charts. Published organization charts are in fact, often so inaccurate in depicting the actual relationships and relative authorities within the company that they are of little use to the management analyst.

Companies that have developed product-division or other forms of decentralized organization have maximized the delegation of responsibility and authority, but they have not reduced the need for clear understanding of them throughout the organization. For the most part, corporations decentralize after the lines of authority have been well established: but at times, even large corporations have suffered as the result of a breakdown in the acceptance or exercise of authority.

Health of Earnings

The evaluation of earnings is concerned with the historical and comparative aspects of corporate income formation, not merely with the income itself. The category Health of Earnings must determine whether the profit potential of the corporation's assets has been realized in full. (By assets are meant not merely company-owned net equity but, in addition, the assets represented by whatever debt is included in capitalization—the net capital invested. These capital factors are represented in the production process by fixed assets in the form of land, plant, and equipment, or by more liquid assets including actual cash or, more remotely liquid, inventories. No matter what form they take, the paramount question is whether they have been employed at the optimum for the full realization of their potential.)

For both manufacturing and non-manufacturing companies the fruitfulness of capital can be determined by a study of the risk assumed in the employment of resources, in the profit return upon their employment, and in the nature and distribution of the assets among various categories. Industrial enterprises are particularly suited to this analysis. Although the actual value of their assets (in particular, of their patents and processes) cannot always be determined exactly, one can at least trace the cost of their acquisition, the rates at which they have been depreciated, and the extent to which they have been employed profitably or unprofitably. While prepared information is seldom available for other categories of the management audit, the information required on health of earnings is usually on public record in a company's annual reports and in digests of its financial structure. Eastman-Kodak has the best of all records in this category.

Service to Stockholders

Appraisal of a company's service to stockowners rests chiefly on a three-part mandate that stockholders give the board of directors of corporations: *first,* that their principal not be dissipated or exposed to unnecessary risks: *second,* that the principal be enhanced as much as possible through the sound use of undistributed profits, and *third,* they they receive a reasonable return on the principal in the form of dividends, while their ownership interest is protected through pre-emptive rights. How well a company satisfies these three requirements determines its *fairness* to stockowners.

In addition, the appraisal covers the obligation that every company has today to provide service to its shareowners—primarily, to keep them well enough informed so that they can evaluate the progress of their investment in the company and participate in decisions that are likely to affect that investment. Even the financially inexperienced shareholder can review his own relationship with the company to determine whether or not the essentials of stockholder service are present. And while stockholder relations are less vital than sound dividend policies, they indicate a management conscious of its responsibilities—a fundamental of excellent management in any company.

For the specifics of analyzing fairness to stockowners, companies and industries differ too widely in what earnings they can pay out as dividends to set optimum ratios of dividends to net income or other absolutes. Rather the ultimate return and capital appreciation are the important determinants of fairness to stockowners, be any particular or current percentage.

Research and Development

Because adequate research efforts over a period of years can assure company growth and improvement of its Industry position, evaluation of company research policies in crucial to a management audit. Giant corporations, almost without exception, know the importance of research as a continuing activity, regardless of how well they pursue it. Too many smaller corporations, however, still look upon it with fear, and often do not undertake meaningful research at all. They could benefit immeasurably by greater boldness—if they boldness is based on a clear concept of what research is and can do and a realistic approach to budgeting and evaluating it.

Evaluating research results can show how well the research dollar has been employed, but it does not show whether or not management has realized the maximum from its research potential. For this reason, research must be examined comparatively and historically—in dollars expended, in the number of research workers employed, in the ratio of research costs and staff to total expenses and personnel, in new ideas, information, and products turned out. These expenditures, examined with past research results, provide an estimate of management's willingness to employ research for *future* growth and health.

Some companies establish an arbitrary payout period to evaluate their own research results. This arbitrary system focuses attention on the need for research profitability, but it may actually discourage future research. The Management Institute's analysis of research success depends on no formula; it attempts, rather, to determine what part of the company's past progress can properly be credited to research and how well research policies are preparing the company for future progress.

Directorate Analysis

The company directorate selects and guides operating management in the interest of the business owners and the public. In appraising its effectiveness, three principal elements are considered:

(a) The quality of each director and the contribution he makes to the board.

(b) How well the directors work together as a team—whether they complement and stimulate each other. This, of course, is a principal test, since it is the board's action as a group that affect the company.

(c) Whether the directors truly act as trustees for the enterprise.

The trusteeship responsibility of the directorate can best be examined in those areas in which a partial conflict of interest exists between a company's executives and the business owners and public. One of the clearest of these is the area of executive incentives. How well the directorate resolves compensation and other incentive problems provides an excellent key to its quality. American Telephone & Telegraph excels in this category.

Fiscal Policies

While the fiscal history of a company—the result of all management activity expressed in measurable money terms—is appraised in the category Health of Earnings, past and present financial policies are appraised directly in fiscal policies. This category includes three areas of study: the company's capital structure; its organizations for developing fiscal policies and controls; and the application of these policies and controls in different areas of corporate activity. The key problems are providing, controlling, and husbanding funds. Eastman-Kodak excells in this category.

Production Efficiency

Evaluating production efficiency has obvious importance in appraising a manufacturing company. What is not so widely understood is that production efficiency or its equivalent, *operating* efficiency, is equally vital to non-manufacturing companies, whether they are in banking, insurance, transportation, communications, electric or other power, or any other field in which the end product is not a tangible good. Virtually all companies which are not merely agents for other companies must obtain and process some good or service before marketing it. This is the field of a company's overall operation evaluated in the category Production Efficiency.

The analysis of present-day production management must be divided into two parts. The first of these may be terms the appraisal of *machinery and material management,* since it evaluates the mechanical production or processing of the company's products. This one part is often overemphasized, so that management's mastery of its machinery appears the major factor in production efficiency. However, a second aspect of production evaluation, that of *manpower management*, is equally important. This facet of operations properly includes all personnel policies and practices for non-sales and non-executive employees developed by management. Only when both aspects are analyzed can overall production in operating efficiency be appraised. General Motors excels in this category.

Sales Vigor

Within single industries and even within single companies sales practices can very broadly enough to represent different marketing principles. Between different industries the variations are often still greater. Yet the comparative appraisal of sales vigor must encompass all the forms that marketing can take.

Sales vigor can, of course, be appraised despite these variations, but only after the marketing goals of each subject company have been determined and assessed. These goals, in turn, must be appraised in terms of the over-all goals of the entire organization. Then, as with other categories of the management audit, historical and comparative evaluations become possible—namely, how well past sales potential has been realized and how well present company sales policies prepare it to realize the future potential. The treatment of sales personnel usually belongs in this category. Procter & Gamble excels in this category.

Executive Evaluation

Executive Evaluation is the most important single appraisal category of the ten that comprise the management audit. To a degree, of course, the other categories in this system of management appraisal also evaluate the organization's executives, since they appraise the results of executive thinking and action in each management function. But the quality of the executives themselves, their management philosophy, and the appropriateness of both to the purposes of the organization must still be appraised directly.

The American Institute of Management has found three personal qualities—ability, industry, and integrity—to be the essential elements for the business leader. These provide a framework for his evaluation in the management audit and should also be the criteria of the organization's leaders in selecting and advancing executives. Excellent management requires that executives work together in harmony, each with specific tasks contributing to the total effort, conscious that he is participating in this effort with men who command his respect. As a group, the executives must regard the continuity of the corporation as an important goal, assuring it by sound policies of executive selection, development, advancement, and replacement. A key problem is to assure sound succession in depth.

Universality of Evaluation

The principles of the management audit remain valid regardless of the nature of the enterprise. All human activity is confronted with the same management problems. When two or more individuals get together in any common endeavour, wanting the best possible result, they must ask. "What shall we do, and how shall we do it?" In order to get good results, whether they are aware of it or not, they must follow fundamental tenets of management, which can be appraised.

Social Function. Whatever the undertaking its impact upon the public welfare must be helpful rather than harmful. In the affairs of a church society, for example, this value may be termed *social function*. In an educational institution, it is *academic function*. The principles of evaluation remain the same.

Organization. The activities of two or more individuals—members of a management team once they unite in a common venture—create lines of authority and responsibility. They may be adjusted as the organization grows in size and consequence and progresses with its undertakings, but the extent to which authority and responsibility are made clear provides a basis for evaluation.

Growth. The enterprise must exhibit growth of facilities, whether these come from gifts or profits derived from merchandising goods or services. The health of that growth can be appraised.

Membership. Members, shareowners, or proprietors of an enterprise are encouraged to cooperate and contribute, whether through dividends or less material rewards. How this is done is a matter of techniques peculiar to the kind of enterprise and varying with circumstances and time. But that it shall be done activates fundamental management principles and permits evaluation of its effectiveness.

Research. Management of whatever kind seeks the most reliable, comprehensive, accurate, and up-to-date information available. Research and development includes study of any phase of group activity, with a view to betterment of either principles or techniques.

Fiscal Policies. The financial and other resources of any group effort are the life blood of its activity. Where they are obtained—and obtained in proper quantity—the enterprise can continue to exist and grow. How well resources are found and used can be appraised. Fitting financial policies and practices to the immediate and long-term needs that experience indicates, and then altering them as the result of study or alertness, is a management principle closely related to survival.

Trusteeship. Whether called trustees, directors, or guardians, those overseeing an undertaking have the responsibility of determining its leadership. In this way they exercise the power of the organization. Appraisal can be made of how well they recognize that their authority needs the sanction of morality and creates obligations to assume responsibility for the welfare of the total enterprise, including the public and all individuals concerned.

Operations. The operation of an undertaking has a degree of effectiveness no matter what the product, service, or purpose. This is true even within the area of charitable, social, political, and spiritual endeavors. Every organization then has production or operating problems, just as it has a research need; it must understand and solve these problems to be well managed.

Sales. Everyone must be able to persuade others to accept him (her), and his services, products, or ideas, whether doctor, lawyer, merchant, or priest. Every group activity must be sold or merchandized if the enterprise is to grow and prosper. The techniques to accomplish this vary with the enterprise, the occasion, and the purpose, but they can be assessed in terms of how well they persuade prospective purchasers, joiners, or whomever

Leadership Quality. The quality of leadership in any enterprise is the most important single aspect of the activity. The success of the executive group and the activity may depend on their integrity, ability, and industry, their devotion to the enterprise, their acceptance of responsibility, and their foresight in providing continued leadership after themselves. These qualities, all of which can be appraised, are not limited to the profit making corporation—they are fundamental wherever individuals join together for a common purpose, whatever the inspiration and the motive.

In conclusion, administrative evaluation must recognize that for an organization to be well managed, it must have sound purposes and use good techniques. To be excellently managed, it must fit these techniques and practices within the framework of true administrative principles.

MANAGEMENT CONSULTING

Omnibus use of the term "management"—as evidenced by the scope of this Encyclopedia—makes it difficult to define, with any degree of exactitude, the term *Management Consulting*. Indeed, the field of management consulting is so broad that many who do not call themselves management consultants use the same skills, techniques, and knowledge to accomplish the same management goals and objectives (systems and methods experts, top executives, and staff specialists).

The Association of Management Consulting Firms (ACME, Inc.) defines management consulting as: "The service performed for a fee by independent and objective professional persons—or a group organized as a firm—who help managers analyze and diagnose management and operating problems." ACME further limits such counsel to upper management—goals, objectives, policies, strategies, administration, organization, and principal functional or operating areas—although this limitation would probably not be agreed to by most practitioners in the field.

The management consultant is concerned with change and improvement, not merely with facts, but people and systems...and the profession is as much art as science. And, though born in industry, management consulting has transcended its original boundaries to become accepted today in various institutions of society—from nonprofit organizations to those providing services to government itself.

History

Management consulting had its origins in the then new "industrial engineering" and "time and motion study" pioneered in the United States by Frederick W. Taylor in the 1890s. The fathers of this new "scientific" management thinking—Taylor, Gantt, Frank and Lillian Gilbreth, Harrington Emerson, Carl Barth, H.K. Hathaway, and others—were themselves the first management consultants. Their work was largely connected with straightening out production problems in factories, and the increasing demand for their services soon outgrew their ability to satisfy it. This void inevitably attracted many inept and unethical practitioners, and a number of self-styled "efficiency experts" of the World War I era, by their inexpert attempts to handle a variety of problems they did not truly understand, had an unfortunately adverse effect on the professional standing of all management consultants—a condition that in some measure still prevails today.

In the 1920s, consulting spread increasingly to other functional areas of business, though it was still far from widespread in application or acceptance. In the 1930s, however, another generation of management consultants evolved: the generalist who could put specialized services in perspective and provide manager-clients with needed objectivity. Thus, Edwin Booz (a psychologist), James O. McKinsey (a professor/accountant), and others like them built acceptance for the profession and broadened its scope. It was in this period, too, that a major new area of activity opened: financial reconstruction and reorganization of companies in difficulty because of the Depression. The role of consultant thus became associated with the saving of "sick" businesses. This association, too, still persists to some degree today, even though management consultants actually make their greatest contributions in furthering the objectives of essentially healthy and well-managed organizations.

Despite a return to specialization demanded by the exigencies of World War II, management consulting emerged in the early 1950s as a prime aid to organizations making the transition to a peacetime economy...and it was in this period that the profession experienced almost meteoric growth.

Emerging Professionalism

In the 1980s, management consulting, though still a generation behind the accounting profession, is increasingly recognized as a valid (though still sometimes controversial) service to managers in almost every environment. Firms have proliferated, individuals have entered by the thousands, and the professional associations are trying to self-regulated against the specter of bureaucratic control.

As the "Who's Who" of management consulting professional groups reveals, eight organizations of varying impact and quality currently serve the management consulting profession. While several of the professional groups have attempted over the years to define exactly what a management consultant is, or what he or she should know, perhaps the most concise presentation is the following summary prepared by the Institute of Management Consultants as a part of its Body of Knowledge for the accreditation of management consultants:

All management consultants should possess certain knowledge in common, and they should also possess substantially greater amounts of knowledge in one or two of a group of specialties or functions.

Knowledge in Common: (1) management consulting as a process and a profession, and (2) general knowledge. The first covers the processes by which consultants apply their knowledge in the context of real-life situations to the solution of their clients problems. Sheer possession of knowledge about how organizations are managed and specific functions operate is not enough: the consultant's role as analyst, recommender, and implementer of change is often crucial.

The "general knowledge" expected of all consultants covers the nature of the management process and the principal technical and functional areas: the legal, political, and social backgrounds within which entities operate: and the major common and differentiating characteristics of business, not-for-profit, and governmental institutions.

Knowledge of functional Areas of Management: These include (1) general management; (2) operations; (3) marketing; (4) logistics, materials management, and physical distribution; (5)

research and development; (6) finance and accounting; (7) human resources; (8) electronic data processing and systems, (9) management science.

It should be noted that many experienced executives fail as consultants: the shades of difference in philosophy and approach between doing and advising far transcend and closet parallel, i.e., the normal differences between line and staff functioning.

Types of Management Consultants

Four basic types of management consultants may be identified:

1. *Independent consultants* function in large firms, mid-sized firms, small firms, and as individual practitioners. They have no connections with other business services or suppliers and can offer the ultimate in objectivity.

2. *Accounting-firm consultants.* These professionals, usually called MAS (Management Advisory Services), operate within a CPA firm (such a firm is typically organized into Audit, Tax, and MAS departments). While these MAS departments burgeoned in the 1970s, serious questions have arisen over possible conflicts of interest (or the appearance thereof), although critics have been hard-pressed to cite specific cases.

3. *Professor/consultants.* Literally thousands of business-school professors work part-time as management consultants. This enriches their experience and can make them better teachers, and it also enables them to supplement faculty salaries. Some universities are concerned about possible diversion from academic thrusts. Professors typically consult in "soft" areas such as organization and training, but this is not always the case. They are accused, too, of an "ivory tower" approach, but this criticism, too, is not always valid.

4. *Internal consultants.* Originally spurred by the high cost of consultants, many organizations have established their own management consulting departments. Little uniformity exists in these functions when viewed from the outside: in one firm it might be a glorified industrial engineering group, in another the thrust might be Management by Objectives, in another an assemblage of systems and procedures specialists. Few mini-general management; consulting operations are found, and the groups—because they are internal—are rarely called upon for reality top-level organiza-

tional counsel. Increasingly, however, internals become the focal point for an organization's use of external management consulting assistance. In such cases the internals aid in selection work with the externals during their assignment, and help to assure implementation of recommendations after the outsiders have gone.

Selection of Management Consultant

(1) Prepare a statement outlining the nature, general scope, and purposes of the proposed assignment. Do this before contacting any consultants, but be ready to accept the outsider's redefinition of the "problem" in more objective terms later.

(2) Achieve a consensus within the organization that seeking outside assistance is a reasonable alternative. Nothing can destroy a management consultant's effectiveness faster than internal dissension on whether or not the outsider should have been retained.

(3) Make a "long list" of management consultants who appear to have the qualifications to assist you. Use the associations, directories, personal recommendations: spread your net wide. Then write to these individuals or firms and ask for literature describing their firm and their services. Consider only the firms who respond as requested.

(4) Develop a "short list" of consultants and invite them in for preliminary discussions. Ask those who survive this step to submit proposals.

(5) Study the proposals carefully and check references. Consider the qualifications of personnel who will actually be working on the project.

(6) Ask for modifications of the proposal as necessary, and make your selection.

Remuneration of Management Consultants

Among the more common methods of compensation for professional management consulting services are: (1) per diem or hourly fee; (2) bracket quotation; (3) lump sum or fixed amount; and (4) retainer. Management should beware of consultants who attempt to secure assignments by offering free services, guaranteeing results or savings, or proposing a fee contingent upon the findings or results of services: such inducements are not compatible with sound professional practice. Reputable management consultants make their professional experience available to clients and serve them to the best of their ability and skill; those who promise more may be unfaithful to best interests of clients.

Knowledgeable clients know that they really cannot get services for nothing and that they make it difficult for the consultant to be objective when they request free surveys; for once the consultants has made an investment in free survey time, he (she) may well feel obligated to recommend the further use of his services whether needed or not in order to recover his investment. Additionally, many professional people and businessmen feel that the consulting services offered by equipment manufacturers should be viewed with caution, for obvious reasons of objectivity. On the other hand, when a professional management consultant works for a client, it may be part of his service to help the client evaluate competitive bids on equipment. The client can then expect effective implementation at a fair price.

Professional Conduct of Management Consultants

The interplay of relationship between client and consultant brings into focus specific responsibilities to the client which have been set forth in the ACME standards of professional conduct and practice, covering the following points (among others):

- ☐ Placing client interest first.
- ☐ Always being impartial and independent.
- ☐ Not serving competitors without their knowledge.
- ☐ Not overstanding competence.
- ☐ Accepting only engagements for which qualified.
- ☐ Performing each engagement in an individualized basis.
- ☐ Training client personnel.
- ☐ Maintaining appropriate files.
- ☐ Not interfering in another consultant's work without permission.
- ☐ Charging reasonable fees.
- ☐ Not paying commissions.

TECHNIQUES IN MANAGEMENT DEVELOPMENT

In the learning process by which a manager is made aware of new relationships, as a result of which he modifies his behavior, he goes through the following phases:

(1) Awareness of the problem area and dissatisfaction with the status quo.

(2) Recognition of alternative solutions to the problem.

(3) Selection and practice of a new behavior.

(4) Feedback from a reliable source.

(5) Generalization and integration of the new behaviour pattern into his established frame of reference.

The instructor plays a major role in the first second and fourth phases. He often creates the initial dissatisfaction by making the participant aware of the need for change. This is particularly critical with experienced executives for whom a departure from existing habit patterns represents insecurity and the risk of disapproval or resentment from superiors, associates, and subordinates. After creating dissatisfaction with the status quo, the instructor may reveal alternative solutions, and then create an environment in which the executive-students can experiment with them. He is also in a position to offer feedback and to help the participants understand its meaning by analysis, synthesis, and interpretation. Thus, the essence of learning can be thought of as guided self-discovery

Educational techniques should be chosen to create the best environment for this learning experience. Many techniques are available today, ranging from on-the-job methods such as job rotation, to classroom devices such as role playing and the case study. Advantages and disadvantages of the techniques in current use appear below.

The success of any single technique depends on its relevance to the subject matter discussed and the principles to be illustrated; its emotional and motivational impact; the assistance it can offer in providing an environment for testing and evaluating various approaches; the degree to which it relates training with the job situation; and its suitability for the particular caliber of the participants in the program. In the final analysis, however, the skill with which the instructor *uses* the techniques is obviously the greatest factor in its success. Sensitivity to the needs of the training group, flexibility an desire to help the learner discover himself or herself, and an understanding of the training process are critical to the success of any training technique. A lecture on human relations by an effective speaker may be more successful than a poorly structured role-playing session, although the latter provides certain unique benefits for such a subject when properly employed.

On-the-Job Teaching Techniques for Executives

Since the primary objective of business education is to modify behavior on the job, many companies feel that the most effective training must take place there. On-the-job techniques are relatively inexpensive since they involve little loss of productive time and rarely need the assistance of a professional training director On the other hand, the pressure of daily operations, the lack of time for analysis and reflection, and the absence of skilled direction often make on-the-job training programs ineffective for many teaching purposes.

Three on-the-job techniques are in common use today:

The Coaching or Guided Experience Method. Many businessmen maintain that there is no instructor as effective as an inspiring superior. By delegating authority, counseling, building mutual confidence, evaluating performance, and assigning meaningful tasks, there is no doubt that an executive contributes greatly to the development of subordinates. However, it is rare for a manager to devote sufficient time to these obligations, and it is even rarer for him or her to convey effectively to subordinates a feeling for the complexities and interrelationships of decision areas, or some of the more theoretical aspects of economics and sociology.

Job Rotation. By enabling a manager to move from job to job according to a specially designed schedule, many companies endeavor to create a well-rounded individual who has proven adaptability. At the same time, the advocates of job rotation point out that the new incumbent often brings new ideas to the job, introduces an element of competition, broadens his or her contacts, and becomes better able to judge his (her) own abilities. On the other hand, when a successful manager is rotated out of a department, the move can disrupt operations and make the subordinates insecure. Also, the method may be costly in terms of the errors which the new manager may make, and the attention required of his or her immediate superior. As with the guided experience method, there is no guarantee that the lessons learned are correct or desirable and, even if they were, they are often learned much too slowly.

Off-the-Job Teaching Techniques

Formal educational programs off-the-job are increasing in scope and number because they seem to be the most effective way to develop the managers needed in industry today. They offer an escape from office pressures, eliminate in-breeding, enable participants to experiment with new ideas away from the critical eyes of their peers, and provide an opportunity for instruction by experts. The main problem with off-the-job training has always been insuring the transfer of the learning to on-the-job behavior. Motivation is often a problem since many mangers resent the implication that a classroom instructor can teach them how to perform their jobs better. Off-the-job training also means lost productive time and the need for competent instructors and suitable facilities.

To motivate managers in an off-the-job teaching session, and to involve them in the learning process, many companies seek techniques which involve a great deal of individual and group participation. Such participation helps trainees to select their own educational goals, teaches respect for other people's ideas, assists in self-analysis, helps them to forget their own immediate problems, and permits them to benefit from the breadth of experience of their classmates. By participating in describing and analyzing a problem situation, and by proposing, criticizing and defending solutions to it, the trainee usually carries away more new ideas and habit patterns than he or she could absorb by a passive experience such as listening to a lecturer. It is entirely possible such as listening to a lecturer. It is entirely possible for people to listen to lectures, and even take extensive notes, without ever reflecting upon what is being said. Worse is that lectures give no opportunity to experiment with new behaviors in a safe environment.

PROFESSIONAL MANAGEMENT EDUCATION

Top managers of business, consulting, and engineering firms, and officials in the higher administrative ranks of government, health care, and institutional management, are increasingly holders of professional management degrees from graduate schools of business and administration. Similarly, corporate recruiters for management programs designed to develop potential top executives are increasingly showing preference for holders of such degrees. In recent years, university degree programs for Master of Business Administration, MBA, have been vying with medical and law schools for the attention of the brightest and most ambitious college graduates.

Most of the graduate programs requiring the GMAT for admission are described in the annual editions of the "Guide to Graduate Management Education." This publication, prepared for the Graduate Management Admission Council by Educational Testing Service, Princeton, N.J., also discusses many aspects of graduate management education and possible careers to which an MBA or similar degree might lead. In addition, it contains an authentic GMAT, including actual directions, time limits, and scoring instruction. The book also includes information about test-taking strategies, guessing, and the various types of questions that may appear in the test. It is sold in many university and commercial bookstores.

The *MBA program* provides a comprehensive foundation in basic subject areas: accounting, taxation, business law, computer application and information systems, economics, finance, management and organizational behavior, marketing, and quantitative analysis, and may require 68 credits.

The *MS in Management or Administration* provides a business base or management core for professionals in engineering, sciences, statistics, computer applications, and public policy, who may then wish to concentrate upon their area of interest.

Advanced Professional Certificates designed to meet the special professional and growth needs in business and government are also offered by graduate schools of business and management. A number of graduate business schools also offer doctorate programs.

MANAGEMENT GAMES

A Management Game is a dynamic training exercise utilizing a model of a work situation. Players, usually managers, grouped into teams representing a manager or the management of one of several competing organizations, make the same type of operating and policy decisions as they do in real life. The word "game" is perhaps an unfortunate one, since it has an implication of fun, and fun is seldom associated with education. Many prefer to speak of "simulation exercises" or "dynamic decision-making sessions." The term "game" however, has won currency. Management games, though serious in intent, *are* also fun.

Objectives

Management games are used for several training purposes. They provide practical experience and the opportunity to experiment. Because they bring rapid feedback on the results of a decision, they can sometimes show cause and effect relationships that may be blurred during the much longer period that elapses in real life situations. At the same time, management games provide opportunities for exchange of ideas with peers. All this can bring much heavier personal involvement, greater attention, and greater retention of new concepts or of ideas that have been acquired.

Preliminary research at the Western Behavioral Sciences Institute and more thorough work at the Center for Social Organization of Schools at the John Hopkins University have confirmed that games will indeed bring better retention, not necessarily of facts, but of concepts. There also is some evidence that learning with games will bring enhanced ability to relate concepts to one another and to the work environment.

Broader Perspective

Management games represent only one technique that has gained wide acceptance in the search for more effective training technologies. The original type of management game, the model-based business game will be described in greater detail in the remainder of this article. Other techniques include:

(1) Analysis of, and greater attention to the needs of the adult learner who wants to apply his or her experience immediately in the learning situation and who wants learning to be highly practical. This has led to much wider use of cases, to development of various methods of role playing and other simulations, as well as

to the adaptation of pure games and toys such as three-dimensional tic-tac-toe and tinkertoys to serious learning designs.

(2) Programmed simulations, where one decision after another is presented to the learners in a structured, programmed form so that they must follow the steps that have been prescribed, and analyze one segment of the situation after another, in partial isolation, so that concepts can be seen or applied more precisely.

(3) Role plays, which are special forms of simulations. These have become more sophisticated with more precise direction and evaluation.

(4) Finally, pure games are used to dramatize topics such as careful planning, decision-making, and communication processes in groups.

It might be worthwhile, at this point, to clarify the distinction between certain words: (1) situation (or case); (2) simulation; (3) game.

(1) A *situation* or *case* is the description of an environment, either real or hypohthetical. Obviously, such a description does not consider all the factors which influence reality, but it attempts to describe those that are most pertinent to the purpose for which the situation or case is to be used.

(2) A *simulation* occurs when somebody uses the case to ask questions like: "What would happen, if..." A simulation requires an analysis of what would happen to the situation if a particular variable were changed, such as if inventory were increased or computers were installed, or another facility were purchased. It also allows exploration of the impact of external events such as changes in the interest rate, or withdrawal of a competitor, or increased activity by competitor, or other changes in the market such as major new inventions. Tracing the impact of these decisions or events is a simulation of what would occur in a real situation.

(3) A *game* exists when an individual or teams of people are in competition either against one another or against the situation, or against both people and the situation. Games against people can either be win-win or win-lose. Win-win means that all teams can win, for example, in a game invironment in which the market can grow if the actions of participating companies are appropriate. The game in which everyone can win could also be one in which

everyone who completes a certain task by a certain time is a "winner." A win-lose game can be zero-sum or other than zero-sum. In a zero-sum game, one team wins exactly as much as another team or combination of teams loses. In a non-zero sum game, the winnings and the losses are not equal.

A Typical Game

It may be helpful at this point to give a brief description of a typical model-based game play. (The mechanics of play for most model-based games are somewhat alike.)

The game session begins with a briefing. At this time the instructor describes for the participants what they will do in the game, whether it is to manage an entire company, or a sales force, or build a bridge or tower. The scope of their authority, the decisions to be made, and the information they will receive are all discussed. In addition to the mechanics of play, the purpose of the exercise and the manner in which it relates to the entire educational program are covered.

After the briefing the participants meet with the other members of their management team. In a typical game, there would be two or more teams, each with four to eight members. The team members all play the same role, though sometimes a leader or "president" is chosen. In a well-run game, teams may be asked to decide on objectives such as achieving highest net profit, net worth, or ROI, of all playing teams, or building a bridge within a specified amount of time, or building a tower of a specific height.

Model-based games are played in periods, each period being the equivalent of a day, week, month, quarter, or year, depending on the particular game. In a business game, using numerical information about inventory, market, or financial factors, participants receive operating reports for the past period and begin by making decisions for the next one.

The teams decisions are processed by a computer or a staff member, and operating reports are then returned. In most model-based game sessions, teams have about a quarter hour to a half hour in which to make decisions. In this manner time is compressed, and many periods of operation are covered in a few hours.

In many games there are observers with each team to follow the proceedings so they can provide feedback on the human interactions evidenced. These observers may themselves be members of the training course, they may be "facilitators" (extra instructors), or specially invited social scientists. In some cases, elaborate facilities are used to observe and record the actions of the participants. This is especially the case when the game is used for evaluation of participant skills, as in assessment centers.

At the end of the game play, team decisions are compared during a discussion session. This "critique" session is held to focus attention on the ideas and concept which were to be learned. The participants have an opportunity to compare their performance with that of other teams, and to receive feedback from the game, the administrator, and observers. Very often the critique takes the form of a report and is guided along specific channels by a previously prepared check list.

The game experience itself provides many learning opportunities but, as an educational device, a well-run briefing and critique are essential for a participant to obtain the full benefit.

Role of Computers

While there were many attempts, particularly at the General Electric Company and by R. L. Sisson and Jay R. Greene, in addition to the one by Andlinger, to make games independent of computers, the early surge of business game development during the sixties was greatly aided and stimulated by the availability of computers. Computers brought to business games a vastly greater ability to include more variables, and even to include incidental events such as shut-down of individual plants, or fire, or strikes, or major competitive activities. They also made it much easier to simulate changes in business conditions such as the probably impact of additional marketing, research and development expenditures, or changes in inventories or production methods, or locations of plants and warehouses, etc.

However, while computers brought many benefits to simulation and games, they also brought with them the seeds for the decline of wide use of model-based business games in training and education, particularly for in-house training in individual organizations.

There are three primary reasons for this decline:

(1) The trend sparked by business games, toward more involving training, led to evaluation of alternative methods. It was then found that extensive involvement of learners and the benefits of business games could be achieved in many other and often less costly ways than with model-based business games. As a matter of fact, business games diffuse, to some extent, the cause-and-effect relationship because of the many variables they present simultaneously. Programmed simulations, role plays, structured problem solving sessions, and incident process (where some of the information is withheld until needed and requested) all have taken over a large share of the potential use of model-based business games in education and training.

(2) The use of computers brought with it the potential for making simulation and business games so highly realistic that they would approximate reality. The lure of such realism is almost irresistible. Adult learners, particularly experienced adult learners, want to apply their knowledge and capabilities to situations with all the variables of realism, they frequently suspect the underlying model to be less then fully applicable and reject it as a foundation for a realistic learning experience. They may refuse to accept the assumptions of the model as appropriate, demanding consideration of more variables. Combined with the difficulty of tracing cause-to-effect when complexity increases, is the high cost of design.

(3) Besides the potentially huge costs of higher fidelity, one additional difficulty arises when a business simulation is made more complex in an attempt to make it more realistic. The amount of knowledge that is required to understand the situation and the skill needed for simultaneous consideration and evaluation of the impact of many variables is of such a high level that only very competent managers can effectively work on such a game. The less experienced members of the team therefore rely heavily on the more competent ones and fail to achieve significant new learning. In effect, the game is too challenging for it to be a useful learning experience. The more competent managers may gain something from it but for them the benefits of playing the game may not compensate for the amount of time they have to devote to

it. Straight simulations, when needed to solve business problems, can be more productive learning experiences for such managers.

Present Outlook

Games have a tendency to go through cycles. While many different techniques were developed during the seventies, toward the end of that decade and going into the eighties there appeared to be a resurgence of interest in model-based business games. In view of the negative factors mentioned above, the cause of this renewed interest is a matter for speculation.

What at this writing appears to be happening is that managers charged with human resource development are making use of the participative learning techniques which were developed during the early sixties and seventies. They are now seeking ways to provide learners with comprehensive experiences that will enable the learners to apply, simultaneously, the principles or skills acquired or sharpened in preceding training experiences. This search often leads to more streamlined, more realistic games which serve as a supplement to other training. The development of such simulations is easier today because comprehensive data bases exist now as part of the more sophisticated management information systems in place, providing data that are more relevant to the success of the enterprise. These simulation games, therefore, represent a new generation of learning tools that are more economical than their precursors, but are nevertheless more useful as learning tools.